DISGUSTED LADIES

DISGUSTED
LADIES

THE WOMEN OF TUNBRIDGE WELLS WHO FOUGHT FOR THE RIGHT TO VOTE

ANNE CARWARDINE

Matador
9 Priory Business Park,
Wistow Road, Kibworth Beauchamp,
Leicestershire. LE8 0RX
Tel: 0116 279 2299
Email: books@troubador.co.uk
Web: www.troubador.co.uk/matador
Twitter: @matadorbooks

ISBN 978 1788032 889

British Library Cataloguing in Publication Data.
A catalogue record for this book is available from the British Library.

Printed and Bound in the UK by 4Edge Limited
Typeset in 11pt Minion Pro by Troubador Publishing Ltd, Leicester, UK

Matador is an imprint of Troubador Publishing Ltd

For Christine, Willow and Amber Carwardine,
with love

Contents

Abbreviations

NLOWS
National League for Opposing Women's Suffrage. (Founded in 1910, as an amalgamation of the existing men's and women's anti-suffrage societies)

NUWSS
National Union of Women's Suffrage Societies. (Founded in 1897. Led by Millicent Garrett Fawcett. Campaigned for the vote using non-militant methods)

NUWW
National Union of Women Workers. (Founded in 1895 as a network of women and associations committed to public service. Renamed National Council of Women in 1918)

WCA
Women Citizens Association. (Founded in 1917 as a network of societies to equip women to become active citizens)

WFL
Women's Freedom League. (Founded in 1907 as a breakaway from the WSPU, over concern at its lack of democracy and increasing militancy)

WLA
Women's Liberal Association. (The Tunbridge Wells WLA was founded in 1890)

WLF
Women's Liberal Federation. (Founded in 1887, to link up local associations)

WSPU   Women's Social and Political Union. (Founded in 1903. Led by Emmeline Pankhurst. Campaigned for the vote using militant methods)

WTRL   Women's Tax Resistance League. (Founded in 1909. Promoted withholding tax as a way of campaigning for the vote)

Foreword

It is a summer's day and the weather seesaws between bright sun and heavy rain showers. I sit upstairs in a café, looking down onto Five Ways, a busy junction in the centre of Tunbridge Wells, and watch the people below. Two young women in strappy tops, one with a tattoo at the base of her neck. A stout gentleman wearing red trousers and a panama hat. A family – mother and daughter in matching pink peaked caps and little boy dressed as Superman. Shoppers with carrier bags. Office workers talking into mobile phones. Coffee drinkers chatting at outside tables.

I have done some of the reading, thinking and writing for Disgusted Ladies at this spot and sometimes what I see below is overlain with imagined images from the long-gone past. Today I think back to another sunny day, in April 1912.

Instead of coffee chain cafés, Five Ways is dominated by the huge Waymark department store (on the corner of Mount Pleasant and Calverley Road), which has been selling drapery and furnishings here for almost forty years. On other corners are Sydney Jones (a smaller drapery), John Harrington (a confectioner), Williamsons (a grocer) and the Grosvenor Tavern. It is a busy road junction, where motor cars and horse-drawn carts jostle for space. On the pavements are the same mixture of old and young, of shoppers and office workers, of the leisured and the busy, although in 1912, the women are dressed in long, straight skirts, jackets gathered at the waist and (in some cases) large hats, while many of the men wear boaters.

A crowd has gathered on one corner. Most are passers-by who have stopped to see what is going on. But scattered throughout are women wearing sashes and ribbons in purple, green and white – colours which identify them as suffragettes. A lady dressed in the same manner stands on a small platform at the centre of the crowd, making a passionate speech. Her subject is not something shoppers and office workers would expect to hear about in the course of a normal day. She is describing the horror that local woman Olive Walton is being subjected to in Aylesbury Prison, where she is on hunger strike and being force-fed. The audience show a mixture of reactions – idle curiosity, shock, or indignation (if they believe Olive has brought this treatment on herself). The speaker urges her listeners to bombard the Home Secretary with demands that he release Olive immediately or, failing that, treat her as a political prisoner rather than a common criminal.

A century ago, Tunbridge Wells was home to an extraordinarily active Votes for Women campaign, including both militants (prepared to use any means necessary, including window-breaking and arson) and non-militants (who believed in using only peaceful forms of protest). I first became aware of these women in 2013, at an exhibition entitled 'Inspiring Women', which was organised jointly by the University of Kent and the Tunbridge Wells Museum and Art Gallery. I had long believed that I owed a debt to those who campaigned for the vote, but up to that point what I knew of them was restricted to a few sketchy details about Emmeline Pankhurst, Emily Wilding Davison's Epsom Derby protest and hunger strikers.

Inspired by the exhibition, I began researching local campaigners in more detail and learnt the stories of a fascinating series of women, who campaigned from the mid-nineteenth century onwards. In uncovering their lives, I also tried to understand their experiences. What was it like to be a woman in their time? What impact did their campaigning activities have on the rest of their lives? What motivated them and kept them going? How did other people react to them?

In some cases I was lucky enough to be able to read the campaigners' own words. At the Women's Library I looked through Amelia Scott's papers, including the notes for a stirring speech she delivered in 1913. The Museum of London hold a diary by Olive Walton, in which I read about the time she spent in Aylesbury Prison and her experience of being force-fed. Annette Matthews' diary, at the Imperial War Museum, gave me a detailed picture of what life was like for a woman living in Tunbridge Wells during World War One.

Through reading and researching local stories, I have also learnt about the national one. The activities and experiences of the Tunbridge Wells women mirror those of many others elsewhere. (They were exclusively middle class, so their experiences differed from those of suffragettes in the textile cities of the north, or the east of London, for example. But the majority of those who campaigned for the vote came from similar backgrounds to theirs.) In addition, many of the national women's suffrage leaders spoke at meetings in Tunbridge Wells and, with London only a short train journey away, local campaigners took part in most of the major events in the capital.

The idea for the book's title came at an early stage. In the 1920s and '30s, letters from an anonymous correspondent appeared in the columns of the Tunbridge Wells newspapers. 'Disgusted of Tunbridge Wells' took aim at a range of targets, from the Salvation Army bands making a racket on the Common, to heavy traffic thundering along on the roads. He (or perhaps she) has come to be identified as the stereotypical Tunbridge Wells resident. The ladies of Tunbridge Wells who feature in this book were also disgusted, although their anger had a single focus – the government's continued refusal to give them the vote.

Chapter 1

Guerrilla Warfare

It was a peaceful spring night in Tunbridge Wells. Moonlight bathed the stuccoed terraces, the Pantiles colonnades and the sandstone rocks scattered across the Common. Church bells sounded out the hours. Lamplighter Mr Love cycled slowly through the empty streets, stopping to extinguish each of the town's gas lamps. At around 4am he heard a dog barking and saw a red glow coming from the direction of the Nevill Cricket Ground. Love raced to the Pantiles and used the alarm telephone to summon the fire brigade. Soon clattering hooves and rumbling wheels broke the peace, as horses hauled two fire engines to the Nevill, where firemen found the pavilion enveloped in flames and the air thick with smoke. They connected their pumps to a hydrant and aimed their hoses. Water hissed and steam rose, but the fire continued roaring like a furnace, as rafters fell, one by one. By the time a press photographer arrived on the scene later that morning, all that remained was a steel frame and a twisted, blackened roof.

Nevill Pavilion Fire

© *March of the Women Collection/Mary Evans*

Throughout the day a stream of people – curious neighbours, anxious insurance agents and angry sportsmen – came to take a look at the damage. (It was not just the pavilion that had been destroyed; valuable equipment belonging to local sporting clubs had also been lost.) Word spread around town as quickly as the fire had consumed the building. 'Have you heard? They found copies of *The Suffragette* on the ground nearby, with a picture of the Pankhurst woman on the front page.'

The newspaper left at the scene was published by the WSPU (the Women's Social and Political Union) whose members, known as suffragettes, had a militant approach to campaigning for the vote. Their campaign of destruction had arrived in Tunbridge Wells.

By 1913, women across the country had been fighting for the vote for almost fifty years. Over that time they had gained many new rights and opportunities. These days, a woman could vote in municipal and county elections. She could be a local councillor, mayor, poor law guardian, or member of an education authority. (Tunbridge Wells did not have any female councillors yet, but there were four female guardians and four women on the Borough Education Authority.) Access to the professions, apart from teaching or nursing, was still difficult, but with determination, persistence and sufficient financial resources, a woman could become a doctor, dentist or lawyer. Yet, despite all this, in a general election she was not allowed to enter a voting booth and put a cross on a ballot paper. And the prospect of doing so seemed as remote as ever.

It was not surprising, therefore, that some women, frustrated that peaceful campaigning had achieved nothing, had come to believe drastic action was required. Over the last few years, suffragettes had marched through the streets, disrupted public meetings, heckled cabinet ministers, broken windows and chained themselves to railings. A number of them (including several from Tunbridge Wells) had ended up in prison.

Many people had been sympathetic, especially when they read newspaper accounts of police brutality at demonstrations and of hunger strikers being force-fed with appalling violence. The previous November, when local newspaper the *Courier* reported on a visit to Tunbridge Wells made by Sylvia Pankhurst (daughter of WSPU leader Emmeline), the article ended '[she] has not shrunk from paying part of the terrible price which England demands from her own women today, as a price of their liberty.'[1]

In early 1913, the suffragettes adopted more destructive campaigning methods, extending to arson and even bombs. They aimed to cause as much disruption as possible and were deadly serious. WSPU leader Annie Kenney (who spoke at a meeting in Tunbridge Wells in February 1913) wrote of this time in her memoir: 'we were no longer the happy, joking crowd we had been in earlier days.'[2] In hers, Emmeline Pankhurst described militant actions as 'guerrilla warfare' and observed:

*...we had to make England and every department of English
life insecure and unsafe. We had to make English law a failure
and the courts farce comedy theatres; we had to discredit the
Government and Parliament in the eyes of the world; we
had to spoil English sports, hurt business, destroy valuable
property, demoralise the world of society, shame the churches,
upset the whole orderly conduct of life.*[3]

Suffragettes damaged or destroyed railway buildings, shop
windows, and telephone wires. They vandalised the orchid house
at Kew Gardens, set fire to the refreshment house in Regent's
Park and smashed a display case in the Tower of London's Jewel
House. Sports clubs, unoccupied at night, made especially good
targets; they used acid to scorch slogans such as 'No Vote No
Golf' on putting greens, set fire to a bowling club pavilion in
Newcastle and burnt down the grandstand at Ayr racecourse.
As their actions became increasingly extreme, public sympathy
evaporated.

On 2 April, Emmeline Pankhurst went on trial at the Old
Bailey, accused of inciting WSPU members to plant the bomb
which had damaged a house being built for Home Secretary
David Lloyd George. She was sentenced to three years' penal
servitude and dispatched to Holloway Prison. Despite being in
poor health, she immediately went on hunger strike. Suffragettes
everywhere followed Emmeline's trial closely and her example
inspired many of them to further actions.

On 11 April, it was Tunbridge Wells' turn to experience the
suffragettes' anger. They were looking for ways to hit men where
it hurt and what better target than an all-male institution such
as a cricket club? The game had been played in the town for
almost 200 years and annual cricket weeks had been held there
since 1874. Each year the town was festooned with bunting
and strings of coloured lights. Shops decorated their windows

with elaborate and inventive cricket-themed displays. Amateur theatrical groups and brass bands provided entertainment and large crowds attended matches at the Nevill Ground. When the fire happened, preparations were well underway for the 1913 event; the pavilion had been redecorated, bands booked, ticket prices set and matches scheduled. But now, with cricket week due to take place in only three months' time, it seemed unlikely it would go ahead.[a]

For some time after the fire, Tunbridge Wells remained in a state of alarm, with widespread rumours that further incendiary devices had been planted. In the early hours of 23 April, a loud bang woke residents in the Mount Sion neighbourhood, convincing many that the suffragettes were at it again. However, it turned out that the Grove Bowling Club, anxious to prevent any damage to their pavilion and green (which had recently been 'brought to the pitch of perfect') had rigged up an ingenious device, consisting of concealed wires. If disturbed by an intruder, it would trigger a mortar explosion to warn the groundsman and the blast had been a test to make sure it was working properly.

Suffragettes would frequently leave literature behind after their attacks and the discovery of their newspaper at the scene of the fire, together with recent events elsewhere, was enough to convince most people they were responsible. (Although the police investigation would be inconclusive and, as some people pointed out, with the gates locked each evening, the only way to get in was by climbing over a high fence. This seemed an unlikely thing for women to do.)

An *Advertiser* reporter headed down to the WSPU office at 11 The Pantiles. This was a narrow shop decorated in their colours – purple, green and white – which stood out among the grocers, butchers and fishmongers lining the promenade.

---

a In the end the Nevill Pavilion was re-built in time for Cricket Week, which went ahead as usual.

He found committee member Violet Matthews on duty, who informed him that most of their members had been in London the previous evening, for a meeting at the Albert Hall, and had not yet returned. Violet was in a defiant mood, refusing to either admit or deny that members of her organisation had started the fire. But she expressed strong support for such actions which, she said, were evidence of how serious suffragettes were. 'Men rioted for the vote in the past,' she pointed out, 'and women are just doing the same.'[4]

The person most widely suspected of setting the fire was Olive Walton, a slim, dark-haired, boyish twenty-six-year-old who was the local WSPU secretary. Olive had gained notoriety the previous year when she was arrested for breaking windows in London's West End and sentenced to four months in prison, where she went on hunger strike. Just a month ago she had hidden overnight under the stage at the Tunbridge Wells Opera House and burst out in the middle of a Liberal Party conference, demanding Votes for Women.

When a reporter tracked Olive down at her home, she refused at first to account for her whereabouts on the night of the fire. On being pressed, she claimed that, after attending the Albert Hall meeting with other local suffragettes, she had spent the night in Highgate. 'The fire could have been the work of a lady from Glasgow, or anywhere else,' she said. 'These things are happening all over the country and it is about time Tunbridge Wells woke up.'[5] (Olive was probably not responsible – evidence suggests most such attacks were the work of a small group of women travelling from place to place). However, Olive defended the arson, whoever had committed it. 'There is a time when patience can hold out no longer.' The reporter asked her whether she thought tactics like this would get women the vote. She was adamant they would and that the government would not allow the arson to continue.

Wherever property was damaged or destroyed in support of Votes for Women there were strong reactions and conservative Tunbridge Wells proved no exception. An article on the fire in *The Standard* (a London paper) stated: 'From the chief citizen to the humblest inhabitant the people [of Tunbridge Wells] feel intense and bitter abhorrence of the outrage, and their one demand is rapid and effective government action.'[6] Cricket represented a treasured tradition to many local people, which is why they reacted so fiercely to the fire. Many of those who had previously been indifferent to the suffragettes, or sympathetic due to the way they were being treated by the government, now turned against them. They were not intending to hurt anyone, it was conceded. But what if someone had been injured, or even killed, by accident? And how could women who wanted a say in making the country's laws be so brazen in breaking them?

The Mayor of Tunbridge Wells, Councillor James Silcock, who lived close to the Nevill Ground, was incensed, describing the town (with some exaggeration) as a hotbed of militants. 'Bats, nets, bows and arrows have been sacrificed, shamelessly sacrificed,' he declared. 'Can one wonder at the high feeling that has arisen? The whole business is as ill-considered as it is criminal... the perpetrators of the crime have won for themselves the anger and detestation of all classes of the community.'[7]

The author of the 'Jottings' column, which appeared each week in the *Courier*'s sports pages, expressed his anger in extreme fashion.

The numerous good sportsmen who have been hard hit through the destruction of the Nevill Ground Pavilion have my utmost sympathy. If it were not inciting a breach of the peace, we males might retaliate.

Once safely under lock and key, they should there remain. Let them "hunger strike". Prison authorities should place on

one side of the cell a loaf, on the other side a coffin, and if
suffragists elected to starve – well let 'em. Who cares.[8]

The Reverend Charles Storey, Vicar of Christ Church, appeared at the WSPU office and informed Violet that her organisation could no longer use the parish room for an 'At Home' they had been due to hold there in a couple of weeks' time. He claimed not to have realised that they had made the booking, despite the fact that the meeting was due to be hosted by Princess Sophia Duleep Singh, the late Queen's goddaughter and well-known for being a suffragette.[a] Many of his parishioners had been amazed and disgusted, he said, when they heard about the meeting. He was not cancelling the booking because he feared a disturbance, but because he believed the suffragettes' whole policy was morally wrong. 'How on earth can you do these things?' he said to Violet. 'How on earth can we not?' she replied.

The Vicar was widely commended for his action, which was in line with what was happening elsewhere. The Albert Hall meeting Olive and her friends attended on the evening of the fire was the last the WSPU was allowed to hold there.

---

a The meeting went ahead at the Pump Room on the Pantiles.

Chapter 2

Righteous Indignation

Reading the newspapers and listening in on conversations around town, it might have seemed there was only one group of women campaigning for the vote in Tunbridge Wells. But in reality the majority of campaigners, here as elsewhere, were suffragists rather than suffragettes and used only non-violent campaigning methods. Local members of the NUWSS (the National Union of Women's Suffrage Societies) collected signatures on petitions, lobbied politicians, held 'drawing room' meetings, wrote letters to the press and took part in peaceful marches. But they would never have dreamt of breaking windows or setting fire to anything. Actions such as the pavilion arson horrified them and they were concerned that both MPs and the public in general were being turned against the idea of women getting the vote.

The NUWSS had a high level of support in Tunbridge Wells. The local branch's 1913 Annual Report stated that they had just over 400 supporters, including 243 'Friends' (who could not afford to subscribe, but had signed a pledge). This was many more than the local WSPU (Women's Social and Political Union) branch, which probably had around fifty supporters at this time.ᵃ At a national level the difference was even more pronounced, with the NUWSS's membership of 50,000 or so dwarfing the WSPU's, which was around 2,000.

The *Advertiser* dispatched a reporter to the NUWSS office on Crescent Road, which was decorated in their colours – red, green and white. Gertrude Mosely, the fifty-five-year-old joint secretary, told him that she disapproved strongly of militant tactics and did not consider that destroying property served any useful purpose. 'The only way in which [women] can really get their end,' she said, 'is by educating public opinion, and showing the inherent justice of the matter.'[9] She agreed women had been exasperated when the latest Votes for Women bill failed, but believed violent methods could do nothing to advance the cause. On the contrary, they might do a great deal of harm. However, Gertrude also said she knew Olive and other local suffragettes personally and thought it unlikely they were responsible for the fire.

There was a third group of activists in the town – the opponents of women's suffrage were just as committed, organised and vocal as the supporters. One of the loudest voices in the chorus of disapproval that followed the fire belonged to fifty-four-year-old Margaret Backhouse, vice-president of the local branch of the NLOWS (the National League for Opposing Women's Suffrage). A regular newspaper correspondent, Margaret wrote to the *Advertiser*, protesting at the continued sale of *The Suffragette* (the WSPU's weekly newspaper), which she described as crime-instigating and anarchist. She also reported that, since the fire, members of local cricket clubs had been flocking to join the Tunbridge Wells branch of her organisation, which now had almost 300 members.

---

a   This figure is an estimate, based on information such as records of donations. The organisation did not have membership by subscription, so donations provide the best available indication of numbers.

Margaret and the NLOWS committee, together with the Blue Mantles Cricket Club and other pavilion users, decided to hold a protest meeting, to condemn the suffragettes' destruction. They booked the Great Hall, opposite the station, placed advertisements in the papers and invited well-known local author Sir Arthur Conan Doyle to take part. Colonel Alfred Simpson, a solicitor and member of the Cricket Week organising committee, agreed to act as chair.

Great Hall, Tunbridge Wells
© *The Author*

The non-militant suffragists of Tunbridge Wells, who no doubt became tired of explaining they were not suffragettes and did not approve of burning buildings, wanted to clear up any further misunderstanding that might arise at the meeting. Their president, celebrated authoress Sarah Grand, and vice-president, churchgoing philanthropist Amelia Scott, sprang into action. They arranged for two large posters to be printed, declaring their organisation's opposition to violence, and employed a man to carry them around the town on sandwich boards. Leaflets were produced for handing out at the meeting and members encouraged to attend, wearing their membership badges. Sarah and Amelia sent a letter to Colonel Simpson, which they copied to the *Courier*, making clear their position.

> *In consequence of the confusion existing in the public mind between our Society and the [militants, we] ask you in fairness to put before your meeting the fact that thousands of those who advocate the enfranchisement of women regret as keenly as any who attend the meeting the acts of violence that have recently occurred.*[10]

The Great Hall meeting room was a hundred feet long, with ornate plaster decorations and a huge gilt chandelier that held sixty-three gas jets. On the morning of 28 April every one of its 600 seats was taken and every inch of standing room occupied. Along the panelled walls stood lines of cricket players, acting as stewards, their muscular appearance intended to deter any disruptive women who might be aiming to cause trouble. There was a buzz of anticipation and a mood of righteous indignation. On the platform, which was decorated in the anti-suffrage colours – white, rose and black – sat Colonel Simpson, Sir Arthur, and a selection of solicitors, councillors, businessmen and retired military officers. There were also several women, including Margaret Backhouse.

The Colonel rose to his feet. He had presided over many meetings in Tunbridge Wells, he said, but never one as enthusiastic as this. It had been organised to express indignation at the actions of 'a certain small section of the community who seek to gain their ends by violating every law of civilisation and debasing themselves actually by crime.' His words were greeted with cheers and applause, which also punctuated the rest of meeting. He read out letters of support from prominent local people, including the town's MP, Captain Spender-Clay, and then introduced the first speaker – Gladys Pott, national secretary of the NLOWS.

Gladys had visited Tunbridge Wells only a few months earlier, to address an anti-suffrage meeting in the town hall. She was a mannish, rather plain-looking woman, described by a suffragette who heard her speak elsewhere as 'harsh, repellent and unpleasing.'[11] However, she was eloquent and the audience, mostly disposed in her favour, drank in her words. The suffragettes, Gladys said, were fanatics or criminals. 'I don't care which,' she added, 'but I do not want life governed by either!' Women who cut signals and telephone wires risked causing horrible tragedies. In contrast, 'anti-suffragettes' such as herself were out for the good of humanity and the stability of womanhood. She concluded by proposing a resolution:

That this meeting, believing that the vast majority of women do not desire the vote, is further of the opinion that in the light of the abominable outrages committed by militant suffragettes, any extension of the franchise to women would be against the best interests of women themselves and of the Empire as a whole.[12]

Colonel Simpson introduced Sir Arthur, a slim, elegant, middle-aged man with an impressive moustache. The author was unwell, the Colonel explained, but was taking part in the meeting, contrary to doctor's orders, because he felt so strongly about recent events. Sir Arthur rose to his feet and recounted some of the militant acts committed by women throughout England who had 'let down the fame and dignity of our Englishwomen [who are] justly admired through the world.'[13] They were 'female hooligans' and their tactics 'malicious monkey tricks.' Echoing the fears of the suffragists, he said that two years ago women might have had a chance of getting the vote, but now – as a result of the suffragettes' actions in Tunbridge Wells and elsewhere – they would not get it within a generation.

Sir Arthur seconded the resolution, which was carried by a large majority. Another was then passed, calling on the government to make suffragettes liable for the damage they caused, and it was agreed copies of both should be sent to the Prime Minister, the Home Secretary and local MPs. After several more speeches, the meeting came to an end. Mrs Conan Doyle and another lady went round the room, holding out long rods with nets on the end, and collected donations towards the cost of replacing the sporting equipment destroyed in the fire.

Whether or not local suffragettes had started the fire, they intended to capitalise on the event. Unable to gain access to the Great Hall (the police had been on guard since the early hours to keep them out), Olive Walton and two friends joined the large crowd that gathered outside. As they pushed their way through, handing out leaflets, it was easy to spot the three of them – they were holding placards and wearing purple, white and green sashes, lapel badges and ribbons on their broad-brimmed hats. When the speeches began (Gladys Pott and Sir Arthur addressed the crowd from the balcony above) the suffragettes interrupted, shouting out questions.

At first people were tolerant and simply asked them to give the speakers a fair hearing. But they persisted and were soon being jostled and jeered. Rotten eggs were thrown at them. Their hats were knocked off and their clothes torn. Banners and leaflets were snatched from them and thrown on the ground. Finally the police intervened and insisted on escorting the three women to the station on Calverley Road. Some of the crowd followed and remained outside for half an hour, hissing, booing and shouting insults. Finally they dispersed and the suffragettes were able to go home.

The next day, Olive was more than happy to talk to the *Advertiser* again. She described the people who had attacked her and her friends as irresponsible and not decent. The reporter suggested perhaps being there at all had been asking for trouble. 'Well,' responded Olive, 'we never meant to interrupt. It was only when [one of the speakers] misrepresented our whole policy and brought Mrs Pankhurst's name into it that we felt it to be our duty to. It was beyond ordinary endurance. And when he said he was not going to be interrupted by us he was practically inviting the crowd to riot. They began to hustle us, but we stood our ground.'[14] She claimed that, while they were at the police station, the group had spent the time talking to the chief constable. 'I venture to think we rather opened his eyes as to what our movement really meant.'

There is no record of what Chief Constable Prior actually thought. But the *Advertiser* was clear that most men and women in Tunbridge Wells shared the opinions expressed at the meeting. 'It was obvious that the public mind has been deeply stirred to indignation at such wanton and malicious acts, which, it is equally evident, have converted even friends of the suffrage movement into opponents.'[15] The paper's commentary section said women already had influence in local government, an area in which they had knowledge and expertise, but that was enough. 'It is, one can be as certain as is possible to be, that not ten percent of women take an intelligent interest in political matters, and [women] do not want the vote... Politics and petticoats do not blend.'[16] All this from the more liberal of the town's two newspapers. Clearly there was still a long way to go to win hearts and minds over to the cause of Votes for Women.

* * *

The 'disgusted ladies' of Tunbridge Wells had a great deal in common. They were all committed to improving the world they lived in. They were all middle-class and mostly single, which meant they could devote time to the cause (more difficult for working women with jobs or married women with families). They also shared enthusiasm, organisational skills and a willingness to step outside the behaviour and environments most people considered appropriate for women. And when they encountered opposition and ridicule, as they frequently did, they were not intimidated or deterred.

However, their approaches to campaigning differed as (in some cases) did their views on the whole issue of Votes for Women. Suffragettes Olive and Violet (who were in their twenties) believed the vote would only be won by direct and drastic action – window-breaking, arson and hunger strikes, for example. Suffragists Gertrude, Sarah and Amelia (in their fifties) had a more conservative outlook. They believed only reasoning and a peaceful, law-abiding campaign would win MPs over. And anti-suffragist Margaret was convinced women did not need, and should not have, the vote.

The 'disgusted ladies' of 1913 were the latest in a long line of committed local campaigners, stretching right back to Matilda Biggs in 1866.

Chapter 3

Denied a Voice

One day in April 1866, in an elegant classical-style villa in the centre of Tunbridge Wells, Matilda Biggs wrote her name on a piece of paper. Matilda did not march in processions. She did not break windows and get herself arrested. She was not sent to prison and did not go on hunger strike. But Matilda was typical

Matilda Biggs
Drawn by Katharine Harper

of women – in Tunbridge Wells and elsewhere – who supported the Votes for Women cause in the mid-nineteenth century. There were no organisations for them to join and, for the most part, they expressed their support through individual rather than collective actions. But by the private act of adding her name to the first national petition calling for women to be given the vote, Matilda played a small part in the beginning of the campaign.

The second daughter of solicitor William Ashurst and his wife Elizabeth, Matilda was born in north London in 1819. She and her three sisters had an unusual upbringing for the time; their parents ensured they received a good education, encouraged them to think independently and brought them up to believe men and women were equal, both socially and politically. William supported many liberal causes (including Chartism and the Anti-Corn Law movement) and a collection of radicals, who became known collectively as 'the Muswell Hill Brigade', met regularly at the Ashurst home. As a child, Matilda would have heard opinions such as those of her father's friend, the social reformer Robert Owen, who looked forward to a time when 'Women will be no longer made the slaves of, or dependent upon men... They will be equal in education, rights, privileges and personal liberty.'[17]

Matilda and her sisters, who called themselves 'the Clan', grew up to be exceptional women. They engaged in lively political discussions, campaigned on issues such as slavery and Italian liberation and shared a belief in 'the perfect equality of the sexes, morally, intellectually and politically.'[18] Their unconventional behaviour even extended to smoking cigars, something many people commented on. Matilda, who was well-read and fluent in several languages, was said to be the brightest of the sisters, who were all very intelligent. She was a reserved character, sceptical (especially about religion) and inclined to be critical, although she could also be kind and generous.

In 1837, when she was nineteen, Matilda married twenty-eight-year-old Joseph Biggs, who ran the glove-making branch of his family's hosiery business in Leicester. Whatever the young couple's view of marriage, from their wedding day onwards Matilda, like all wives at that time, ceased to exist in a legal or economic sense. Any property she had previously owned passed straight to Joseph and any money she might earn from that day on would be paid direct to him. The celebrated writer Elizabeth Gaskell found herself in the same position; between 1848 and 1865 all the revenue from her bestselling novels was paid to her husband, a church minister, who passed just 'pin money' on to her.

As a married woman Matilda could not incur a debt, sign a contract or write a will without Joseph's consent. If she and Joseph had separated or divorced after the birth of their daughters Elizabeth (in 1838) and Caroline (in 1840), she would have had no say in where the girls lived or how they were educated. In a happy marriage, as the Biggs' seems to have been, this inequality did not cause any great problems (although, given her upbringing and political beliefs, Matilda would no doubt have considered it unjust). But when things went wrong, a woman was virtually powerless.

Matilda's life was restricted outside as well as inside her home. As a middle-class woman, she could not have worked (although it is unlikely she would have wanted to), nor could she engage in any political activity (which she might well have wanted to do). The main campaign in which middle-class women played an active part was for the abolition of slavery and even then their involvement was mostly confined to fundraising. The limited nature of their role became apparent to Matilda when she attended the first World Anti-Slavery Convention in June 1840.

On a sunny summer's day, pregnant with her second child, Matilda arrived at Freemason's Hall on Great Queen Street in London, together with her father and older sister Eliza. William Ashurst went to take his seat among the hundreds of official delegates, who packed every corner of the huge hall's floor, under the stern gaze of the former masons in paintings and sculptures above them. His daughters, on the other hand, had to go and sit in a gallery above. From this vantage point women were permitted to listen to proceedings, shielded by a curtain which was intended to preserve their respectability and prevent them from distracting the male delegates. Before the day's business had begun, a group of American ladies joined Matilda and the others. These were seasoned anti-slavery campaigners, sent as representatives by one section of the American abolitionist movement. But when they arrived and presented their admission tickets, they were directed to the gallery.

It had not occurred to the Convention's British organisers that women might want to take part and most of the first day was spent debating whether or not this should be allowed. Women should not step outside their natural sphere, a series of male delegates argued. Permitting women to participate would be 'not only a violation of the customs of England, but of the ordinance of Almighty God,' thundered one American cleric. Other speakers feared this divisive issue would distract from the event's main purpose – to extend the abolition of slavery across the world – or that if women took part, it would bring the proceedings into disrepute.

Listening to the debate, Matilda became increasingly angry; her daughter Caroline would later write that she was 'roused to white heat' by what she heard.[19] It was all the more infuriating when, at the same time as opposing the American women's participation, speakers also praised them and their English counterparts in fulsome terms. 'I will yield to none in the high estimate which I form of female talent, female genius, female kindness and female accomplishments,' said one, while denying these paragons the right to play any active part in the proceedings.

A few delegates, including Matilda's father, argued that the American women should be allowed to participate. However, when a vote was taken, a substantial majority were against it and over the next twelve days they were forced to observe proceedings from behind the gallery curtain. This was the first public debate on the principle that women should only be observers in politics and the first time a major campaigning organisation had made a ruling to that effect. In the following months and years, women's exclusion from the Convention was discussed in private homes, at public meetings and in newspaper and magazine articles.

The experience had a powerful impact on many of the women who were present that day. One of the American group later observed that it had 'stung many women into new thought and action' and 'given rise to the movement for women's political equality both in England and the United States.'[20] In America it was not long before the first women's rights conference took place, at Seneca Falls, New York in 1848. In Britain it would be a while before there was any organised campaigning, but some of the women who had attended the Anti-Slavery Convention, and shared Matilda's outrage, began acting individually.

In 1847 Matilda received a letter from sixty-one-year-old Anne Knight, a Quaker from Chelmsford. Like Matilda she had been deeply affected by events at the Convention. From that time onwards she raised women's suffrage at peace and temperance meetings, wrote letters to any person or organisation she thought might be swayed in favour and produced pamphlets on the subject. In her letter, she asked for Matilda's 'hearty co-operation in demanding justice for all, whether gowned or coated, so that all might have a voice in the affairs of their country.'[21] She enclosed a packet of leaflets on women's suffrage, which Matilda circulated amongst her acquaintances in Leicester. One of them opened with the words:

'NEVER will the nations of the earth be well governed, until both sexes...are fairly represented, and have an influence, a voice, and a hand in the enactment and administration of the laws.'[22a]

a This is thought to be one of the earliest leaflets on women's suffrage, possibly the first.

Most women were far from having an influence, a voice or a hand in public life at this time. On the contrary, by the mid-nineteenth century opportunities for middle-class women such as Matilda had contracted. Teaching and medical care were professionalised, requiring training women could not access. Care of the poor was undertaken by poor law unions, who had no female members. Women who had no father or husband to support them and needed to earn a living had few options, apart from becoming a governess, dressmaker or writer. Most of those who would previously have worked in a husband's or father's business, were now expected to devote themselves to managing the home and caring for their children. Women's lives had become increasingly focussed on the domestic sphere.[a]

By 1851 Matilda could not have worked, even if she had wanted to. Her health was deteriorating and it had become clear she was suffering from tuberculosis. This may have been why, in that year, Joseph Biggs swapped manufacturing in Leicester for hop growing in Kent (a profitable business given the demand generated by London's breweries) and the family moved to live at Barden Farm, a few miles outside Tunbridge Wells. Perhaps the Biggs hoped the climate there was healthier than in industrial Leicester, or in London, where coal fires belched smoke and sewers poured effluent into the Thames, raising an unhealthy stink. While Tunbridge Wells' heyday as a fashionable spa was long since over, it remained a popular destination for those who believed taking the water and enjoying the fresh country air would benefit their health.

Life in Kent was difficult for Matilda. Her health worsened steadily and during the next four years she suffered the loss of her mother, her father and a baby son, who died at only a few

---

a Historians differ on the extent to which women and men lived in separate spheres in the mid-nineteenth century.

weeks old.[a] Country life made her feel isolated – she had never been as outgoing as her sisters and now became prone to low moods, feeling neglected by friends and family. Letters she wrote indicate that she formed few, if any, friendships in the Tunbridge Wells area and, given her scepticism about religion, she would not have had the church connections that provided many women with a social network. However, she was not completely cut off. With London only an hour away by train, family and friends visited her frequently, especially once travelling became more difficult for her.

Despite ill health, Matilda continued to take an interest in women's suffrage. She believed that to get the vote for themselves, women needed to take part in men's campaigns and so, in 1859, she applied to become a member of the Northern Reform Union. The secretary wrote back that, while they were happy to accept her donation, their campaign was restricted to obtaining the vote for men. Matilda might have reluctantly accepted the need for patience, but word reached her of a speech made at a Union meeting in Newcastle.[b] The large audience had applauded when the speaker declared the franchise should not be granted to women, the insane, or criminals. Women did not need the vote, he had said. Men could speak for them and if they were given more rights, this would cause dissension in domestic life.

Matilda took up her pen and wrote a long letter to the *Newcastle Guardian* expressing her frustration. 'I live in a small town in the south of England,' she began, 'removed by various circumstances from any active intercourse with the general progress and welfare of mankind.' She went on to describe her application to the Union, their reply and what she had heard about the meeting in Newcastle. Responding to the suggestion

---

a More happily, she gave birth to two further daughters, Maud in 1857 and Ada in 1860, both of whom thrived.

b It is likely that she heard of the Newcastle meeting from her brother-in-law MP James Stansfield, who was present at it.

that giving women the vote would lead to dissension she demanded, 'What is the worth of the "peace" which comes from preventing the legitimate expression of opinion?' Matilda continued:

> *I have never given my rights to be merged in those of any other person, and I feel it an injustice that I, who am equally taxed with men, should be denied a voice in making the laws which affect and dispose of my property, and made to support a State wherein I am not recognized as a citizen. I consider that a tyranny which renders me responsible to laws in the making of which I am not consulted.*[23]

Matilda signed herself 'one of the unrepresented.' Soon other like-minded women, who also believed that they were denied a voice in matters that affected them, would begin demanding the vote.

Chapter 4

The First National Petition

During 1865, Matilda would have heard from close family friend Clementia Taylor[a] about a new debating society which began meeting in the elegant drawing room of a large house in Kensington. Its members, including Clementia, were intelligent and articulate women, who were committed to improving the world in general and women's lives in particular. Some of them had overcome huge challenges to take up paid employment (in education and medicine, for example) and move into spheres dominated by men. Yet, society continued to restrict their lives, just as tightly-laced corsets and cumbersome crinolines restricted their bodies. At meetings of the Kensington Society (as it became known) these women had a rare and welcome opportunity for mutual support and open discussion.

At their second meeting, in November 1865, the Society turned its attention to the issue of Votes for Women and debated the question 'Is the extension of the parliamentary suffrage to women desirable, and if so under what conditions?'

---

a Clementia's husband had succeeded Matilda's brother-in-law as MP for Leicester in 1862.

The 1832 Reform Act had extended the vote to more people, but used the term 'male person', which made the exclusion of women explicit for the first time. Now the government was proposing further voting reform, but in parliamentary debates, public meetings and newspaper coverage, there was never any suggestion women should be included. The prospect of more men being able to vote, while women still could not, seemed a glaring injustice to the members of the Kensington Society, which is why they chose this as one of their first subjects (and why the arguments in favour were so heartfelt). Members believed the inequalities suffered by women would only be tackled if they had the vote and the debate concluded with a decisive vote in favour.

Following the meeting, some of the Society's members decided to send a petition to Parliament. Huge numbers of petitions were presented in the mid-nineteenth century; there were around 10,000 to 15,000 in each parliamentary session between 1828 and 1858[24]. They had little or no direct impact in bringing about change, but were a way to bring issues to the attention of MPs. There had been previous petitions calling for women to be given the vote, but this was the first national one. There was reason to believe some MPs would look on it favourably. For example, back in 1848 Benjamin Disraeli (then a back-bencher, now a leading Conservative) had said that, in a country governed by a woman and with women landowners, he could not see why women did not have the right to vote.

When considering whom they should ask to present the petition, there was one obvious candidate. From his speeches, his writings and their personal knowledge of him, Kensington Society members knew sixty-year-old MP John Stuart Mill would be sympathetic to their cause. In 1860 he had written that a person's gender was as irrelevant to political rights as height or hair colour[25]. So they wrote to him, asking for his support. His stepdaughter responded on his behalf, saying success was unlikely and they should prepare themselves for failure. However, if they could collect at least one hundred signatures on a petition, he would be happy to present it.

A suffrage committee was formed and (after some discussion about whether to demand the vote for all women, or just for unmarried ones) a petition was drafted which made the following request:

> *Your Petitioners...humbly pray your honourable House to consider the expediency of providing for the representation of all householders, without distinction of sex, who possess such property or rental qualification as your honourable house may determine.*

First National Petition, 1866

Women's Library, LSE

In April 1866, using the same 'chain letter' system some of them had employed in previous campaigns (for other causes), committee members sent out hundreds of letters, each with a copy of the petition enclosed. They also encouraged friends, family and neighbours to sign. Given their political views and their close connection with Clementia Taylor, it is not surprising that, down in Tunbridge Wells, Matilda Biggs and her two eldest daughters, Elizabeth (28) and Caroline (26) put their names to the petition.

The Biggs family had moved into the centre of Tunbridge Wells towards the end of 1864. Their new home, Calverley Lodge, was one of a number of properties designed by celebrated architect Decimus Burton and constructed during the building boom that took place in the town during the 1820s and '30s.

With her liberal political views and belief in women's suffrage, Matilda was not a typical Tunbridge Wells resident. Retired army and navy officers, clergymen, merchants and colonial administrators who had enjoyed summering there in the past were now making it their home in retirement. Church attendance was well above the national average and the prevailing political opinion strongly in favour of the Conservative Party and the status quo.

Maltilda also made no mark in the town's history. This was due principally to her illness, combined with the fact that her main connections were with family and friends in London. However, it was also the case that, at the time she lived there, women were not highly visible, here or elsewhere.

At the start of the nineteenth century there had been a small number of women who played a prominent role in the town. In 1802 impresario Sarah Baker had a new theatre built on the Lower Walk, which she managed with great success until her death in 1816. In 1803, Elizabeth Shorey, Lady of the Manor of Rusthall, had a new bath house built, which she also managed personally. But by 1866 there were no equivalent women in the town's public life. Local newspaper columns were filled with the affairs of men – the Town Commissioners struggling to sort out the water supply, magistrates presiding over petty sessions, poor law guardians controlling access to assistance and working-class members of the Saturday Half Holiday movement campaigning for improvements in conditions. When women did feature, it was generally as brief references in the births, deaths and marriages columns, or in lists of the officers of charities. The only women to appear in any detail were victims, witnesses or perpetrators of crime.[a]

Yet in reality, despite their relative invisibility, the population of Tunbridge Wells included a higher than average proportion of women. This was due partly to the number of cooks and maids employed by the town's wealthier inhabitants and partly to the high number of all-female households, headed by unmarried women and widows. The lack of any public activity or voice makes it difficult to know what these local women thought about not having the vote. It is likely most of them gave the matter little or no consideration, although there were at least a few who, like Matilda, believed in the need for change.

Matilda could not do much to publicise the petition; her tuberculosis was now well advanced and she was confined entirely to home. However, her daughters Elizabeth and Caroline seem to have canvassed for support amongst friends and acquaintances in the Tunbridge Wells area and, as a result, a handful of local women signed. These included Jane Ashby, a friend of Elizabeth's, and the wife and daughter of the corn merchant who had taken over Barden Farm when the Biggs moved to Calverley Lodge.

---

a In April 1866 the local newspapers were full of the story of Ann Lawrence, who murdered her young son and attempted to murder her lover.

Over a period of two weeks, women from Falmouth in Cornwall, to Lerwick on the Shetland Islands, wrote their signatures on scraps of paper and sent them to the petition organisers in London. They came from all classes of society, although middle-class women (whether their husbands were gentry, professionals or in trade) predominated. And they represented a large number of other women who also wanted the vote but, for whatever reason, did not declare it publicly. According to an article in the *Westminster Review*:

It is not going too far to say, that for one woman who can and will pronounce openly on such a subject, there must be at least ten whom family hindrance or habitual timidity will prevent from expressing an opinion, even if they have formed any. And the number must be still greater of those whose minds are only partially prepared for any ideas on such subjects...[26]

Caroline Biggs travelled up from Tunbridge Wells and spent hours in the library of Clementia Taylor's west London home, pasting the signatures onto a long scroll. When this task had been completed and the names were counted, there were 1,499 in total. Many petitions had more than this, but collecting so many in just a fortnight was a significant achievement. And the number was far higher than John Stuart Mill had suggested was required.

Kensington Society members Emily Davies (an education campaigner) and Elizabeth Garrett Anderson (who had recently succeeded in qualifying to practise medicine) delivered the petition to Mill at Westminster. He presented it on 7 June 1866 and spoke about it in the Commons a few weeks later. The petition had been compiled by women, without the involvement of him or any other man, he said, and provided clear evidence that their sex did want the vote.

The press were divided in their reporting of the petition. The *Daily News* was favourable: 'Having given to the question much thought, and with the help of much experience, we are unable to suggest a single sound objection to the claim of female householders to vote.'[27] An article in *The Spectator*, on the other hand, warned against giving the vote to the ninety-nine out of a hundred women 'who have no political nature, and no political wishes and no political insight.' The writer continued that, for the most part, 'the influence of women in political discussion is thoroughly bad – unreal, tawdry, dressy.'[28]

What were Matilda's thoughts, as she lay confined to her bed and close to death? She would no doubt have been concerned for her daughters' future. However, she would have heard from Caroline how many petition signatures had been collected in such a short time and she probably believed that it would not be long before women gained the vote. So, although little had changed for women since her marriage in 1837 and the Anti-Slavery Convention in 1840, there was cause for optimism. She would also have hoped that there would soon be changes to women's legal and financial rights, so that if her daughters married, their position would be better than hers had been.

Certainly most of the Kensington Society's suffrage committee believed they would soon have the vote. In the autumn of 1866 Emily Davies wrote to another member: 'I am very inclined to think that our victory is not far distant.'[29]

Matilda did not live long enough to find out what happened next. On 15 October 1866, aged forty-eight, she died at Calverley Lodge. Clever, capable, eloquent and with convictions just as strong as later campaigners', the first 'disgusted lady' is representative of women who supported the Votes for Women cause up to the mid-nineteenth century. Their actions included writing letters, circulating pamphlets, discussing the issue (in private) and signing petitions. All of this was done largely in private. Where women did participate in male-led organisations, such as the Anti-Slavery Society, they were not allowed to hold office or speak at public meetings.

On the other hand, women such as Matilda were not entirely isolated. They belonged to informal networks, based around family, friends, church and other shared interests. Through these they could engage in a certain amount of political activity, on suffrage and on other issues. One-off actions (such as signing a petition) and small-scale organisations (such as the Kensington Society) had a cumulative effect and women such as Matilda prepared the ground for organised campaigning in London and other major cities to begin with, and then in towns such as Tunbridge Wells.

Chapter 5

Organised Campaigning Begins

On 20 May 1867, almost a year after John Stuart Mill had presented the national petition, the Reform Bill had its first reading. A small number of women were there to watch proceedings. Just as they had been relegated to a curtained gallery at the Anti-Slavery Convention, they were confined to the Ladies' Gallery in the House of Commons. This was a dark, low-ceilinged, airless room, high above the Speaker's chair, with space at the front for just sixteen or so women to press against a heavy, latticed brass grille. Through this they could catch a glimpse of MPs below and listen to debates (although it was sometime difficult to hear what was being said).

Matilda's daughter Caroline may well have been in the Gallery that day. (She would later be a familiar figure in the Central Lobby, waiting to collar MPs and press them on Votes for Women.) One woman definitely present was Millicent, younger sister of Kensington Society member Elizabeth Garrett Anderson. This short, slightly-built nineteen-year-old, who had married blind MP Henry Fawcett a month earlier, would go on to become one of the foremost leaders in the women's suffrage campaign. In her autobiography she described the headache-inducing experience of peering through the brass grille as being like wearing a pair of gigantic, ill-fitting spectacles.[30]

After four and a half hours, the debate reached clause four. Mill rose to his feet and proposed an amendment replacing the word 'man' with 'person', which would include women and give them the vote on the same basis as men. MPs listened attentively as Mill demolished each of the principal arguments against women having the vote – that they did not want it, that they suffered no inconvenience by not having it, that they were not as wise as men and that being involved in politics would be detrimental to their characters. Millicent listened with pride as her new husband spoke in support.

The debate concluded with a proposal that the bill remain unchanged and MPs headed to the division lobbies. Up in the Gallery, the women heard laughter, as the number entering the 'No' lobby (in support of Mill's amendment) was far greater than expected. Nevertheless, the amendment was rejected and the debate moved on.

When the Reform Act became law in August 1867, it doubled the number of men who could vote to around two million (around one in three), including many working-class men. But, to the disappointment of those who had organised and signed the petition, the right was not extended to any women. Nevertheless, seventy-three MPs (more than a quarter) had voted in favour of women having the vote and some campaigners saw this as further confirmation that success was not far off. The following year, Manchester-based campaigner Lydia Becker wrote: 'I do believe that if we are thoroughly bent on our point, and play our cards well, we may see women voting at the next election.'[31]

Lydia's confidence was shared by many women at the heart of the campaign. They believed that, since their cause was clearly a just one, they were bound to succeed before long. However, they based this on what they heard in their homes and in discussions with other like-minded women. They seem not to have appreciated that most people were still opposed to women having the vote. Yet reports of Mill's speech in some sections of the press gave clear indications of this. The *Morning Herald* observed, '[His] speech was as feeble and halting as his proposal was abhorrent to the almost universal instinct of mankind,' while *The Globe* stated, 'There is as much difference between the intellectual powers of men and women as there is in their physical strengths; consequently women are unfit to possess the suffrage.'[32]

In 1869, the government passed the Municipal Franchise Act, allowing women ratepayers to vote in local elections. This right was only given to single women or widows who owned property, but it felt like a significant step towards women being allowed to vote in parliamentary elections too. In 1870, after the first Women's Suffrage Bill passed its second reading, John Stuart Mill wrote to another MP: 'I am in great spirits about our prospect, and think we are almost within as many years of victory as I formerly thought decades.'[33] Mill was wrong. The bill failed at the committee stage and it would be decades rather than years before the Votes for Women campaign achieved its aim.

Active campaigning was soon underway in London and other large cities, although in towns such as Tunbridge Wells, it made a slow start. In 1869, MP Peter Taylor (husband of Matilda's friend and Kensington Society member Clementia) presented a petition to Parliament with thirty-one signatures 'from certain inhabitants of Tunbridge Wells in favour of extending the suffrage to women.'[34] This was just one of many petitions presented that year calling for women's suffrage, and very small compared to ones from northern towns such as Bolton and Scarborough. But it showed that, even in a conservative place such as Tunbridge Wells, there were people who believed women should have the vote. Further suffrage petitions from the town's residents were presented in 1872, 1873 and 1881.

On 6 October 1873, the first public meeting on women's suffrage in Tunbridge Wells was held at the Great Hall (which had been constructed three years earlier and was used for lectures, concerts and meetings). There was an audience of around one hundred, a good number, but well short of the venue's capacity. The speaker was Amelia Arnold and her subject 'The Political Disabilities of Women.' She argued that, since women had many hardships to complain of, they should have a share in the political voice of the nation.

Amelia, originally from Ireland, was one of several women touring the country around this time to promote women's suffrage. Matilda's daughter Caroline was another. This took a great deal of nerve on their part. Most of their audiences had come to make fun of them, or out of curiosity at this strange new phenomenon – a female public speaker. Few were genuinely interested in hearing what they had to say. Emily Davies wrote in a letter: 'People notice our manners more than our arguments.'[35]

Some people thought women were 'unsexing' themselves by engaging in politics. Campaigner Lilias Ashworth later recalled the reactions on a tour she and Caroline made in North Wales:

It was evident that the audiences always came expecting to see curious masculine objects walking on to the platform, and when we appeared, with our quiet black dresses, the whole expression of the faces of the audience would instantly change.[36]

In 1873, a political commentator referred to:

Certain celebrated women who have flung themselves with ardour into the vortex of politics…[and have necessarily sacrificed]…conjugal happiness, the welfare of children, domestic peace, reputation, and all the amenities of the gentle life.[37]

The meeting Amelia addressed in Tunbridge Wells did not feature any ridicule or abuse, but the *Courier* observed that the audience were not very enthusiastic. When local Unitarian minister Robert Crompton Jones appealed at the start for one of the gentlemen present to take the chair, he met with complete silence and eventually the speaker's husband – a radical newspaper editor – had to take on the role. (A female chair was apparently still a step too far.) Commenting afterwards, the paper did not consider there was much potential for a campaign in the town:

Judging from the number of persons present and the general tone of the meeting, we do not think it at all probable that the advocates of women's suffrage will look very hopefully on their prospects as far as Tunbridge Wells is concerned.[38]

Six years passed before the next local women's suffrage meeting took place. In February 1879, a letter appeared in the *Courier*, announcing one that was to be held in the Great Hall on 6 March. The author, who signed herself as 'A Woman Householder and Conservative,' observed that, while one in seven of all householders were women (and probably more in Tunbridge Wells 'where many pretty villas were owned by widows and spinsters') they had no representation. The letter-writer continued by pointing out that it was said women would not use the vote if they had it, yet large numbers of them been voting in school board elections.

Local solicitor Nehemiah Learoyd opened the meeting, saying he was sure it would not be long before women would have the vote, and introduced the speaker. Fifty-two-year-old Lydia Becker from Manchester did not appear very impressive to her audience. She was dressed severely, had a bun of thick plaited hair, wore narrow, steel-rimmed glasses and stood stiffly, due to chronic back pain. She read her speech hesitantly from notes and it was clear that public speaking did not come naturally to her (although she was more confident than she had been when she began addressing public meetings ten years earlier).

The title of Lydia's speech was 'The Political Disabilities of Women Householders.' It was appropriate to be speaking about women's suffrage in Tunbridge Wells, she commented. A high proportion of the landowners and ratepayers in the area were women and anyone who had a house or property and paid tax should have a vote. 'Just imagine the spectacle of a lady of Tunbridge Wells riding in state in her carriage drawn by two horses,' she said, 'and the coachman, who drove, being the only political unit in the whole concern.' The audience laughed when she added: 'Sometimes it has been said that women are not sufficiently intelligent to exercise a vote, but [not] all men are very intelligent.'[39] In conclusion she stated that:

> She firmly believed that as the combined intelligence of women and men were brought to bear on a solution of social and political problems, a wider and higher solution would be attained than could be by men or women separately.[40]

In 1884, electoral reform came to the fore once again, as Parliament debated another reform bill, which would extend the vote still further. In June of that year, MP William Woodall proposed an amendment, by which all references to men would also include women. At first it seemed to have a chance of succeeding; London-based campaigners estimated there were 249 'known friends' of women's suffrage in the House of Commons, compared to 236 'known opponents.' But Liberal Prime Minister William Gladstone (who had been expected to support women's suffrage) was concerned that, if women were given the vote, they would cast it for the Conservatives. He instructed his party's MPs to vote against the amendment and it was defeated. After that there was no further suggestion of including women.

The Tunbridge Wells newspapers gave the Reform Bill extensive coverage, but made only one brief reference to women's suffrage. On 1 August, the Marquess of Abergavenny entertained around 4,000 local people at Eridge Park (just outside town) for a lavish event, which included a procession, a picnic, fireworks and speeches – a cross between a celebration and a political rally. The issue on most people's minds that day was not the exclusion of women from the Reform Bill, but the fear that, if it was passed, the votes of agricultural labourers would outnumber those of urban workers. However, in reporting the event, the *Courier* (the more right-wing of the two local newspapers) noted the large number of women who had taken part and commented:

Women's suffrage is no doubt looming in the not very far off future, and what could be wiser we ask than for the sympathy of the women to be enlisted on the side [of the Conservative Party] which can boast of always having been true to the principles of real, civil and religious liberty, and rendered Old England great, glorious and free.

When Parliament passed the Representation of the People Act (known as the Third Reform Act) later in 1884, the electorate was increased to around 5.5m, which meant that two-thirds of all men now had the vote. Yet women – along with criminals, the disabled and the inmates of lunatic asylums – still did not, even if they owned a substantial property, or held a responsible position. Some of them found this situation unacceptable, including a few in Tunbridge Wells; in 1886 and 1887, further Votes for Women petitions from the town were presented in the House of Commons by local MP Robert Norton.

A specific example of local women who believed they should have the right to vote was Mary Moberly, the headmistress of the Tunbridge Wells High School for Girls. Mary was highly respected in the town and described as having 'high intellectual power.'[41] Yet, following the Third Reform Act, she still did not have a vote, while the coal merchant and chimney sweep living in the houses on either side of her school on Mount Sion did. Mary evidently considered this an injustice and, in 1889, she and two of her staff were amongst 2,000 women who signed *A Declaration in Favour of Women's Suffrage*.[a] As well as teachers like Mary, a wide range of women, including titled ladies, writers and businesswomen, signed the declaration, which argued that giving women the vote would bring their political status 'into harmony with changes which have already taken place in their social, educational, and industrial status.'[42]

Mary was not typical and the declaration was an exception. Most women seem not to have been troubled by being left out of the Reform Act, believing that their exclusion from the franchise reflected the natural order of things. As a result, women's suffrage was not generally considered a high priority issue over the remainder of the nineteenth century; there was only a limited amount of campaigning on it and far more attention was focussed on issues such as home rule for Ireland, free trade and labour relations. National and regional women's

---

a   The declaration was in response to an earlier anti-suffrage declaration. Details of this can be found in Chapter 20.

suffrage organisations continued to exist, but there were frequent arguments and splits. Local societies were not very active and often only short-lived.

While the Votes for Women campaign had faltered, in the late nineteenth century women began to have more political influence through the two main parties. They had been involved in fundraising and networking for many years previously. However, after the 1883 Corrupt Practices Act made it illegal to pay canvassers, both the Liberals and the Conservatives began making more use of volunteers (especially at election time), and many of these were women.

From 1884 onwards, women were allowed to join the Primrose League, the organisation for Conservative Party volunteers founded the previous year.[a] This helped improve their political knowledge and gave them a role in canvassing and fundraising activities. At a meeting of the Nevill Habitation (the Tunbridge Wells branch of the League) in April 1886, the chair acknowledged the contribution being made by lady members, saying:

> …*the great position which the League had attained…was very much owing to the kind exertions of the ladies, who, although [they did not] possess any vote in the return of members to Parliament…[did] in their families, in other circles, and in various other ways exercise a great influence in the elections which were carried on in this country.*[43]

In August 1891, several hundred people attended a Primrose League fete in the spacious grounds of Fairlawn House on Mount Sion. Light refreshments and entertainment (including coconut shies, comic singers and a military band) were followed

---

a There was a strong local connection with the Primrose League, through its founder the Marquess of Abergavenny, who lived in Eridge, close by.

by speeches. Edith Milner, a League organiser from Yorkshire, delivered a stirring address, which was greeted with loud cheers. She spoke about women's mission as politicians and said that, while she could not advocate women's suffrage, it was every woman's duty to study the politics of her country.

Around the same time as Conservative women in Tunbridge Wells became involved in the Primrose League, women who supported the Liberal Party were also organising themselves. Early in 1890, a local Women's Liberal Association (WLA) was established, affiliated to the Women's Liberal Federation (WLF), a national organisation which had been set up three years earlier. Founder members included suffrage campaigner Laura Crompton Jones, whose husband had taken the chair at the women's suffrage meeting back in 1873.

Unlike the Primrose League, the WLA was a women-only organisation and focussed on issues which particularly affected or concerned women, such as women's wages and employment conditions, reform of the marriage laws and child welfare. Members believed women had an important role to play in public life and should be involved in shaping policy in the areas that concerned them.

There were many individual Liberal and Conservative women who believed that their sex should have the vote. However, their national organisations took differing positions. The Primrose League was unwilling to come down on either side of an issue which had the potential to be divisive. When asked if the Ladies' Grand Council would consider supporting women's suffrage, founder Lady Borthwick replied that they could not 'enter into questions of contentious politics.' The WLF, on the other hand, supported women's suffrage, adopting this as an official policy in 1892.

In line with their national organisation, members of the Tunbridge Wells Liberal women were strongly committed to

Votes for Women. One of their first meetings, which was held on 12 June 1890 at the Bethel Chapel in Hawkenbury (on the edge of town), included a talk on women in politics and a debate on whether women should have the vote. For some years after this, their meetings were the main local forum for discussing and promoting the issue.

Whether or not their members believed women should have the vote, the activities of the Primrose League and Women's Liberal Associations in towns such as Tunbridge Wells helped strengthen the case for women's suffrage. Opponents had previously assumed women could not understand, and had no interest in, politics. As they attended meetings, canvassed in elections and took on other responsibilities, women proved both assumptions wrong. They also acquired knowledge and skills which equipped them to campaign for the vote.

And, while women were as far away as ever from being able to vote in national elections, they were beginning to break down barriers and participate in other areas of public life. One way they did this was through voting in local elections. By the end of the nineteenth century, women could vote in elections for municipal councils, county councils, school boards and boards of guardians. These polls generally were considered to be an appropriate sphere for women, as they dealt with aspects of life that could be classed as 'domestic'. Women were keen to exercise their right; when municipal elections took place in Tunbridge Wells in 1896, 144 out of 165 (87%) of the eligible women in Tunbridge Wells used their vote, compared to 516 out of 976 (53%) of the eligible men.[44]

Another way that women participated more in public life was by taking on the public roles that were now open to them. The 1870 Education Act allowed women stand for election as members of the new school boards and Lydia Becker, Elizabeth Garrett Anderson and Emily Davies were all elected to their local boards with substantial majorities. It was claimed that when she stood to represent Marylebone on the London board, Elizabeth received the highest number of votes any candidate (male or female) had ever received in any form of local election.

As a result of the 1869 Municipal Franchise Act, women were also able to stand for election as poor law guardians. In 1893, the Tunbridge Wells WLA gave their support to the first woman to stand for election as a guardian in the local union – workhouse campaigner Louisa Twining.

Chapter 6

More than Housekeeping

The Tonbridge Union workhouse, located in the village of
Pembury just outside Tunbridge Wells, was a haphazard

collection of red brick
buildings with 'prison-like'
windows and a commanding
view over the fields and hills
beyond. On a mild April day in
1893, a carriage drove through
the gates and up the drive to
the entrance, where the driver
reined in the horses, bringing it
to a standstill. An elderly lady,
in a black dress and bonnet,
climbed out. Louisa Twining
was agitated; she was late for
her first meeting as a poor law
guardian on the Tonbridge
board. The workhouse master

Louisa Twining (1906)
Elliott & Fry, via Wikimedia
Commons

welcomed her and conducted her to the board room, where the meeting was already underway. To her surprise, the twenty or so men around the table rose to their feet, making her even more flustered. She had been up in London on business the previous day, she explained, and had missed the fast train back earlier that morning. Louisa, who prided herself on her punctuality, hated being late. She was shown to a seat beside the chairman and the meeting continued.

To the gentlemen on the board their new colleague, with her nervous manner and old-fashioned clothes, would not have looked likely to cause them any trouble. But they had good reason to know that, in her case, appearances were deceptive. They might have read her letters to *The Times* and some of her numerous books and pamphlets. They would certainly have been aware of her experience as a workhouse visitor and poor law guardian and of her formidable reputation in the field of workhouse reform. They were wary of her and of the 'feminine' improvements she might try and impose on them.

Born in London in 1820, Louisa was the youngest child of wealthy tea merchant Richard Twining and his wife Elizabeth. She was educated at home by her mother and older sister and enjoyed a range of rich experiences while growing up. These included hearing Michael Faraday lecture at the Royal Institution and Mendelssohn play the organ at St Peter's Church, Cornhill. Her family were noted for their charitable works – especially her father, who was a member of the first board of management at King's College Hospital and supervised a free local dispensary.

In her thirties, Louisa visited an elderly acquaintance at the Strand Union Workhouse and a crossing sweeper (who had operated close to her family home) at the St Giles Workhouse. She was shocked by the conditions she encountered in both places, which included overcrowding, poor sanitation, filthy bedlinen, inedible food and inadequate medical care. Louisa made further visits and soon came to believe that the key to improving workhouse conditions (as well as the moral and spiritual welfare of inmates) was visiting, especially by women. Boards and workhouse masters, were resistant. They saw visits as meddling interference and, in some cases, had reason to fear what might be uncovered. So, while Louisa frequently gained admission for herself, she failed to get individual workhouses, or the Poor Law Board, to agree to formal arrangements for other ladies to visit.

Her response was to set up a campaigning organisation. In 1858 she helped establish the Workhouse Visiting Society, with a committee that included doctors, barristers, clergy, leading politicians' wives and members of the aristocracy. Louisa became honorary secretary and from this time onwards devoted herself full-time to workhouse reform. She gave lectures, wrote articles, pamphlets and books and sent frequent letters to the newspapers. She also continued to visit workhouses, travelling all over the country to do so. (She later claimed she had visited more than half of the workhouses in Britain.) By 1861, Louisa's reputation was such that she was asked to give evidence to a House of Commons select committee on the poor laws. Appearing before parliamentary committees and royal commissions was one of the few ways women could make their voices heard during the mid-nineteenth century. Fellow reformers, including Elizabeth Fry, Florence Nightingale, Octavia Hill and Mary Carpenter, also did so.

After Louisa's parents died (her father in 1857 and her mother in 1866), the usual course of action for a single woman in her forties would have been to move to live with one of her married siblings and help care for some of her many nephews and nieces. Alternatively, she could have set up home with her older sister Elizabeth, who was also unmarried. However, the substantial inheritance Louisa received from her parents gave her a private income, allowing her to live independently and to continue her involvement in workhouse reform, rather than being confined by the demands of family life.

A logical progression from visiting workhouses was for women to become poor law guardians and Louisa believed women had a distinctive role to play in this. In guidance for women guardians she would later write: 'Nearly all the details of the vast institutions which come under the care and supervision of guardians are such as women would naturally control in their own households.'[45] The details she referred to included clothing, bedding, diet, schooling and midwifery, as well as temperance and the salvation of souls.

Louisa became a trustee of the Society for Promoting the Return of Women as Poor Law Guardians, after it was founded in 1881. Another of the organisation's founders was Caroline Biggs (Matilda's daughter). In 1875, Caroline had run a highly efficient campaign which resulted in her friend Martha Merrington being elected as the country's first female poor law guardian, in Kensington. In 1884, Louisa followed in Martha's footsteps and was elected to the Kensington board, where she served as a member for six years.

In 1892, just after her seventy-second birthday (and two years since she had retired from the Kensington board), Louisa moved to Tunbridge Wells – a town she had visited several times as a child and where she had friends – and set up home on St James's Road.

Louisa considered her life's work was almost complete and did not anticipate playing an active role in the public affairs of her new home town. Besides, it appeared there were plenty of other local people with leisure and capacity for philanthropy and she was told repeatedly there was nothing for her do in Tunbridge Wells. The workhouse in particular had no need of her input. It was said to be perfect – a 'model for all England' – with an excellent master, who had been in post for twenty-seven years.[46] So for the first few months Louisa occupied herself writing her autobiography. It was not exactly a quiet retirement, however, and she continued travelling to London for workhouse reform meetings, writing letters to the newspapers and publishing pamphlets.

Men were still in charge of business and public affairs in Tunbridge Wells, just as they had been thirty years earlier when Matilda Biggs lived there. A municipal council, elected by ratepayers, had replaced the Town Commissioners in 1889, but its membership was still all male. On the day Louisa attended her first meeting at the workhouse, the *Courier's* columns were full of meetings and dinners held by all-male organisations, including the Borough Improvement Association, the Co-operative Society, the Ratepayers Association, and the Equitable Society. Women's participation in the town's public life was still mainly through their involvement in local charities.

For years the workhouse had been run by an all-male board of guardians, with the same men in office year after year and no thought ever given to appointing a woman. However, when a vacancy arose in August 1892 following the death of draper Ebenezer Waymark, some local women decided here was an opportunity to nominate one of their sex to play a role beyond charitable works. With her background in the workhouse movement, the town's new resident made an ideal candidate. Agnes Drummond, secretary of the local Brabazon Scheme[a], called on Louisa and asked her if she would consider standing for election.

Louisa's initial reaction was to refuse. She had come to Tunbridge Wells intending to retire from public service, she said,

---

a The Brabazon scheme was a charity which organised such activities as knitting, embroidery and lace-making for older workhouse inmates who were too infirm to do manual work.

and considered that her life was drawing to its close.[47] She later admitted to another reason – she was reluctant to take part in an election, in which she might defeat a popular local candidate or, worse still, suffer defeat herself. Faced with insistent requests, and on being informed she would be the only candidate, she changed her mind, counting it 'a privilege and honour to be allowed to help in a national work, and to start in a fresh place the cause of women workers under the Poor Law.'[48]

There was some opposition to Louisa's nomination. One of the guardians was quoted as saying the board were unanimously against it and there were rumours of the unpleasantness she could expect if elected. The *Courier* published a letter from a correspondent calling himself 'Diogenes', who suggested that Louisa would be better employed as a visitor and continued:

> *I fail to see on what ground Miss Twining seeks our suffrage. It is not, I presume, to superintend those operations in bricks and mortar, farming, buying and selling and sewage disposal, which constitutes the chief work of the gentlemen who meet fortnightly at Pembury. It is, I suppose, to look after the inmates. May I suggest that when we have tender-hearted guardians, who are rebuked by the Local Government Board Inspector for being too lavish with outdoor relief, and a Brabazon Committee which looks after what I may call, without offence, the 'coddling' of the old people, I do not see what room is left for Miss Twining, although her presence would adorn the luncheon table.*[49]

Most people though, including (contrary to what one of them had claimed) the majority of the guardians, looked on Louisa's candidacy favourably. She also had the backing of the local Women's Liberal Association (WLA) and of the *Courier*. An article in the paper commented that it was 'an important change and one in accordance with the spirit of the times, when women are coming forward to take their share in the work and responsibility of public life.'[50] The *Courier* also pointed out that Louisa was well qualified, was supported by voters of all political shades – 'from the local ruler of the Primrose League to the most radical of our Town Councillors' – and was best placed to represent the needs and claims of female inmates. She was elected in April 1893 and attended her first meeting later that month.

The board she joined was made up of farmers, clergymen and tradesmen, several of whom were also local councillors. Louisa had encountered hostile guardians and workhouse managers previously and not been daunted or deterred. But she found the Tonbridge board intimidating initially. Perhaps this was because, unlike in Kensington, she was their first and, at this stage, only female guardian. (It was still unusual to have women in this role – out of over 20,000 guardians in England in 1893, only 119 were women.)

However, the Tonbridge board turned out to be more enlightened than many and Louisa found the majority of her colleagues ready to listen to suggestions 'which came from her womanly standpoint.' There were exceptions, though, and some of the rural guardians did not take kindly to what they saw as her 'new-fangled ideas'.

Louisa had to find a way of dealing with her male colleagues, especially those who did not want her there. She did not try to act like a man, or play on her femininity, neither of which would have suited her character, nor gone down well with the other guardians. One tactic she did use was to find allies amongst her colleagues, who would support her proposals and defend her when she came under attack. Another was to wait until she was well-informed, so that when she made observations and proposals, she could back them up. At her first meeting she was assigned to carry out the next fortnightly inspection and although, when she did, she found plenty that needed to be addressed, she confined herself to describing the facilities as 'extremely satisfactory'. After that she held frequent meetings with the master and other workhouse officials, to learn from them and ensure that, if possible, they would endorse any proposals she made.

The guardians did not make it easy for Louisa to participate fully in the board's business. They met from 11am to 1pm, and then broke for lunch. Etiquette dictated that it was inappropriate for a single lady, even one of her age, to take lunch with the male guardians, and she would leave at that point. (So she did not 'adorn the luncheon table' as the *Courier* correspondent had suggested.) To her frustration, a great proportion of each morning session was taken up with considering applications for outdoor relief (financial assistance to people not admitted to the workhouse, which rose steeply during the hop-picking season).[a] As a result, the business that interested Louisa most and which she considered to be of greatest importance – the management of the workhouse itself – was dealt with in a hurry, or postponed to the afternoon, when she was no longer present. One guardian suggested putting the lunch break back to 1.30pm, but others disagreed. The farmers amongst them had been up and working since early morning and did not want to wait any longer for their lunch. Of course the current arrangement could also have provided an opportunity for them to exclude their new colleague from discussions.

In August 1893, when she had been a guardian for some months, Louisa began to make her presence felt. At the board meeting, she proposed the appointment of a lady to visit young girls who had been placed into domestic service. This was

---

a Louisa described this as 'The Ever Open Hotel', commenting that many of the applicants were better dressed than she was.

common practice in many unions, but some of the guardians saw it as unwarranted interference and were strongly opposed, so Louisa had to withdraw her proposal. As a compromise, it was suggested she should carry out visits in a personal capacity, without the board's authorisation, and she did so on around a dozen occasions over the following months.

At a meeting in late October, guardian Thomas Manwaring challenged Louisa about these visits, which he described as objectionable and done without the board's authority. A wealthy hop farmer and owner of Marle Place (a substantial property in the nearby village of Brenchley), Manwaring was a longstanding board member. Of all the guardians he was the most hostile to Louisa. In response to his accusations, she referred to the informal agreement given at the earlier meeting. In the acrimonious debate that followed, several other guardians came to her defence. Following the meeting, Louisa continued her visits, claiming that, with only one exception, she was received 'cordially and thankfully' by mistresses of the households where the girls had been placed.

In November 1893, when she was appointed to carry out the fortnightly inspection for the second time, Louisa was feeling more confident. Instead of the usual cursory two lines in the report book, to the effect that everything was satisfactory and in good order, she wrote two whole pages of recommendations. These included installing a stove in the girls' bathroom (which was very chilly), a separate laundry for the infirmary (linen was being washed in the bathrooms) and the creation of a dining room for the nursing staff (who had to eat meals in their bedrooms). She worried that there would be a storm of opposition, but most of her suggestions were eventually carried out.

Early in 1894, the issue of visiting girls in service arose again. Louisa presented a report in which she recommended, amongst other things, visiting some and sending others to an 'industrial training home'. Thomas Manwaring launched into a lengthy attack on her proposals, which he described as 'interference', and a heated debate amongst all the guardians followed. It ended with them voting, by eleven votes to five, to allow Louisa to visit the girls on a year's trial (although the board refused to appoint a paid lady visitor).

Louisa showed an extraordinary level of energy and drive in her role as guardian, especially given her age. She was described around this time as having a 'trim, energetic figure and keen searching eyes' and as being 'acutely sympathetic, tender and kind-hearted' towards the deserving poor.[51] (She was much less sympathetic to those she considered to be undeserving.) Throughout the three years she remained in post, she constantly pressed for improvements, from major ones such as modernising buildings and employing qualified nurses in the infirmary, to minor ones, such as providing hairbrushes for residents (which helped prevent the spread of infestation and disease).

Opposition to Louisa and to her many suggestions was not as great as might have been expected. Nevertheless, she did meet with extreme hostility from some of the other guardians, especially Thomas Manwaring, who on one occasion dismissed her as an 'old lady', despite the fact that they were born in the same year. How much of this was due to her sex? It is difficult to be sure. It could have been just as much down to her being an outsider who came in and proposed changes to a workhouse which some considered did not need improving, or to the number and nature of the changes she suggested. However, Louisa certainly felt that as a woman she was treated differently. When a male guardian resigned, after attending only three meetings, she wrote:

I could not help thinking what would have been said if a woman guardian had acted thus! Truly there is in more than one department of life a different standard for men and women![52]

Board minutes cannot convey the tone of meetings and it is likely much more was said than was reported there or in the press. Louisa was extremely upset by allegations made against her and by the vitriol directed at her by Manwaring and other opponents. At a meeting on 8 June 1894, which she could not attend, the clerk read out a letter in which she responded to 'unfounded accusations' made against her at the previous meeting. These related to the arrangements she had made for several young girls to be sent to a training house in Maidstone, away from the corrupting influence of the workhouse. Louisa added in a postscript that she had seriously considered resigning, having been misunderstood and misrepresented. In the end, however, she decided to stand her ground.

When she died in 1912, at the age of 92, an obituary in the *Courier* said of Louisa's time as a poor law guardian in Tunbridge Wells:

Miss Twining proved quite capable of holding her own in debate, and her intellectual power as well as her obvious philanthropy soon earned her...the grudging respect...of those opposed to a woman venturing not only to enter their administrative sphere, but to question the wisdom of their administration... [53]

Louisa's most significant achievement in Tunbridge Wells was not the changes she brought about – they had been needed, but the workhouse was by no means among the worst in the country and improvements were not solely down to her. It was the barrier she broke through in becoming the board's first female guardian. In 1893, when she stood for election, the more conservative guardians (and other local people who did not want a female in the role) could not deny that she was well-qualified. Once appointed, she proved herself more than up to the job, making it easier for other women to follow in her footsteps.

In December 1894, the Women Guardians Association held a public meeting in the Tunbridge Wells Town Hall, on Calverley Road, to promote the election of female guardians to the Tonbridge board. Louisa and schoolteacher Anne Ludlow both spoke and a number of local councillors, clergymen and doctors attended to support them. Early the following year the two women were elected to the board, with the highest numbers of votes (which pleased their supporters, but surprised some of the older board members). From this time onwards the Tonbridge Poor Law Union always had at least two female members.

While workhouse reform was her main priority, Louisa had supported the Votes for Women campaign for many years by the time she arrived in Tunbridge Wells. Like many female reformers, she believed women had a distinctive contribution to make in politics, just as they did in the management of workhouses, schools, hospitals and prisons. Having the vote, she believed, would allow women to influence Parliament's decisions on the social issues which affected and concerned them.

In 1872, Louisa joined the committee of the National Society for Women's Suffrage, acting as their vice-president for many years, and in 1889 she signed the *Declaration in Favour of Women's Suffrage*, along with Tunbridge Wells headmistress Mary Moberly.

Suffrage campaigners frequently pointed to the fact that women such as Louisa, who held responsible positions and had achieved so much, could not vote, while illiterate and uneducated men could. In 1872, one leading suffrage campaigner wrote:

*When we find among the disfranchised such names as those
of Mrs. Somerville, Harriet Martineau, Lady Burdett Coutts,
Florence Nightingale, Mary Carpenter, Louisa Twining,
Emily Davies, and many others scarcely inferior to those in
intellectual and moral worth, we cannot but desire, for the
elevation and dignity of the parliamentary system, to add
them to the number of electors.*[54]

In October 1893, six months after she had been appointed to the
Tonbridge board, Louisa was on the platform at a meeting held in
the Sussex Assembly Rooms in Tunbridge Wells on the question
of women's suffrage. The main speaker was Millicent Fawcett.
Since listening from the Ladies' Gallery in 1867, as John Stuart
Mill proposed his amendment to the Reform Bill, Millicent had
been at the heart of the women's suffrage campaign, especially
after her husband's death in 1884. Bright-eyed and alert, she
had a small build, but an enormous strength of character. She
spoke quietly and in a dry, straightforward manner, which was
not very inspiring, but got her point across effectively. On this
occasion she pointed out that women were landowners, farmers
and employers but, while their shepherds and other employees
had the vote, they did not. It was argued that giving a woman the
vote would deprive her of her womanly qualities, she said, but
dropping a paper in a ballot box would not do so.

In July 1897, after she had finished her second term as
guardian and moved away from Tunbridge Wells, Louisa wrote
a letter to *The Times* expressing her belief that women should
have the vote. She queried why they were classed with paupers
and lunatics, as incapable of making a decision and a judgement
on matters of vital importance, and concluded:

*I can quite understand the opinion to which some still cling
that women are only meant to be the housekeepers and the*

home-managers of their children and servants, but I am
quite unable to understand or believe that a majority of the
advanced thought in England advocates such a theory.[55]

Three months later, the National Union of Women's Suffrage
Societies (NUWSS) was founded, as a loose federation of around
seventeen local associations, with Millicent Fawcett as their
leader. At the start, the NUWSS had little power and limited
funds. However, unlike previous campaigning organisations,
they would manage to avoid arguments and splits and to attract
widespread support. The NUWSS would remain at the forefront
of the Votes for Women campaign through to its conclusion.
There would not be a branch in Tunbridge Wells for some years,
however. When one was finally formed in 1908, a driving force
behind it would be Amelia Scott.

Chapter 7

A Share in Striving

The 'disgusted ladies' of Tunbridge Wells were a formidable series of women – none more so than Amelia Scott (known to her friends and family as Milly).

The Scott family moved to Southborough (on the edge of Tunbridge Wells) in 1861, a year after Amelia was born. Her father was an accountant and they were comfortably off. When she was three her father died, leaving her mother Ellen a widow with seven children aged between three months and eleven years. In 1873 Ellen married James Darnell, a Church of England minister twenty-five years older than her, and the couple moved to Canterbury. Twelve-year-old Amelia and two of her sisters stayed living in Southborough,

Amelia Scott (c1930)

Women's Library, LSE

with their aunt and grandmother, an arrangement that continued even after their mother and stepfather returned to Tunbridge Wells on his retirement a few years later. As adults Amelia and her sister Louise set up home together. They had each inherited a share of their father's estate, which meant that, although not wealthy, they could live independently and spend their time campaigning and doing good works.

In November 1892, Amelia, aged thirty-one, had an experience which proved life-changing, challenging her beliefs and prompting action. She was visiting a friend in the Bristol area when she heard that a conference was taking place nearby and decided to attend. The conference was the third one which had been organised by the National Union of Women Workers (NUWW) and its aim was to provide an opportunity for sharing information and ideas. Amelia joined around 250 other women and heard talks from some of the country's foremost female philanthropists on ways of helping the disadvantaged. A key theme was the distinctive role women had to play. It is possible that she also attended a meeting which took place in a private home, alongside the official conference programme, where Millicent Fawcett spoke on women's suffrage. Men would not listen to women unless they got the vote, Millicent said, and having the vote would give support and impetus to the areas of work covered in the main conference sessions.

What Amelia heard in Bristol, from a series of inspiring speakers, challenged her view of the world. She would later write: 'In those days in Tunbridge Wells, we lived in our own small self-satisfied circles, both in religion, politics and class.'[56]

Even an affluent town such as Tunbridge Wells had areas of poor housing and households living in poverty, and in the late nineteenth century there were numerous local societies working to help (and often improve) the poor. The Mendicity Society, for example, aimed to keep beggars off the streets, by offering assistance to those in genuine need and exposing fraudsters. The Girls Friendly Society gave practical help to unmarried girls and young women, as well as encouraging them to live moral lives. However, these societies were not working well together, which led Amelia and other women to decide that a local branch of the NUWW was needed, to co-ordinate those which were run by and supporting women.

On 16 May 1895, Amelia and her sister held a drawing room meeting at their home on Belvedere Terrace, attended by representatives of around fourteen different societies working across Tunbridge Wells. Louisa Twining took the chair and Emily Janes, national organising secretary of the NUWW, spoke. 'Women have been called the reserve force of humanity,' she said. 'It is time they took their share in striving to solve some of the many problems of our complex civilisation.'[57] At the end of the meeting the names of anyone interested in forming a local NUWW branch were collected. When it was established, a couple of months later, Louisa was appointed as president and Amelia as honorary secretary. The Tunbridge Wells organisation joined a network of around thirty local societies, each with their own rules and character but united by a common purpose: 'to promote the social, moral and religious welfare of women.'

A few months later, on 25 November, the new branch held a 'social gathering' (more like a conference) at the town hall, which was attended by almost 200 women. Louisa was in the chair again and representatives from a wide range of charitable organisations attended, as well as individual women, including Agnes Drummond (the Brabazon Scheme organiser who had promoted Louisa Twining's appointment as a poor law guardian).

Louisa opened the meeting, welcoming the NUWW's potential to promote co-operation between the numerous local private charities and the Poor Law Union. The first task the

branch set themselves was to compile a list of charities working
in the town and tackle the duplication between their activities.
For example, it had been identified that there were at least sixteen
different mothers' meetings and one woman was even said to be
receiving assistance from five of them at the same time.

Emily Janes, back in Tunbridge Wells again, spoke next and
highlighted the NUWW's aims, which included:

> *To enable existing societies to co-operate with each other, or
> at the very least to learn of each other's existence and modes
> of usefulness...[and]...to increase knowledge, to cultivate a
> habit of careful consideration and to make our alms-giving
> less a matter of often self-indulgent feeling and more a matter
> of true and thoughtful charity.*[58]

Over a period of six months during 1897, Amelia and five other
local NUWW members travelled up to London once a week, to
do social work training at the Southwark office of the Charity
Organisation Society (COS). Years later she would speak about
one of the people she encountered during that period:

> *...a working woman I had the honour to know, who kept
> herself, a drunken husband and five children by collar-stitching
> for a factory in Bermondsey. The collars were a speciality used
> by Eton boys. By working her hardest she could only earn 2/6d
> a day. She died of a terrible disease brought on by sitting for
> such long hours together.*[59]

By December 1899, the Tunbridge Wells NUWW branch
had 125 members, who between them represented fifty-six
local societies. Their annual conference, held that month, was
addressed by Edith Lyttleton, a member of the national executive
committee, who spoke on women in local government. She

called on her audience to 'insist that women shall take what part they may in local government... as poor law guardians, urban district, rural district and parish councillors.'[60]

At the end of 1900, Amelia and her sister Louise, along with local Quaker businesswoman Sarah Candler, set up the 'Leisure Hour Club for Young Women in Business' at a small house on Upper Grosvenor Road. The club's purpose was to provide girls of fifteen and older who were working in shops, factories and laundries with 'amusement and relaxation when the business of the day is done.' A subscription of 1s per quarter was charged and the entertainment on offer included singing, needlework and basket work (in the winter) and collecting wild flowers, cottage gardening and outdoor pursuits (in the summer).

In 1901, on Louisa Twining's advice, Amelia followed in her footsteps and joined the Tonbridge Union as a poor law guardian. Many years later she would write of the impact the role had on her:

Here [in the maternity ward] we women guardians often stood face to face with tragedy about human life before which our own protected and sheltered lives cried out against any conceit or pride in our own virtue.[61]

Her experiences as a guardian challenged her prejudices and informed her views, some of which were unconventional for a middle-class churchgoer. Amelia wrote of two lessons she learned from her experiences with unmarried mothers at the workhouse:

The first, that the girl who has a child and loves it is worlds removed from the immoral girl who knows how to prevent motherhood and deliberately evades it. And the second –

that the shades of guiltiness are so varied that no sweeping accusation can be made by us fellow mortals.[62]

A key aim of the NUWW and its members (nationally and locally) was to support women in taking on public roles such as poor law guardian, local councillor, sanitary inspector or prison officer, which had previously been restricted to men. In Tunbridge Wells there were other women, as well as Louisa and Amelia, who moved into new areas of work around the turn of the century.

When Relieving Officer Frank Hoptroff (who was responsible for collecting the poor law rates in parts of Tunbridge Wells) died in 1890, his forty-six-year-old widow Ellen was one of ten candidates to replace him (she had already been doing the job for some time, during her husband's illness). Ellen, who was described as 'a highly respectable and a good woman in every sense of the word,' was given the job and continued in the post until 1909.[63] (This was in addition to looking after their eleven children, who were aged from three to nineteen when she was widowed, and succeeding her husband as licensee at the Greyhound public house in Langton Green.)

In 1895, fifty-five-year-old Jane Escombe was elected as a parish councillor in Penshurst (a village near Tunbridge Wells) a year after the Local Government Act first allowed women to become parish and district councillors. Jane conducted a vigorous campaign to get houses for working people built locally, piling pressure on private landlords, the Sevenoaks Rural Development Council[a] and Kent County Council, who all constantly blocked her efforts. Eventually she wore them down and six houses were completed in December 1900. Jane was also the driving force behind the campaign for a local isolation hospital and succeeded in securing a clean water supply for her village.

---

a Although Penshurst is close to Tunbridge Wells, it lies within Sevenoaks District.

When the first higher and primary education committees were established in Tunbridge Wells, following the 1902 Education Act, they had four female members: Anne Ludlow (who had been elected as a poor law guardian, along with Louisa), Mary Whitrow (a former head teacher), Mary Louisa Bishop and Edith Abbott.

The increasing involvement of women in public life made not having the vote even more of an anomaly and NUWW members such as Amelia became increasingly frustrated by this situation. On 8 May 1905, Amelia attended a public debate on the subject of Votes for Women which was organised by the local NUWW branch and held in the Christ Church parish room. The speaker, prominent Scottish suffrage campaigner Lady Frances Balfour, said that, despite the advances in women's rights since the 1866 petition, 'a woman owning property in three counties, and considered fit to present thirty livings… has not the responsibility which is granted to her gardener and her dustman.'[64] However, she also pointed out that all the political parties had women's branches and women were being used for canvassing at election time, sometimes venturing into rough areas where men would not go.

The next speaker, a Mrs Wilson Lloyd, argued the case against women having the vote. Women already had more power and influence than they would get through the vote, she said. In any case, they did not want it; she travelled round the country a great deal and rarely heard the subject mentioned at all. The *Courier* reported that she continued by outlining some of the other main arguments put forward against women's suffrage:

Woman was created to be a helpmeet for man, not his rival, and she could not be this if she insisted on having the same rights. Women were too carried away by feeling. If the suffrage were universal, as there were more women than men, the

government of the country would practically be in the hands
of women...it would cause great unhappiness in families;
husband and wife, parents and children, would vote against
one another. Women were not as a rule the breadwinners, or
heads of households, and they ought not to have the vote.[65]

In the debate that followed, Amelia spoke up in support of Votes
for Women. She said that her experiences in her social work
training and as a poor law guardian had changed her view on
women's suffrage and convinced her that women should have
a say in laws relating to morality. This meeting proved to be
another turning point for her (leading on from her experience
thirteen years earlier in Bristol) and she later described her
contribution to the debate as a 'public confession' in support
of the cause. Her use of religious language indicated both the
strength of her views, and the beliefs that influenced them.
When a vote was taken at the end of the meeting, only a few
of those present voted, with twenty-seven in favour of women
having the vote and eight against.

This was also a significant time in the national campaign,
when it moved up a gear and became more visible. In autumn
1906, when the NUWW held their annual conference in
Tunbridge Wells, it would prove a significant event, focussing
attention on women's suffrage and challenging some of the
individual women who attended.

Chapter 8

The Tide Turns

When a general election was called for January 1906, members of the Tunbridge Wells Women's Liberal Association (WLA) campaigned enthusiastically for their party's candidate, thirty-nine-year-old Alfred Paget Hedges, owner of the Benson and Hedges cigarette company. Around one hundred women, in Tunbridge Wells, Southborough and Pembury, did clerical work, distributed leaflets and canvassed door to door. They had a major task on their hands – the town had been represented by Conservative MPs for the past fifty years.

The Liberal women were campaigning on behalf of a candidate they would not be able to vote for on Election Day. However, they were hopeful that, if a Liberal government was elected, it would do something to change that situation. After all, women's suffrage was in line with the party's commitment to equality and democracy and many of their MPs, including Alfred Hedges, had previously pledged support. On 8 January, a deputation from the Tunbridge Wells WLA went to see Alfred, to hold him to his promise. Both the women and the candidate took great pains to disassociate themselves from

the extreme methods which some campaigners had begun
to adopt. Alfred said that in his view these had resulted in a
severe setback for the cause and deterred previously lukewarm
supporters.

Conservative Arthur Griffith-Boscawen, who had been the
town's MP for the past fourteen years, took a different position
from Alfred on the issue of suffrage, claiming that he was not
in favour of 'any further tinkering with the suffrage.'[66] The
Conservative women of Tunbridge Wells do not seem to have
canvassed activelyon his behalf. (Perhaps they assumed the
result was a foregone conclusion and Tunbridge Wells would
elect their party's candidate as usual).

When the election results were announced, on 19 January,
the Liberal Party had won a landslide victory. With the
support of his female canvassers, Alfred had been elected as
MP for Tunbridge Wells by the substantial majority of 1,283 (a
significant swing from the previous Tory majority of just over
2,000). Local Liberals celebrated his victory with a torchlight
procession around the town and surrounding villages, with
the MP and his wife transported in a carriage pulled by male
supporters. In a speech on 25 January, Alfred reaffirmed his
commitment to women's suffrage, declaring that, as members
of a community, women should have a voice in representing it.
It was absurd, he said, for the government to appoint women
as officials, but allow them no voice in electing the government
itself.

The first clue that campaigners' optimism had been misplaced
and that the Liberal Party might not give women the vote came on
19 February, when there was no mention of it in the King's Speech.
Then in early March, the Franchise and Removal of Women's
Disabilities Bill, which had been tabled by MP Charles Dilke, was

talked out before it could be referred for its second reading.[a]

In the same month, a commentator in the *Advertiser's* 'Current Comments' column suggested that Alfred Hedges might not be going to deliver the support for women's suffrage some of his constituents had hoped for. 'If I were elected MP,' ran the article, 'I should adopt Mr Hedge's plan of campaign. I should say nice graceful things [to women's suffrage campaigners] and support the principle, but when I got returned, I should keep a free hand, and go by the merits of the arguments in the House. And they might be against it!'[67]

The *Advertiser's* commentator considered most MPs would not vote for women's suffrage. He himself was not confident in women's ability to understand, or take an interest in, political issues like taxation. 'The great majority,' he pronounced, 'take more interest in Blouses and Babies than Politics.'[68]

When he spoke at a WLA reception held at the Great Hall in early April, Alfred did not mention suffrage specifically, although he thanked the Liberal ladies for the work they had done during the election and were prepared to do in the future. The chair of the meeting, however, expressed the hope that women would be voting at the next election and the ladies themselves continued to be optimistic. The WLA's 1906 annual report (which was presented at the same meeting) commented positively on the election success, on their new MP's commitment to women's suffrage and on having a government in power 'inspired by a new spirit and new ideals and led by a prime minister in whom we have absolute confidence.'[69]

---

a A bill's first reading is its formal introduction to the House of Commons. The second reading is the first opportunity that MPs have to debate its main principles and vote on it. The bill then proceeds to committee stage, where detailed examination takes place. Most bills are dealt with in a Public Bill Committee (previously Standing Committee). However, a small minority are referred to a Committee of the Whole House, in which case the committee stage consists of a debate by all MPs on the floor of the House of Commons. The report stage and third reading follow, after which a bill goes through the same steps in the House of Lords.

In May 1906, when a deputation of around 400 women representing the main national suffrage organisations went to see the new Prime Minister, they were disappointed. Henry Campbell-Bannerman conceded that their case was 'conclusive and irrefutable' but, with his cabinet divided on the issue of women's suffrage, he could not give them any commitment. All he could do, he said, was advise them to carry on pestering and to exercise the virtue of patience.[70] It appeared he was afraid (just as William Gladstone had been back in 1884) that, if property-owning women were given the vote, they were likely to use it for the Conservative Party.

It was against this background of disillusionment with the Liberal Party and its failure to deliver Votes for Women, as had been widely hoped, that the National Union of Women Workers (NUWW) held their annual conference in Tunbridge Wells in October 1906.

Amelia Scott and the other ladies of the Tunbridge Wells branch, one of the most active in the country, were delighted when their offer to host the conference was accepted. In the months leading up to the event, they suspended all other activities to concentrate on making arrangements for the 400 or so delegates who were expected. They set up committees, booked the Opera House and opened a temporary office just round the corner, in the Colonnade on Monson Road. A total of 174 hosts were found, to provide accommodation for delegates, fifty-four stewards recruited and arrangements made for light refreshments, literature stalls and floral decorations. A programme was printed and distributed as widely as possible, and tickets were sold – 3/6 for delegates and 4/- for non-delegates. The task was a huge one; it was reported later that in the four months leading up to the conference, office volunteers sent out 1,694 letters and 2,800 postcards.

Opera House, Tunbridge Wells
© *The Author*

On the morning of Monday 22 October, delegates took their seats for the opening session. The Opera House, which had been constructed four years earlier, was an ornate theatre, with light blue and gold mouldings, deep crimson upholstery and burnished brass light fittings. With seating for 1,200 people, it was used mainly for entertainments – pantomimes and matinees of London plays, for example. A month before the conference, the Moody-Manners opera company had staged eight different operas there in one week, including *Carmen*, *The Marriage of Figaro* and *Tannhauser*.

Attendance was good and the stalls, boxes and dress circle were soon full. The chairwoman Edith Griffith-Boscawen (local NUWW president and wife of the Tory MP who had lost his seat earlier in the year) welcomed delegates to Tunbridge Wells and called on them to realise the influence they held in the universe. Even in this first session, Votes for Women featured. In her opening speech the NUWW's national president referred to suffrage campaigners' disappointment at not receiving more immediate help or redress from the Liberal government. She also made a sideways swipe at women who were adopting more militant methods, saying 'some women, feeling desperate, have taken an unusual method of showing their fitness for responsibility and their capacity for wise decisions.'[71] Although she recognised the strength of feeling driving them:

> *Women are charged with all the responsibilities and anxieties of citizenship, yet without political power to protect them, and to assert their rights, they are bound, in their weakness, to be driven to the wall.*[72]

The conference proceeded, with a series of sessions on subjects such as 'The Domestic Servant Problem' and 'Parental Control and the Development of Individuality within the Home' (in which the speaker advocated that all girls should be brought up to earn their own living). However, there was soon a distraction for delegates, when word began to arrive from London of a protest which had been mounted by members of the Women's Social and Political Union (WSPU).

The WSPU had been established in Manchester in 1903, with the motto 'Deeds Not Words.' Its members were frustrated that it was taking so long for women to get the vote and did not believe the passive approach that campaigners had adopted so far was ever going to succeed. They soon began to attract members and their charismatic leaders, Emmeline Pankhurst and her daughter Christabel, inspired hero worship and devotion.

At first the WSPU campaigned by peaceful methods. However, in October 1905 Christabel and former millworker Annie Kenney were thrown out of a Liberal Party meeting at Manchester's Free Trade Hall, arrested, charged with assault and imprisoned in Strangeways for three days. From that time on, the organisation's campaigning methods became increasingly militant. They disrupted meetings, heckled government ministers and protested in the streets. In return they were manhandled by the police, taken to court and imprisoned when they refused to pay fines. In January 1906 the *Daily Mail* described WSPU members as 'suffragettes.' It was meant as an insult, rather than as a compliment, but the women treated it as a badge of honour and started using the term themselves.

Through 1906, as it became clear the new Liberal government was not going to give women the vote, the WSPU stepped up their campaign still further. On the afternoon of Tuesday 23 October (the first day of the new parliamentary session and the second day of the Tunbridge Wells conference) a group of suffragettes mounted a protest in the Central Lobby at the Houses of Parliament – waving flags, climbing onto benches and making speeches. They were ejected, shrieking and screaming, and continued their protest outside. The police arrested ten women, including Adela Pankhurst (Emmeline's youngest daughter), and charged them with insulting or threatening behaviour likely to lead to a breach of the peace. On Wednesday morning they appeared in Westminster Police Court, where they were fined £5 and bound over for good behaviour. On refusing to pay their fines, they were sentenced to two months in prison. There was widespread shock at the unprecedented length of their sentences. (Although one MP wrote to the *London Daily News* to protest at the magistrate's leniency, which he said was 'as good as encouragement to them to repeat their scandalous misconduct.')[73]

Down in Tunbridge Wells, NUWW delegates would have heard about these events by word of mouth and read some of the extensive coverage in the daily newspapers. *The Times* described the Central Lobby protest as a 'disorderly scene' which 'had something of the nature of a tumult.' The headline of the *Pall Mall Gazette's* account of the court hearing was 'Pandemonium in the Police Court.' Interest in the issue of Votes for Women, which had already been considerable, was heightened. When Thursday's session on that subject began, every seat in the Opera House was taken and the orchestra pit filled with newspaper reporters.

Millicent Garrett Fawcett was in the chair. She opened by saying it was of 'little use the state appealing to women, when it treated them as below the felon, the pauper, and the lunatic with regard to the franchise.' For women to try and bring about change without the benefit of the vote, she said, was 'like pulling at a bellrope without a bell at the other end.' Millicent referred to the advice the Prime Minister had given the delegation back in May, that women should be patient. 'I don't think patience is what we need,' she said. 'We have been working for forty years… it is time something more was done to rouse the House of Commons and the Country to the importance of the subject.'[74]

After two papers on women's suffrage had been read, delegates were invited to contribute to the discussion. All heads turned as Elizabeth Robins, a well-known American actress and novelist, stepped onto the Opera House stage. She had been shocked to discover that women at the conference were accepting press accounts of the suffragettes, she said, when she knew these to be completely untrue. When she had met these women in the past, she had found them to be earnest, sincere and self-sacrificing. In addition, she had been in court the previous day and none of the accused had been wild or hysterical, as had been reported in the press.

Millicent brought the session to a close, saying that it was against NUWW rules to send an official message of sympathy to the protestors, but please would Elizabeth convey the tone of the meeting to them?

The following morning, Amelia and members of her committee took down the floral arrangements, cleared the refreshment tables, packed away any unsold pamphlets and vacated the Opera House. By evening, the venue had reverted to its usual form of entertainment, with a production of the comedy *Pilkerton's Peerage*, staged by an amateur theatre company.

The conference was generally considered to have been a great success. (A few months later the committee presented Amelia with an opal pendant, in recognition of her hard work organising it.) It also seems to have been a significant point in the national Votes for Women movement. Amelia would later write about a chance meeting she had with Millicent Garrett Fawcett in a London square, long after the conference, when the campaign leader said to her:

> *I felt I must speak to you for I want to tell you that I always felt that meeting in the Opera House at [Tunbridge Wells] was of historical value in the history of the granting the vote to women. Until then I felt we were rowing against the tide; but at that great meeting I knew that the tide had turned, and that we should win.*[75]

The conference was also a turning point for some individual women who were present. Journalist Evelyn Sharp, sent by the *Manchester Guardian* to report on proceedings, had been especially affected by Elizabeth Robins' words and soon became one of the WSPU's most active members. She would later write: 'The impression she made was profound… From that moment I was not to know again for twelve years, if indeed ever again, what it meant to cease from mental strife…'[76]

Some Tunbridge Wells women had also been stirred to action, although the non-militant approach of the NUWSS (National Union of Women's Suffrage Societies) had more appeal for them. A few weeks later, a letter appeared in the *Courier*, which read:

...to convince Parliament and the public that women are really anxious to obtain the Suffrage, a committee has been formed in Tunbridge Wells. Its object is to receive the signatures of women employed in various forms of work, who resent the injustice of being excluded from a voice in the government of the country.[77]

Signatories to the letter included Amelia Scott, seventy-three-year-old Laura Crompton Jones (who had attended the first local suffrage meeting over thirty years earlier), poor law guardian Anne Ludlow and two of the other women who sat with her on the town's education committee.

Over the next few months, the petition, which included the words: 'I am desirous that women should vote at Parliamentary Elections on the same terms as men,' was made available for signing at shops and other places, across the town. The signatures collected were sent to London and incorporated into a national petition compiled by the NUWSS, which eventually had 250,000 signatures.

The Tunbridge Wells suffrage committee seems to have existed specifically to promote the petition and nothing was done to set up a local NUWSS branch at this stage, although occasional Votes for Women meetings were held over the next couple of years.

Nationally, however, the NUWSS was becoming increasingly active and visible. On 9 February 1907, around 3,000 women, representing forty societies from all over the country, marched from Hyde Park to Exeter Hall on the Strand, with Millicent Garrett Fawcett at their head. The banners they carried reflected the NUWSS's non-confrontational approach. 'Gentle but Resolute,' read one, and 'We Appeal to Reason,' another. (There is no record of any Tunbridge Wells women taking part, although it seems likely some did. The Tunbridge Wells WLA were still campaigning actively on Votes for Women and may have marched with other members of their organisation.)

Rain poured down on the procession, which stretched for half a mile and was soon nicknamed 'The Mud March', due to the state of the participants' shoes and skirts by the end. All of London looked on as they passed – cabbies waiting for fares, ladies doing their shopping, club members on their balconies, drinkers standing outside public houses. This was the first time middle-class women had appeared on the streets en masse and it took courage to risk their reputations and expose themselves to being ridiculed or sworn at. The general appearance of the march, however, was impressive and dignified.

When the NUWSS organised a further march the following year, on 13 June 1908, Amelia Scott took part as a representative of the NUWW and carried one of their banners from the Embankment to the Albert Hall. She later recalled that, as the procession paused on Piccadilly, a man on a crowded omnibus shook his fist at her and called out, 'Who'll mend my socks?' There may have been other local members NUWW and of the WLA taking part in that march as well as Amelia.

THE SCENE INSIDE THE ALBERT HALL

NUWSS Rally at the Albert Hall (photo from *The Sphere*)
© *Royal Albert Hall*

Suffragist leaders addressed the marchers from the Albert
Hall platform, which was decorated with banners to the rear
and flowers to the front. Lady Frances Balfour (who had visited
Tunbridge Wells three years earlier) described the prime minister
as 'squeezable.' Millicent Fawcett said '[the march] brings within
measurable distance the day of our final triumph.' When she had
finished speaking, thirty or so local societies presented her with
bouquets, in tribute to her forty years' service to the cause, and
the organ accompanied everyone present in a rendition of 'For
He's A Jolly Good Fellow.'

Finally, in October 1908, a Tunbridge Wells NUWSS branch
was formed. Amelia was appointed vice-president and their
president was novelist Sarah Grand.

Chapter 9

A New Woman

Sarah Grand was born in 1854, in County Down, Ireland, and christened Frances Clarke. Her father, an English naval lieutenant, died when she was seven, after which her mother moved the family to Yorkshire. As a teenager, Frances attended the Royal Navy School in Twickenham, where she formed a club to support Josephine Butler's campaign against the Contagious Diseases Acts. These allowed the police to arrest women in ports and army towns suspected of being prostitutes and subject them to compulsory checks for venereal disease (while taking no action against the men involved). A well

Sarah Grand (1916)
© *National Portrait Gallery, London*

brought up girl was not expected to be aware of such a subject, let alone speak up on it, and Frances's campaign was followed by a sudden exit from school. (Although she later claimed she had not been expelled.)

In 1870, after spending a short time at a finishing school in Kensington, sixteen-year-old Frances escaped an unhappy home life by marrying army surgeon David Chambers McFall, a widower with two sons, who was almost twenty years older than her. The couple had another son, Archie, and spent several years travelling in the Far East, returning to England in 1879.

Frances said that her life at this time was aimless and empty, but that this drove her back to the writing she had loved as a child and led her to write her first novel, *Ideala*. In 1888, having been unable to find a publisher, she paid for it to be published herself (an experience she described as both interesting and useful). The plot, which concerned a woman in an unhappy marriage, reflected her own experience and in 1890, once she had received income from book sales, Frances left her husband and moved to London. (Just twenty years earlier the option would not have been open to her, or certainly not as easy, as any money she earned would have been paid to her husband. However, the 1870 Married Women's Property Act had changed the law, so that women could keep the money they earned or inherited.)

Frances's estranged husband was not happy that his surname had been associated with *Ideala* and its subject matter, so when she published her next novel, in 1893, she did so under the name 'Madame Sarah Grand.' From that time onwards this was the name she was known by. *Heavenly Twins* was the book that established Sarah's reputation as an author and gave her a certain amount of financial security. It told the story of Edith Beale, who contracted syphilis from her naval officer husband, and challenged the double standard by which women alone were blamed for the spread of venereal disease. Another of the book's female characters, Evadne Frayling, reflected on women's lives:

> But that remark of her father's about "all that women are fit for", which he kept well watered from time to time with other conventional expressions of a contemptuous kind...set her mind off on a long and patient inquiry into the condition and capacity of women...by degrees, as her reading extended, it changed its form, and then she asked herself doubtfully: "Are women such inferior beings?" a position which carried her in front of her father at once by a hundred years, and led her rapidly on to the final conclusion that women had originally no congenital defect of inferiority, and that, although they have still much way to make up, it now rests with themselves to be inferior or not, as they choose.[78]

The Heavenly Twins' controversial subject matter meant Sarah had great difficulty finding a publisher. One of those she approached told her no respectable house would touch it and another that it would cause ladies great pain. However, eventually Heinemann agreed to take it on. Reviews were mixed. The book was widely criticised for being too long and over-earnest and received reviews along the lines of one that denounced it as 'a product of hysteria and wilful eccentricity, with something more than a savour of indelicacy'.[79] But it was also described as 'fascinating for all its faults'. The reading public agreed with the latter assessment and *The Heavenly Twins* soon became a bestseller; within a year it had been reprinted six times and had sold over 20,000 copies. This was very similar to the level of sales achieved by another controversial book, published a year earlier – Thomas Hardy's *Tess of the D'Urbervilles*.

As well as telling the stories of women in unhappy marriages, Sarah's novels depicted a new type of woman, who was educated, independent and could earn her own living (if she wanted or needed to). In her journalism, Sarah was the first to use the term 'new woman'. In the March 1894 issue of the *North American Review*, she observed that:

> *The new woman… has been sitting apart in silent contemplation all these years thinking and thinking, until at last she solved the problem and proclaimed for herself what was wrong with 'Home-is-the-Woman's-Sphere' and prescribed the remedy.*[80]

Soon newspapers, magazines and books were full of references to the new woman and other novels were written which featured her. Reactions were both favourable and unfavourable. In many people's eyes, a woman who spoke in public, took up political causes, undertook higher education and entered traditionally male professions, was doing all this at the cost of home life and was therefore unfeminine and improper.

The new woman was ridiculed by those who saw her as mannish, man-hating and man-eating. *The Times* observed that the distinguishing feature of the 'new women' novels was the very poor figure that man cut in them. In May 1894, *Punch* magazine published a nursery rhyme on the subject.

> *There is a New Woman, and what do you think?*
> *She lives on nothing but Foolscap and Ink!*
> *But, though Foolscap and Ink form the whole of her diet,*
> *This nagging New Woman can never be quiet!*[81]

However, Sarah wrote later that one of her chief sources of pride was how her original new woman had 'helped women free themselves from the stupid shackles of the brayers and shouters of the opposite sex and of her own.'[82]

In 1896, Sarah visited Tunbridge Wells for the first time,

when she took a suite of rooms at the Spa Hotel on Mount Ephraim to work on *The Beth Book,* which was published the following year. Like *The Heavenly Twins*, this book covered the subject of venereal disease, with the heroine (Beth) discovering that her husband was employed at the local Lock hospital.[a] It was a semi-autobiographical work and the fictional doctor's circumstances, character, and even name, seemed to indicate he was based on Sarah's real-life husband, giving a clue as to the nature of the relationship she had left. Nevertheless, despite the difficulty of her own marriage, she continued to believe strongly in the institution. After similar experiences to the author's, Beth said: 'My ideal in life is love in marriage and loyal friends.'[83]

In 1898, after the death of her estranged husband, Sarah, now aged forty-four, moved to live in Langton Green on the edge of Tunbridge Wells, accompanied by her stepson and a friend. Newspapers reported her as saying she appreciated the pure country air, which had a beneficial effect on her writing, enabling her to write as much in a month there as she did in three months when in London. It was a relief to settle down; she had been constantly on the move over the eighteen months she was writing *The Beth Book.*

Sarah's new home provided her with a base, but she was in demand as a public speaker (and needed income), so she was often away on tour, in England, Europe and America. Occasionally she gave talks in her home town. In March 1900 she delivered one of her popular lectures at a meeting in the Great Hall organised by the Pleasant Sunday Afternoon Movement.[b] Sarah, an elegant woman with a pale complexion, soft brown hair and grey-blue eyes, spoke with a low and melodious voice on the subject 'Mere Man'. A *Courier* reporter began their

---

a Lock hospitals specialised in treating venereal diseases.
b The Pleasant Sunday Afternoon Movement was a non-conformist initiative to provide improving activities on Sundays.

account of her talk by praising her superb word pictures, dry humour, perfect English and easy grace. She spoke fluently for well over an hour and the audience, mainly women, hung on her words. She touched on what she saw as men's best and worst characteristics and their various attitudes towards women – which could be condescending, grovelling, or social and generous. Overall, she said, she had always found 'mere man' an excellent comrade, who had stood by her resolutely.

Given her high profile (in Tunbridge Wells and beyond), her views on women and her known commitment to women's suffrage, Sarah was an obvious choice as president for the town's first suffrage society when it was formed in October 1908 and, together with Amelia Scott, she would be a key figure in its activities over the next few years.

The two women made an unlikely partnership – one an author of controversial novels who had left her husband, the other a devout churchgoer and committed philanthropist who never married. They also moved in different social circles, although occasionally their paths crossed; in 1903 and 1904 both were present at receptions held by the mayor and in 1906 Sarah was a member of the organising committee for the NUWW (National Union of Women Workers) conference, which Amelia headed. In March 1907 Sarah shared her experiences of Votes for Women campaigns in other countries, at a drawing room meeting on women's suffrage which Amelia probably attended.

Given their different backgrounds and lifestyles, it is unlikely Amelia and Sarah ever became friends and they seem to have remained on formal terms throughout the twelve years they worked together on the local campaign for the vote. However, they had much in common. They both believed that women had an important role to play in society, they had the same fundamental attitudes on morality and they shared a strong commitment to campaigning for the vote by peaceful means.

They also proved to be a formidable combination. Amelia was an organiser and administrator, who added the NUWSS (National Union of Women's Suffrage Societies) to her many other commitments (including as poor law guardian and as an officer of the NUWW, Charity Organisation Society and Leisure Hour Club committees). Sarah made a good figurehead for the local suffragists, but she also regularly chaired and spoke at their meetings.

Through the work of women such as Amelia and Sarah, the national NUWSS continued to grow and extend its non-violent campaign across the country. At the same time, while its membership was much smaller, the militant WSPU (Women's Social and Political Union) was attracting more attention and generating more press coverage. Some younger women in Tunbridge Wells were drawn to their more active approach and a number of them, including sisters Dorothy and May Le Lacheur, attended the organisation's first major rally, when it was held in Hyde Park in the summer of 1908.

Chapter 10

A Magnificent Moving Colour Scheme

In the mid-nineteenth century Matilda Biggs, her cigar-smoking sisters and her daughter Caroline campaigned in support of Votes for Women and other causes. In the early twentieth century the Pankhurst women – the formidable Emmeline and her daughters, Christabel, Sylvia and Adela – were founders and leaders of the militant WSPU (Women's Social and Political Union). At around the same time, Tunbridge Wells had its own family of activists – the Le Lacheurs.

Lydia Le Lacheur[a] and her husband John moved to Tunbridge Wells from Guernsey in around 1879. John was a coffee trader with interests in shipping and insurance, who had also spent many years as Costa Rica's consul-general in London. The couple's new home was 'The Wilderness' on Pembury Road, an eleven-bedroomed gothic-style mansion with extensive grounds and views over the countryside. Lydia and John became

---

a Lydia is a shadowy figure today, compared to some of the other 'disgusted ladies'; no photograph of her is available and there is no record of her words.

involved in the life of Tunbridge Wells and especially in the Congregational Church; in 1889 they funded the building of a new chapel in Hawkenbury, on the edge of town, in memory of their eldest son, who had died a few years earlier. They were a relatively wealthy family; at the 1901 census their household included a cook, two housemaids, a kitchen maid, a parlour maid and a groom.

Lydia and John had twelve children – nine daughters and three sons.[a] In common with the Ashursts (Matilda Biggs' parents) and with Matilda and Joseph Biggs, the Le Lacheurs raised their daughters to be strong, independent women. Two of them studied at Cambridge and several went into business.

Lydia and Nelly, her second eldest daughter, were members the local Women's Liberal Association (WLA) from the time it was founded in 1890. After John Le Lacheur died suddenly in 1904, from an asthma-related illness, Lydia became more actively involved. With her older children having left home, and a number of servants, including a nursemaid who was employed to look after her youngest daughter Mabel (who had learning disabilities), she had more free time. In 1906 she and Nelly took part in the WLA election campaign and they were both members of the delegation that visited Alfred Hedges, once he had been elected as MP, to ensure he remained committed to women's suffrage.

Despite setbacks in March 1906, when Charles Dilke's bill was talked out, and in May 1906, when Prime Minister Henry Campbell-Bannerman advised women's suffrage campaigners to be patient, women such as Lydia and Nelly continued to hope. In their 1907 annual report, the Tunbridge Wells WLA said:

We believe that, notwithstanding some cause for discouragement, the justice of women's claim to the suffrage

---

a The Le Lacheurs' daughter Amy died in 1866, when she was only three, and their son Brealey died in 1884 at the age of 19.

*is more widely acknowledged than ever before, and that the
day is not far distant when women will share with men the
privileges as well as the duties of citizenship.*[84]

Early in 1908, it seemed possible that this optimism was justified;
there had been a majority of MPs in favour of giving women
the vote for some years and when Henry Stanger put forward a
private member's bill in February, it passed its second reading by
a clear majority of 271 to 92 votes.

However, the bill did not progress any further. Still fearing
that if women were given the vote they would use it for the
Conservative Party, the Liberal government referred it to a
Committee of the Whole House. This meant it was effectively
put on hold and would have to wait until there was time available
for the House of Commons to debate it. Then in April the
prospect of women getting the vote suffered a further setback.
Henry Campbell-Bannerman, who had been suffering from ill
health, resigned as Prime Minister and was replaced by Herbert
Asquith, who was strongly opposed to women's suffrage. On 21
May, Asquith told a deputation of Liberal MPs that he would
not give Stanger's bill any support and required evidence that
women wanted the vote.

The WSPU decided to organise their first large-scale rally,
to send Asquith and other MPs a clear message that women did
want the vote, very much indeed. It would take place in Hyde
Park on 21 June and would be an impressive and unprecedented
spectacle – 'a magnificent moving colour scheme, never before
seen in London's streets'[85] – making it impossible for the prime
minister to ignore their arguments. Only the NUWSS (National
Union of Women's Suffrage Societies) Mud March, back in
February 1907, had done anything similar, and this would be on
an even larger scale.

The WSPU leaders recognised the importance of spectacle

and the day's events were carefully stage-managed. New colours were introduced – purple for dignity, green for hope and white for purity – and suffragettes who would be attending the rally were instructed to display them in the form of sashes, badges and rosettes. They were also told to dress in as fetching, charming and ladylike a manner as possible. The WSPU were anxious to counter the impression that their members were drab and unfeminine, an image the press had conveyed in the early days of the campaign. According to an article in their newspaper, *Votes for Women*, 'pictures of women with short hair, billycock hats, and other article of masculine attire were paraded as another argument against women having the vote'.[86]

A huge amount of organisation was undertaken – planning the programme, printing tickets, briefing local branches, recruiting stewards and liaising with the police and the park authorities. The event was also advertised as widely as possible; across London members pasted up posters, distributed handbills, chalked messages on pavements and canvassed door-to-door. Away from London, in places such as Tunbridge Wells, WSPU supporters began publicising the rally and making arrangements to attend it.

Recent setbacks in progress towards getting the vote had drawn more women towards the militant approach of the WSPU. Three of the Le Lacheur sisters – Kate, Dorothy and May – apparently came to the conclusion that the non-militant approach adopted by the WLA and NUWSS (and favoured by their mother and older sister) would never succeed. Far from being a hindrance, as some claimed, they believed that militant action was essential. Over the past year, each of the three sisters had made generous donations to the WSPU. By 1908, Kate had moved away from Tunbridge Wells, but Dorothy (26) and May (23) now began to get more involved in its local campaign.

Dorothy wrote a letter which was published in the
Courier, announcing that a special train had been arranged to
take marchers up to London. 'This demonstration has been
organised,' she wrote, 'in order to show the government that the
movement for the enfranchisement of women is supported by
the women of the country.'[87] On 15 June she hosted a meeting
at The Wilderness. The speaker, forty-three-year-old suffragette
Georgina Brackenbury, had spent time in Holloway Prison
earlier in the year and was now on a nation-wide tour, talking
about her experiences. The *Courier* described her as 'a charming
representative of the "danger corps"' and reported that she gave
a most interesting and convincing address, which her audience
listened to attentively. Georgina pointed to the need for more
vigorous action and newer methods, saying:

> *The militant tactics, disliked by so many, have aroused marked
> attention and interest, and the movement has taken on fresh
> life…It is time to show that women know their own minds;
> that they can work together, and that they possess resolution,
> courage and steadfastness, and will not now draw back.*[88]

Early on the morning of 21 June, May Le Lacheur and two
friends set off from Tunbridge Wells in a motor car owned by
her mother and driven by one of her brothers. A small placard
on the front of the car read 'Votes for Women', a large notice on
the back gave details of the demonstration and it was decorated
with rosettes in the new WSPU colours.

Meanwhile, another group of women, including Dorothy
and sisters Violet and Irene Tillard, caught the train. (Despite
Dorothy's enthusiastic organisation, there were only six of them
altogether.) At 10.15am the group arrived at Victoria Station,
where they were met by a marshall, who escorted them down
to the Thames and along the Embankment, until they found

their allocated place, a short distance beyond the Houses of Parliament. Seven processions would be converging on Hyde Park from different corners of London and theirs was lining up between Westminster and Waterloo Bridges. May and the car party soon joined them, as well as a few other women from Tunbridge Wells who had stayed in London overnight.

The Tunbridge Wells group had to wait some time before heading off, although on a sunny day this was not a hardship. As instructed they were wearing white dresses, with sashes and belts in purple, green and white. They unfurled the banner they had been given to carry, as others did along the line. Theirs read: 'Working women demand the vote.' Hawkers approached them, offering artificial flowers, programmes for the rally and handkerchiefs printed with maps showing the locations of the speakers' platforms. A passing bus driver leant out of his window and called out to them: 'Now, my duckies, come and hang out the washing.' [a]

At one point a short, stout, energetic woman approached the group. She was wearing a peaked cap, gold epaulettes and a sash with the word 'General' on it. With a smile on her face and speaking with a broad Scottish accent, she issued them with instructions for the march.

Flora Drummond had organised the rally with military efficiency. A couple of days earlier, she had boarded a small steam launch on the Thames, called 'Lottie.' It was decorated with banners which read, in bold, black letters: 'Women's Rally', 'Hyde Park Sunday June 21' and 'CABINET MINISTERS SPECIALLY INVITED.' Just as Big Ben struck four, the launch, with a band playing on board, drew up alongside the House of Commons Terrace. MPs, the lady friends they had been entertaining to tea and the waitresses serving them all rushed to

---

a Many of the things shouted to women's suffrage campaigners at demonstrations such as this were rather less polite.

the parapet to see what was going on. The band stopped playing and Flora climbed up onto the cabin roof. 'Come to the Park on Sunday,' she bawled through a megaphone. 'You shall have police protection and there will be no arrests, we promise you.' She continued shouting for several minutes, until police boats approached and the launch sped off. Now, on the day of the rally, Flora was visiting marchers in each of the seven processions, to give them directions and encouragement.

Finally, they were off. Mounted police led the way, followed by a mixture of local branches and overseas deputations. Ahead of the Tunbridge Wells women were representatives from Germany and Sweden and behind them a beautifully-worked banner from South Africa. Four horses pulled a carriage containing elderly protestors and, at regular intervals along the line, there were brass bands, playing rousing tunes.

As they made their way slowly along the Embankment, around the Houses of Parliament, up Victoria Street and along Grosvenor Place, curious spectators crowding the pavements, doorways and windows, looked on. While some comments were shouted – suggestions that the suffragettes should be minding babies, darning socks, or doing the washing, instead of marching – they were surprised how few jeers there were. Some people even cheered.

As the Embankment contingent crossed Hyde Park Corner and entered the park, six other processions arrived from different directions. Railings had been removed to avoid the damage that had been caused at earlier rallies for other causes. In front of them May and Dorothy saw an array of men's straw boaters and ladies' broad flower-trimmed hats, of dark suits and white summer dresses adorned with purple and green. (Sylvia Pankhurst later described the effect as being like a giant bed of flowers.) Scattered throughout the crowd, around 700 banners flapped in the breeze. As well as the huge silk ones which had been carried at the heads of the processions, there were hundreds of finely embroidered and appliqued smaller ones, with messages such as 'We Fight to Win' and 'Keep Pestering.' The sounds of talking and laughter were accompanied by music from forty bands.

WSP Rally, Hyde Park (1908)
© *Women's Library, LSE*

Twenty wagons were stationed around the Park in an oval formation. The Tunbridge Wells contingent had been hoping to hear Christabel Pankhurst, but the crowds around her were so dense they could not get anywhere close. So they made their way instead to Platform Ten, at the northern end of the park, where Adela, the youngest Pankhurst sister, was due to speak. At 3.30pm bugles were blown from a conning tower in the centre and the first speaker climbed onto each platform. Twenty-three-year-old Adela made a passionate speech – despite being only a slight figure, she had no difficulty making herself heard. She was followed on the platform by a nurse, a teacher and New Zealander Frances (Fanny) Parker. The last was another speaker Dorothy and May had been especially keen to hear; she had studied at Cambridge with their older sister Kate and the two women were now running a suffragette dairy in Berkshire.[a]

The crowds were fairly peaceful at most platforms. However, around Emmeline and Christabel Pankhurst's were a number of young men who had come expressly to cause trouble. They cat-called, jeered, blew toy trumpets and rang bells, in an effort to drown the speakers' voices. Some of the heckling was humorous – 'Don't put me on an island with the suffering gettes!' was one cry. Other hecklers were more offensive. The youths kept surging forward, causing alarm and fears that the platforms would be overturned. Eventually the police intervened and cleared a space beside Christabel's platform, where ambulance men could treat women who had fainted or suffered minor injuries. (Two thousand policemen, in uniform and plain clothes, were on duty in the Park that day to maintain order. Apart from this incident, they had very little to do.)

At five minutes to five, the bugles were blown again, the speakers stopped and a resolution was read out at each platform, calling on the government to give women the vote without delay. The bugles sounded one last time and women with megaphones led three shouts of 'Votes for Women.' These were rather ragged, as many found it difficult to hear. However, they were followed by a swell of shouting, cheering and clapping which spread across the park – a huge triumphant din.

Some people stayed on for hours, enjoying the occasion, but most of the huge crowd now dispersed. The surrounding streets became crowded, queues built up at tube stations and any local restaurants that had opened for the day were besieged.

---

a Kate Le Lacheur, who was already an active suffragette, may well have been at the rally too. See Chapter 14 for more on her.

As the Le Lacheur sisters and their friends travelled back to Tunbridge Wells, by train and car, they must have reflected on their experiences that day. They had taken part in an exciting and historic event. Surely the Prime Minister would be convinced and women would soon have the vote? Their feelings may have been similar to the Sheffield WSPU branch president, who wrote:

> We started out...with mirth and laughter, we returned with joy in our hearts because we felt we had done something towards the making of history...We arrived [home] near midnight and although we were tired, we were filled with new zeal and determination to render of our best until we have seen the realisation of our desires.[89]

In her history of the suffrage movement, Sylvia Pankhurst recalled the euphoria and optimism she and other women had felt:

> We were buoyed up by delighted triumph in this success, and belief of an early victory for the cause. Self was forgotten; personality seemed minute, the movement so big, so splendid. What an achievement! This without doubt was the greatest meeting ever known.[90]

There had certainly been a large number of people in Hyde Park. Newspapers estimated that 30,000 took part in the processions and that there were at least 250,000 at the rally, as well forty bands. In their extensive coverage, most concluded that the event had been a success, both as a spectacle and in providing evidence to the Prime Minister of women's desire for the vote.

The *Daily News* said the rally had been 'daringly conceived, splendidly stage-managed and successfully carried out.'[91] The

Manchester Guardian was more measured in its assessment, but came to the same overall conclusion:

> *As an indication to Ministers of popular determination, it was hazy; as a token of the drawing power of the women's movement it was astounding. As an affair of passing resolutions it was negligible; as a way of sharpening up the fight and bringing the cry out into the open, it was splendid.*[92]

Dorothy and May no doubt described the day's events to their mother. What did Lydia think of their involvement in the WSPU? There is no evidence she was ever a member. However, it seems unlikely that Dorothy could have held meetings at the family home and advertised them in the press, if her mother disapproved strongly.

Lydia Le Lacheur and her daughters would continue campaigning for the vote for many years to come. They would need to. The Hyde Park rally, one of the largest political demonstrations ever seen in London, was a success in that it helped counter some of the negative views that people had of suffragettes. It also brought the issue of Votes for Women to the attention of those who had previously been unaware, uninterested, or dismissive, prompting them to discuss it and think about it. But it did not change many people's views and certainly not the Prime Minister's.

Chapter 11

Caravans and Banners

On Monday 29 June 1908, just eight days after the Hyde Park rally, a Romany-style caravan, pulled by a large carthorse, lumbered slowly into Tunbridge Wells. It was on a tour of Kent, Sussex and Surrey, arranged by the Women's Freedom League (WFL) and posters on the vehicle's sides and back proclaimed 'Women's Suffrage' and 'Votes for Women.'

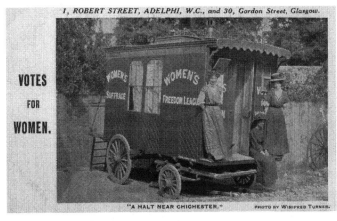

WFL Caravan (1908)
Women's Library, LSE

The WFL had been formed towards the end of 1907, by Charlotte Despard and Teresa Billington-Greig, as a breakaway group from the WSPU (Women's Social and Political Union). They were unhappy at the level of control Emmeline Pankhurst and her daughter Christabel were exercising over the organisation. Things had come to a head in September 1907, when Emmeline cancelled the annual conference and abolished the constitution. In future, she announced, the organisation would be run by a committee, appointed by her personally. The WFL aimed to do things differently and be a more democratic body, giving local branches and individual members a greater say.

The new organisation's leaders were also concerned about the extreme methods some WSPU members were adopting. WFL supporters, who also called themselves suffragettes, took direct, and sometimes illegal, actions (such as protesting at meetings, picketing and refusing to pay taxes). In doing so, they risked imprisonment. But they would not attack property or people.

Soon the WFL had its own colours – gold, green and white – and a network of local branches. (They would launch their own newspaper, *The Vote*, in 1909.) Caravanning was identified as a good way to publicise their cause, recruit members and raise funds. They purchased a vehicle, fitted it out and decorated it with slogans. In mid-May 1908 it set off from Charlotte Despard's Surrey home on its first tour, pulled by a horse named 'Asquith'. On board were Edith How-Martyn (honorary secretary), Lilian Hicks (a long-term suffrage campaigner from Essex) and Muriel Matters, a thirty-one-year-old Australian actress and suffrage campaigner who had moved to England in 1905.

When they arrived in Tunbridge Wells, the caravan party had already spent some weeks travelling through Surrey and Sussex and had experienced a variety of receptions, good and bad, in different towns. Muriel later recalled that as they made their way slowly up the hill towards the town, they were greeted by sisters Violet and Irene Tillard (both of whom had been in Hyde Park just a few days earlier). The latter, a tall, slim figure, would soon become close friends with Muriel.

Violet (who preferred to be known as Till or Tilly) was born in Madras, India in 1874, daughter of army officer George Tillard and his wife Louisa. Her mother died in 1883, her father remarried a year later and she soon had two half-sisters – Georgina and Irene. Having reached the rank of colonel, George retired from the Indian Army and by 1891 the family were living in Devon. At some point during the following ten years they moved to Tunbridge Wells, where they were living when the 1901 census was taken. Violet, meanwhile, trained as a nurse at the Poplar and Great Ormond Street hospitals and in 1904 she travelled to the United States, to care for a paralysed boy. By 1908, she had returned to England and was living back with her parents and sisters.

Violet Tillard
Drawn by Katharine Harper

When she went to meet the caravan party, Violet was already involved in the organisation – she had been one of the first women to join when it was formed the previous year and earlier in 1908 she had been appointed assistant organising secretary. Muriel later summed up her character: 'Courage – sympathy – generosity... shy, elusive qualities accompanying the grim[m]est kind of determination and will.'[93]

Muriel and the other caravanners intended holding a

meeting on each of the three days they were in Tunbridge Wells and, as evening arrived, they set up a makeshift platform on the Common. (Political meetings, religious services, band concerts and cricket matches all took place there on a regular basis.) A crowd began gathering and suffragettes walked among them, handing out pamphlets. The police had been informed of the meeting in advance and several officers were standing close to the stage in case there was any trouble.

By the time Muriel, a slim, lively woman with gold-coloured hair, climbed up onto a chair mounted on top of the platform, a crowd of around a thousand people had collected. Unfortunately they included a number of youths who, according to the *Courier*, were 'distinguished by cigarettes, high collars, straw hats and unintelligent faces'[94] and who were there to make trouble. As with female suffrage campaigners who had spoken in public many years earlier (Lydia Becker and Caroline Biggs, for example), Muriel was not exactly what her audience expected. The *Courier* observed:

> *Probably the hobbledehoys were disappointed to find that Miss Matters was not the suffragette of the comic papers. As she herself put it, she was 'neither a freak nor a frump', but she certainly was a lady of amiable demeanour and a speaker able to put her points with a great deal of force and forensic skill.*[95]

Muriel spoke confidently and fluently, setting out the reasons women should be given the vote. (As a former actress she was used to speaking in front of an audience and making herself heard.) At first she was given a good hearing. When a heckler interrupted her, she advised him to move to another part of the Common, where he would no doubt find himself an audience. When there were further interruptions, she pointed out that no-one was obliged to stay and listen to her. Gradually the crowd grew, with the arrival of more young men who had come specifically to 'bait' the suffragettes. Soon 'ill-mannered' remarks (which the newspapers deemed unsuitable to repeat in detail) were being called out. Every now and then something was thrown at Muriel – an egg, a potato, a banana skin and even a stone. (She later recalled that, when addressing open-air meetings, she used to wear a mackintosh to protect her from bad eggs and rotten fish.) One missile hit her on the face, but she kept on speaking.

The dense crowd became increasingly hot and sweaty and the rougher element began shouting and shoving. Other people appealed to them for calm and 'fair play', but they continued pressing forward and eventually Muriel was knocked off the platform. Luckily a local Baptist minister who was standing below broke her fall. She was keen to climb back up and continue, but Chief Constable Prior insisted on taking her to the station on Calverley Road for her own safety, accompanied by a police bodyguard.[a] A large crowd of young men followed, jeering, yelling and hooting. They hung around outside the station for some time and at one point tried, unsuccessfully, to break in. Eventually Muriel left by a back entrance, choosing to spend the night at the home of one of her new Tunbridge Wells friends, rather than in the caravan.

When a *Courier* reporter went to see her the next morning, Muriel claimed to be none the worse for her experience. He asked if this was her first encounter with hooligans and she replied:

No. I have been through it before and am getting hardened to it now. I do not mind their heckling, but their brutality gets on my nerves...they resembled a herd of buffalo. Once emotion

---

a This was the same Chief Constable whom Olive Walton would try to convince five years later.

crosses them, it is like a wind at which the animals take fright
and these people are really no higher than the animals.[96]

But she also noted: 'I saw many intelligent and sympathetic faces
in the crowd, and… little knots of women cheered us. I think the
women were on our side.'

Tuesday's meeting was moved to the town hall, where only
women, plus a few carefully selected men (reporters, police
or known supporters), were admitted. Women wanted to take
their place in the state and stand shoulder to shoulder with men,
Muriel told her audience. She also said she had been insulted by
women (as well as men) in the streets of Tunbridge Wells. Surely
it was not unreasonable to ask for the freedom of thought and
speech which had been fought for in years gone by? At the end
of the meeting she left by a side door, to avoid the large crowd
that had gathered outside.

On Wednesday afternoon, around a hundred ladies and
just three men met in the drawing room of Grosvenor Lodge
(the substantial home of NUWSS (National Union of Women's
Suffrage Societies) secretary Edith Tattershall Dodd) and that
evening Muriel and her fellow suffragettes returned to the
Common for a final open-air meeting. The crowd was even
larger than it had been two days earlier, but on this occasion
there was only applause, good-natured joking and laughter. The
police dealt promptly with any disruption and afterwards, they
escorted the caravan party away from the Common. An article
in the *Courier* commented that the suffragettes' experience in
Tunbridge Wells had been of little credit to the town, although
it also observed that the disgraceful exhibition of bad manners
had been mainly confined to the younger generation.[97]

For Violet Tillard, Dorothy Le Lacheur and other local
Votes for Women supporters, events in their home town were in
sharp contrast to the triumphant occasion they had witnessed

in Hyde Park only a few days earlier and a reminder that the campaign for the vote was not likely to be straightforward or easy. However, they were not discouraged. A few months later, they invited Muriel back to speak at a meeting in the town hall, which they advertised by chalking details on pavements and dragging a costermonger's barrow, plastered with notices, through the streets. Perhaps the novelty of a woman speaker had worn off, as the audience this time was much smaller and there was no trouble.

On 28 October, Violet travelled up to London to take part in a WFL protest at the House of Commons. At around 8.30pm she arrived at the St Stephen's entrance, together with Muriel and Helen Fox, another WFL member. They said that they had come to see Liberal MP Stephen Collins[a], were admitted and headed for the Ladies' Gallery. Nothing had changed since forty years earlier, when MPs debated Votes for Women for the first time, and this was still the only place from which women could watch the Commons in action. To many campaigners the Gallery's brass grille, known as 'the cage', symbolised women's continued exclusion from national politics.

Once they were able to get a place at the grille, the three women looked down onto the heads of MPs in the half-empty chamber below. As the final item of the day's business, a licensing bill, was being debated, Muriel and Helen produced the chains they had smuggled in under long cloaks, wrapped in cloth to keep them from rattling. They padlocked themselves to the grille and began shouting 'Votes for Women!' At the same time, Violet fed a banner through the grille and lowered it towards the Speaker. A handbill had been pasted onto it, with the headline WOMEN'S FREEDOM LEAGUE-DEMANDS-VOTES FOR WOMEN-THIS SESSION. (In advance of the protest, 5,000 similar bills had been posted on buildings and pillar boxes across

---

a Stephen Collins later claimed to have been completely unaware of their intentions.

London.) Violet also poked handfuls of leaflets through the grille, which floated down into the chamber below.

WFL Ladies Gallery Protest (1908)
© *Illustrated London News Ltd/Mary Evans*

MPs raised their voices and forged on with the debate. 'The women of England demand the vote,' shouted Muriel. 'We have listened behind this insulting grille for too long. We call upon a Liberal government to prove itself liberal.' Her words became jerky and uneven as they were joined by the sounds of House of Commons attendants trying frantically to file through the chains. These proved too strong and eventually the attendants had to wrench whole sections of the grille out of their stone setting and take them, with the two women still attached, to a committee room close by. An elderly MP looked on in disgust as they passed. 'Yes it is perfectly scandalous that we women should have to behave in this way,' Muriel said to him, 'but we must do something vulgar to attract your vulgar attention.'[98] A locksmith was summoned and finally managed to break the chains.

Meanwhile, MPs continued their debate. As they began voting on an amendment to the Licencing Bill, further protests took place in the Strangers' Gallery, at the far end of the Commons. A man shouted, 'Why do not you do justice to women and the unemployed? Votes for Women!' and threw more leaflets. He was removed immediately. A few minutes later another, younger, man began protesting and resisted desperately as six attendants manhandled him out of the building.

Once the day's business had been concluded, MPs expressed their disapproval of the protestors' actions and the Speaker made an announcement.

> *...in consequence of what has occurred, the decencies of the House having been violated and the privileges granted by this House having been grossly abused, and not for the first time, I have felt it my duty, most reluctantly, to order that for a time the Strangers' Gallery and the Ladies' Gallery be closed.*[99][a]

While all this was going on, a number of other suffragettes had staged a demonstration in the Central Lobby. After the police ejected them, they continued protesting in the yard outside, where Violet, Muriel and Helen (who had also been escorted off the premises) joined them. A couple of women climbed up onto the plinth of a statue of King Richard the First and addressed the crowd who had gathered, until they were pulled down. The police arrested thirteen women, including Violet and Muriel.[b] At one point a young man shouted out, 'Shame! Let the ladies alone,' and they arrested him too. The suffragettes and the young man were taken to Cannon Row Police Station, where a large crowd had gathered, who cheered as each of them arrived.

The following morning all those arrested appeared before magistrate Arthur Hopkins in the Westminster Police Court. A number of WFL supporters were present to witness the proceedings, including the organisation's leader, sixty-two-year-old Charlotte Despard. She was a distinctive figure – a tall, elegant, sharp-featured lady, dressed in a long flowing black dress, a Spanish shawl and a lace mantilla draped over her white

---

a The Galleries re-opened the following year, under strict conditions.

b Helen escaped arrest, although she later claimed that this was not by her choice.

hair (in place of the conventional hat).

A respectable-looking young man in a dark overcoat and cap was first to enter the dock. Arnold Cutler, a packer from Kensington, was accused of having swung his belt and shown a threatening attitude. His defence to this charge was that he had a weak heart and had been carried away with excitement. The magistrate ordered him to pay a fine of twenty shillings (which a suffragette paid on his behalf).

After that, the women appeared one by one, each wearing gold, green and white. When Violet's turn came, she was accused of having pushed violently through police lines, found guilty and ordered to pay a fine of £5. She refused, opting instead for a month in prison. Muriel asked for her case to be adjourned for a week. However, the magistrate responded that he was unwilling to agree, if this was just to give her time to prepare a speech. Muriel refused to express regret, or give an undertaking not to offend again, and was also given a one month sentence. All the protestors were dealt with in the same way, with only two exceptions – one woman had her case adjourned and another, who claimed to have been caught up in events by accident, was discharged.

After a short wait in a dark, dirty police cell, Violet was transferred to Holloway Prison in North London. Even the ride – crammed into a narrow, claustrophobic, coffin-like compartment in a horse-drawn Black Maria – would have been a shock to her. Worse was to come at the prison, with an admissions process she would later describe as 'humiliating'. After she had waited for some time in a holding cell, wondering what lay ahead, she was taken to a reception office. There she had to put on a shift, remove her clothes beneath it and pass them to the prison officer, who signed to record what she had handed over. Next she was 'rubbed down' (to check for contraband), her hair examined and her weight measured, before being taken to a bathroom to wash. Finally she put on her prison clothes – an ill-fitting brown serge dress (decorated with broad arrows), a cotton bonnet and a blue and brown checked handkerchief to wear around her neck.

Muriel later recalled her friend's appearance that day:

Tall, slender, delicate, reticent...even in prison clothes – and I see her now that first awful day in Holloway...with the rough boots, long unshapely dress, check apron and harshly-pointed prison cap – yet 'Till' managed to look so graceful. How cheerful she was, how philosophic when many were either 'edgy', 'weepy' with strain, or rebellious.[100]

After a further wait, Violet was given a medical and taken to her cell. The heavy iron door slammed shut, the key turned and she was alone in a small, overheated, stuffy room. A suffragette, who had been in Holloway a couple of years earlier, described the setting:

The cells had a cement floor, whitewashed walls and a window high up so that one could not see out of it. It was barred outside and the glass was corrugated so that one could not even get a glimpse of the sky; and the only sign of outside life was the occasional flicker of the shadow of a bird as it flew outside across the window. The furnishing of the cell consisted of a wooden plank bed stood up against the wall, a mattress rolled up in one corner, two or three tin vessels, a cloth for cleaning and polishing and some bath brick...There was also a stool without a back, and inside the mattress...were two thin blankets, a pillow and some rather soiled-looking sheets. One tin utensil was for holding water, the second for sanitary purposes, and the third was a small tin mug for holding cocoa.[101]

Over the following days, Violet experienced the monotony of prison life, which consisted of long hours in her cell, broken only by daily marches in the exercise yard and chapel services, during which she was not allowed to talk to other prisoners. The diet, which consisted mainly of porridge, potatoes and bread, was also monotonous and in the first four weeks of her sentence, she was allowed just one visit and one letter.

All this was very different from Violet's home life and campaigning activities. In addition, she found it an eye-opening experience to come into contact with women from different backgrounds whose current situation, no matter what crime they had committed, inspired pity. Another suffragette who was in Holloway at around the same time referred to a 'sea of miserable, white, sad faces' and observed that these women probably needed six months in a sanatorium rather than a prison sentence.

Chapter 12

The Resolution and the Great Watch

When Violet and Muriel were released from Holloway on 28 November 1908, together with three other WFL (Women's Freedom League) prisoners, they found their leader, Charlotte Despard, waiting at the prison gate to greet them. The group headed straight to the Cottage Tea Room on the Strand (which claimed to offer 'prompt and dainty fare in pleasant surroundings') where a breakfast was held in honour of the prisoners, who gave an account of their experiences. A couple of days later, Violet and Muriel headed to Chelmsford, to take part in a by-election campaign. Then it was on to Tunbridge Wells, where a meeting had been arranged in their honour.

It was organised by the Tunbridge Wells WFL branch, which had been founded the previous month, while Violet was still serving her sentence. (Around this time suffragists founded the local NUWSS (National Union of Women's Suffrage Societies) branch in the town). The caravan campaign's visit back in June and the participation of a local woman in the Ladies' Gallery protest had raised the WFL's profile and prepared the ground.

(Local women had attended the WSPU's (Women's Social and Political Union) Hyde Park rally and donated to their funds, but perhaps the organisation's increasingly militant approach was felt to be too extreme for Tunbridge Wells at this time.)

Dorothy Le Lacheur, who was appointed secretary of the new WFL branch, wrote a letter to the *Courier*:

> *Dear Sir, I hope that you will permit me, through the medium of your columns, to communicate to the women of Tunbridge Wells interested in the suffrage question that a local branch of the Women's Freedom League has been formed...The Suffrage Bill has passed its Second Reading, and without delay, further pressure should be brought to bear upon the government...We hope that many Tunbridge Wells women will join us, our chief motive being that the needs of numberless women and children demand that their stronger sisters should have the greater freedom and power to help them, which the vote alone can give. The right is demanded because the duty is clear.*[102]

The meeting, which took place in the town hall on 3 December, was well attended – people were curious to see and hear the women responsible for such a daring protest. A small number of men were admitted, but only if they had a ticket, and many had to be turned away. Violet was the first to speak. She had never made a speech before, she said, and after being forbidden to speak in prison, it was strange to be allowed to talk freely again. Her experience had convinced her that the prison system required improving and that women needed the vote to be able to fight against current conditions. She was applauded as she concluded her address, saying, 'I feel that everyone who can go to Holloway ought to.'[103]

Muriel followed, with more fighting talk. 'I've never been in the British House of Commons before, but I hope to go again… and don't be surprised to hear that I have done something very much worse.' She claimed that the newspapers had misrepresented the speech she made during the protest – it was not screamed, it 'rang out.' Muriel finished by appealing for volunteers to come forward and join the movement.

Over the next year, the WFL had an active presence in Tunbridge Wells and Dorothy Le Lacheur threw herself heart and soul into organising their activities. An article in the *Courier* said of her:

She worked with untiring patience and determination at a seemingly impossible task – to introduce such a movement into such a town: but it did not prove impossible, as those who remember her indefatigable efforts…in organising open-air meetings, chalking street pavements, constant propaganda efforts etc. will testify.[104]

In January 1909, just two days after her mother had held an NUWSS 'At Home' at The Wilderness, Dorothy hosted a WFL meeting there. Members discussed the best means of promoting Votes for Women in the town. They agreed to meet every other Friday evening for a discussion (the topic for the first session was 'Women Under the Law') and decided to hold a public event as soon as possible.

This took place on 9 February at the Great Hall and the guest speaker was Charlotte Despard. In her speech she referred to the widespread demand for women's suffrage and the improvements women could bring about if they had the vote. With no prospect of legislation being passed, the time had come to break the law, Charlotte said. If there was no mention of Votes for Women in the King's Speech (which was due a few days later), the resolutions which were being passed all over the country would be taken to the House of Commons. If WFL members had to force their way in (in order to present them) they would just be doing their duty.

At the end of the meeting a resolution was passed, with wording that was being approved at other similar meetings:

This meeting calls upon the Government to include Women's Suffrage in the King's Speech, and to enfranchise women during the present session of Parliament, as the continued denial of political liberty to women is a violation of the principles of justice and humanity and a direct incentive to the use of unconstitutional methods.[105]

On 16 February, campaigners' fears were confirmed when, once again, the King's Speech contained no reference to women's suffrage. Two days later, Dorothy and several other local suffragettes caught an early morning train up to London, to join members of other branches. They headed to Caxton Hall (just off Victoria Street) where they were briefed on how to behave, during the protest, towards the police and in court. The 'danger delegates', who would be the ones attempting to deliver the resolutions to the Prime Minister, were instructed to carry out their work quietly; they should not aim to get arrested, although in practice this was likely to happen.

When the briefing was over, the 'danger delegates' headed off first, to loud cheers from the rest. Amongst them was twenty-eight-year old Olive Ibbotson, carrying the Tunbridge Wells resolution. Originally from Yorkshire, Olive had moved to live in Rotherfield, a nearby village, a few years earlier. In 1907 and 1908, she had taken part in WSPU protests outside Parliament and at Downing Street, for which she received prison sentences. She had joined the Tunbridge Wells WFL branch soon after it was founded the previous autumn.

In the group that followed were Dorothy and twenty-three-year-old Constance Brock, carrying a Tunbridge Wells banner between them. Both women felt very nervous, even though they were not going to be in the front line. To avoid looking like a procession (and risk getting themselves arrested) the suffragettes split into small groups. Dorothy and Constance were heading along Victoria Street, when a policeman stopped them and instructed them to give up their banner. Someone standing nearby offered to take it back to Caxton Hall, which meant they could continue to Downing Street, where around 150 women gathered outside the gates. A police cordon was in position and mounted police rode up and down in front of them.

A superintendent informed the WFL leaders that the Prime Minister was unwilling to see the delegation and that their members would be arrested if they tried to force their way through. As the 'danger delegates' repeatedly tried to do just that, there were shouts of 'Bravo' and 'Hurrah' from some in the crowd and hisses from others. The police arrested twenty-four women, including Olive, for obstruction.

Along with other protestors who had escaped arrest, Dorothy and Constance returned to Caxton Hall. Word came that some of those who had been detained were to appear in court immediately and a deputation set off to the Westminster Police Court to watch proceedings, flanked by a police escort and with costermongers shouting abuse at them as they passed. Other cases, including Olive's, were heard that afternoon at Bow Street Magistrates' Court the third time she had appeared there). Olive was found guilty of obstruction and, rather than be bound over to keep the peace, opted for six weeks in prison.

The following week, the Tunbridge Wells WFL branch held a meeting. According to the chair, Miss Peacock, it had been arranged so that local women with an interest in suffrage could hear an accurate account of the demonstration. Newspaper reports of such events were often very misleading, she said. Sometimes this was out of ludicrous ignorance posing as knowledge and sometimes it was in order to provide amusing copy. As well as speaking at the meeting about her experiences, Dorothy wrote an account for the *Courier*. She claimed that the women involved had been much more orderly than was portrayed in the press and continued:

> *I wish it were in my power to describe graphically to you the proceedings...you could not fail to feel, as we were all feeling, that it is disgraceful for a country to have brought its women to that. You would have felt ashamed for Asquith, the Government, and the country and...you would know that militant methods were more than justifiable.*[106]

On through 1909, women's frustration with Asquith and the Liberal government grew and the WFL intensified their campaigning. In early July, after the Prime Minister refused to receive a deputation of their leaders, they mounted a picket outside the House of Commons, asserting their legal right to petition him. Relays of suffragettes lined up beside the entrances to the Commons, and stood there, in all weathers, whenever MPs were sitting. They were not causing an obstruction, so the police could not arrest them and each day, as MPs arrived for the day's business, they had to walk past a long line of silent protestors. The WFL leaders announced that their protest would continue until Asquith agreed to receive a deputation, or they were removed by force. It became known as the 'Great Watch.' At various times, WFL members also picketed 10 Downing Street, where they were always arrested immediately.

Members of the Tunbridge Wells WFL branch would probably have taken part in the Great Watch, although the only one known for certain to have done so was twenty-two-year-old Irene Tillard (Violet's half-sister). On 19 August Irene and another suffragette, both dressed in gold, green and white, stood on either side of the Prime Minister's residence, waving copies of the petition on rolls of paper. When they refused to leave, the two women were arrested and charged with obstructing the police in the execution of their duty. Six further arrests followed, including WFL leader Charlotte Despard.

The cases against the eight suffragettes were heard at Bow Street on 27 August, in a courtroom crowded with their supporters. They were defended by flamboyant Irish MP Timothy Healy, who did not submit any evidence, but made a lively eighty-minute speech in defence of his clients, during which he described them as 'the women who stand in rain and snow, hail and shine, knocking like beggars at the gates of the fortress.'[107] Healy based his case on the ancient constitutional right to present a petition. In reply, the prosecutor alleged that the suffragettes had not been at Downing Street to present a petition, but to 'foist themselves' on the Prime Minister, forcing him to grant them an interview. The magistrate agreed with the prosecutor and the women were each sentenced to a 40s fine, or seven days' imprisonment. They were prepared to go to prison, but the following January, after an appeal had eventually been heard and dismissed, their fines were paid by an anonymous supporter.

The WFL continued the Great Watch for fifteen weeks, during which time the Prime Minister resolutely refused to meet their leaders or accept their petition. When it finished, at the end of the parliamentary session, they calculated that a total of 14,000 hours had been spent on the protest.

* * *

In Tunbridge Wells, the WFL were not the only suffrage organisation operating through 1908 and 1909. The town's non-militant suffragists had also been busy campaigning and recruiting new members. At their first annual meeting, on 26

November 1909, the local NUWSS branch reported that they had held a total of sixteen meetings over the past year. One of the most successful, which had been held in the Great Hall the previous week, was described as 'the largest indoor gathering ever held here on the suffrage question.' The speeches, including one by Millicent Garrett Fawcett, had been very well received, many badges and copies of *The Common Cause* (the NUWSS newspaper) had been sold and new members recruited. The Society claimed to be well-established and looking forward to its second year with hope and confidence.[108]

The local WLA also continued campaigning on Votes for Women, along with other issues. They passed resolutions in favour of women's suffrage at meetings in October and December 1908 and kept the pressure up on local MP Alfred Hedges. In December 1908, they sent a large deputation to a women's suffrage demonstration held by the Women's Liberal Federation at the Albert Hall.

The only main suffrage organisation *not* represented in Tunbridge Wells at this time was the WSPU. Yet nationally, it was they who were attracting the most attention and generating the most headlines, especially once they adopted more extreme and shocking campaigning methods such as stone throwing and hunger striking.

Chapter 13

Idle and Mischievous Women

When Prime Minister Herbert Asquith's position remained unchanged after the WSPU's (Women's Social and Political Union) Hyde Park rally in June 1908, despite the scale of feeling it demonstrated and the positive public reaction, their members' patience began to run out. With negotiation, petitions and marches all having failed to get women the vote, it seemed to them that more extreme actions were required.

On 30 June 1908, the WSPU convened a women's parliament in Caxton Hall and sent deputation to the Prime Minister. When word reached the meeting that he had refused to see them, suffragettes began heading to Parliament Square in small groups. A crowd had already gathered there, who (according to *The Times*) were made up of idle onlookers, high-spirited youths and a rough element. The suffragettes waved banners and shouted. Some of them climbed up onto railings to address the crowd. At first the police tried to move them on, but this became impossible and, with more and more people arriving, they began making arrests. It was a much less peaceful affair than the Hyde Park rally had been, just nine days earlier. Meanwhile, two women arrived at 10 Downing Street in a taxi and began throwing stones at the building's windows. They managed to break two before being arrested. Attacking government property represented a change of tactics – suffragettes had begun committing violent acts as well as suffering them.

On 13 October 1908, a couple of weeks before Muriel and Violet's demonstration in the Ladies' Gallery, the WSPU encouraged the public to join them in 'the rush' – an attempt to storm the House of Commons. Thousands of handbills were distributed across London, calling on people to join in. On the day, a crowd of around 60,000 gathered in and around Parliament Square. There were also 5,000 or so police, who formed a cordon and, despite repeated attempts, managed to prevent anyone breaking through. Thirty-seven people were arrested and ten taken to hospital. Music hall actress Kitty Marion described her experience, in an (unpublished) autobiography:

...as each of us tried to proceed singly towards the House, petition in hand, two and three policemen, one on each side taking us by the arm and shoulder, quite unnecessarily pinching and bruising the soft under arm, with the third often pushing at the back, would run us along a little distance and fling us, causing most women to be thrown to the ground... Aching in body and soul, I went home at last to find my arms and shoulders black, blue and painful, as were every woman's who had taken part in this rightful, legal, peaceful petitioning.[109]

The Standard took a different view of events and condemned the actions of women such as Kitty:

The disturbances of yesterday and the day before, the utter contempt shown for public decency, the defiance of law, the heavy work thrown on the police, and the temptation offered to the baser elements of the populace, render it necessary to deal with the Suffragist agitation, not as a passing folly, but as a grave menace to the peace of the metropolis. Tolerance and forbearance cease to be possible.[110]

Emmeline Pankhurst, Christabel Pankhurst and Flora Drummond ('the General' who had organised the Hyde Park rally) were arrested and charged with conduct likely to provoke a breach of the peace. When their trial took place, it received a huge amount of attention, especially as Christabel conducted the defence personally, calling Chancellor of the Exchequer David Lloyd George and Home Secretary Herbert Gladstone as witnesses.[a] All three defendants were found guilty and imprisoned when they refused to pay their fines.

Christabel Pankhurst, Flora Drummond and Emmeline Pankhurst at Bow Street Magistrates' Court (October 1908)
Women's Library LSE

---

a Christabel was a trained lawyer, although as a woman she was not allowed to practise professionally.

From this time onwards, the WSPU's tactics became more extreme. Suffragettes chained themselves to railings. They disrupted government meetings, sporting events and church services and made frequent attempts to gain access to the Houses of Parliament. These actions ensured that they featured constantly in the newspapers and that they frequently ended up in prison, where they would refuse to obey rules and regulations, such as the requirement to wear prison dress or remain silent.

In the past, some suffragists (notably NUWSS (National Union of Women's Suffrage Societies) leader Millicent Garrett Fawcett) had taken the view that militant suffragettes were energising the movement and generating support for the cause. In October 1906, just after the NUWW (National Union of Women Workers) conference in Tunbridge Wells, Millicent had expressed support for them. 'Far from having injured the movement,' she wrote, 'they have done more during the past twelve months to bring it within the region of practical politics than we have been able to do in the same number of years.'[111] Two months later she arranged a dinner in honour of released suffragette prisoners at the Savoy Hotel.

Recently, however, as a result of extreme tactics, the divisions between the militants and non-militants had widened and Millicent had become anxious to disassociate her organisation from the WSPU and their increasingly violent protests. In November 1908 she sent a letter to MPs and the newspapers, pointing to their Parliament Square protest in June and 'the rush' in October as a change in tactics. She made clear that, while she understood why women might be driven to such actions, they were wrong and the NUWSS disassociated itself from them.

In the summer of 1909, suffragettes adopted an even more extreme tactic – hunger strikes. On 25 June Marion Wallace Dunlop smuggled an inkpad and stamp into St Stephen's Hall in the House of Commons and used it to print a protest on the wall in indelible ink: 'Women's Deputation. June 29. Bill of Rights. It is the right of the subjects to petition the King, and all commitments and prosecutions for such petitionings are illegal.' She was arrested, tried, found guilty of causing wilful damage and sentenced to a month in Holloway Prison. On being admitted, she sent a request to the prison governor, claiming the right to be treated as a political prisoner and given 'first division' treatment. She would not be eating any food until that happened, she said. Marion's request was refused. She remained in the third division and began a fast in protest.

People imprisoned on political grounds were generally designated as 'First Division' prisoners and allowed benefits not enjoyed by others, including their own clothes, books and newspapers to read and frequent visitors. Suffragettes, however, were being assigned instead to the second or third divisions, where the accommodation was less comfortable and their experience less pleasant. Discomfort was not the main issue though. Hunger strikes were a protest at the fact that they were being treated as common criminals, rather than as political protestors.

After Marion had fasted for ninety-one hours, Home Secretary Herbert Gladstone ordered her release on medical grounds. Other women soon followed her example and were also released early, when their health deteriorated. The government could not continue releasing prisoners, but did not want suffragettes to die and become martyrs. So, from September 1909 onward, prisons began force-feeding hunger strikers, usually through a rubber tube inserted into the mouth or nostril. This painful process caused considerable mental and physical damage, especially to women who experienced it multiple times.

Throughout the autumn, MPs walked past silent WFL (Women's Freedom League) protestors taking part in the

Great Watch on their way into the House of Commons and then debated hunger striking inside the chamber. Labour MP Keir Hardie asked questions about the practice and Gladstone defended it, claiming that the effects had been exaggerated. He was not an opponent of women's suffrage but, while he admitted to admiring the suffragettes' gallantry, he refused to give in to them. '[women's franchise] will not come through violent actions', he wrote in a letter to a government colleague, 'and not through sentimental or cowardly surrender to them.'[112]

There were differing opinions in the press as to whether the suffragettes had been provoked and whether their actions were helping or hindering the Votes for Women cause. Some newspapers published graphic accounts of force-feeding, written by women who had first-hand experience of it. Others played down its impact. The *Daily Telegraph* even said that, while it was initially disagreeable to the person being fed, it soon became tolerable.

The public were generally opposed to the suffragettes and their violent and destructive protests. But people were shocked at the lengthy sentences being given to some protestors and at the brutality with which hunger strikers were being treated.

The WSPU's tactics would have horrified earlier campaigners such as Caroline Biggs and Louisa Twining, who had always been anxious to emphasise their respectability. Even now, in 1909, they did not sit easily with many women and divisions between the different arms of the suffrage movement widened even further. In Tunbridge Wells both the WLA (Women's Liberal Association) and the NUWSS were critical of suffragettes and their activities. The WLA's 1909 annual report included a strong statement to the effect that their work in support of Votes for Women was being made far more difficult by the misunderstanding and prejudice that militant methods were creating. On 19 November, the *Courier* published a letter from Edith Tattershall Dodd, local NUWSS secretary, in which she reminded readers that her organisation, the oldest and most numerous body campaigning for women's suffrage, had consistently and constantly condemned violent methods.

When a general election took place in January 1910, local suffragists had an opportunity to demonstrate their form of non-violent campaigning to the people of Tunbridge Wells.

Chapter 14

Hopes Are Raised Again

In early January 1910, a new shop opened near the top of
Grosvenor Road. It was brightly decorated, in red, green and
white, and an array of eye-catching posters were on display.
When anyone walked past, a lady would emerge from the shop,
hand them a leaflet and ask them whether they thought women
should have the vote. If the response was at all positive, she
would suggest that they come inside and sign a petition. Each
time a cart stopped beside the shop, before descending the short
hill, one of the ladies would take the opportunity to speak to
its driver. In all these exchanges, the suffragists took particular
trouble to make clear that they were not connected in any way
to the militant suffragettes.

With a general election approaching, the NUWSS (National
Union of Women's Suffrage Societies) had launched a national
Votes for Women petition, intended to demonstrate to potential
MPs, and to the new Parliament once elected, the strength of
public feeling on the subject. The Tunbridge Wells branch
decided that they needed a place to collect signatures and co-
ordinate their election campaign and found themselves premises

at 61 Grosvenor Road (just opposite Secretary Edith Tattershall Dodd's home). They furnished and decorated the property and kept it open from 9.30am to 9pm each day.

The NUWSS was the only suffrage organisation campaigning in Tunbridge Wells in the lead up to the election. The WSPU (Women's Social and Political Union) did not have a local branch and the Tunbridge Wells WFL (Women's Freedom League) branch seems to have ended around this time. The last reference to them in the newspapers was in December 1909, when Charlotte Despard made a final visit. In any case the WFL's national organisation focussed most of their energies on campaigning against cabinet members in their constituencies.

The NUWSS did not canvass on behalf of either of the local candidates, but pressed them both to make clear their position on Votes for Women. Liberal Alfred Hedges continued to profess support for women's suffrage and mentioned it in his election address. In contrast, while the Conservative candidate (former army officer Captain Herbert Spender-Clay) agreed that action was needed on voter reform, he did not consider the issue urgent enough to include it in his address.

In practice, women's suffrage was still not a high priority for most male voters and therefore not for most parliamentary candidates. The NUWSS had to work hard to make sure that it had a higher profile than had been the case in the 1906 election, although, now that they had paid staff, a well-organised network of local branches and their own newspaper, *The Common Cause*, the suffragists were able to lobby more effectively.

Despite the local branch's efforts, the petition sheets were only filling slowly, so their members also went out canvassing door-to-door. The national organisation provided identity cards and advised canvassers to wear their colours as well as, given the current cold weather, warm clothes and a hat that would not blow off in the wind. They also suggested carrying indelible ink pencils, a sheet of mackintosh to cover the petition and a thermos flask of hot coffee.

On 11 January the Tunbridge Wells NUWSS branch held a meeting in the town hall, at which the speaker was Helena Swanwick, editor of *The Common Cause*. They sent a report on the meeting to the newspapers, which indicated that, after several years of campaigning, they believed they were beginning to make progress:

> [*The meeting*] *was an unqualified success, the town hall being nearly full, in spite of torrential rain. Numerous regrets for non-attendance have since reached us. Men were specially invited, and were present in considerable numbers for the first time...at a suffrage meeting...We feel we have gained some ground locally. People have come to recognise the NUWSS colours, and to realise what we stand for.*[113]

The suffragists were not the only ones to appear on doorsteps around town in the run-up to the election. The Conservative Party's Ladies' Committee also went out canvassing door-to-door (determined that the 1906 defeat would not be repeated). Their candidate claimed afterwards that they had knocked on every door in the town on his behalf. They were organised by Margaret Backhouse. Her sister Mary had been appointed the secretary of the local anti-suffrage society when it was founded the previous year and Margaret was also strongly opposed to women's suffrage. Not all of her Conservative colleagues shared her views, however. In a letter to the *Advertiser* in November 1909, Edith Tattershall Dodd had pointed out that the NUWSS committee included some staunch Conservatives, as well as Liberals.

When the election took place, on 19 January, Herbert Spender-Clay won Tunbridge Wells back for the Conservatives with a clear majority and it was he and his wife who made a triumphant tour of the area, in a motor car this time. Overall, however, the Liberals just managed to hold on to power.

The suffragists closed their Grosvenor Hill shop straight after the election, but continued collecting signatures on the petition for a few more weeks. By late February, they had collected a total of 954, which they forwarded to their new MP at the House of Commons. (The *Courier* described the number as 'interesting and encouraging news for upholders of women's suffrage'.)[114] The total number of signatures on petitions across the country amounted to almost 290,000, an impressive number.

During the campaign, Prime Minister Herbert Asquith had said that, if elected, the government was prepared to allow a free vote on whether an amendment benefitting women should be included in any future franchise bill. With a clear majority of MPs declared supporters of women's suffrage, it seemed, once again, that women were about to succeed. A Conciliation Committee, with thirty-six members drawn from all parties, was formed to promote women's suffrage, which led the WSPU and WFL to declare a truce and suspend their campaigns in anticipation of legislation coming forward.

Another positive development occurred in March 1910, when Home Secretary Winston Churchill introduced Rule 243a. This stated that suffragettes could be treated in a similar manner to first division prisoners, providing they had not been convicted of a serious offence. Since hunger strikes had been in protest at not being treated as political prisoners, it seemed that they were no longer necessary.

On 14 June 1910, the Women's Franchise Bill (sponsored by the Conciliation Committee and known generally as 'The Conciliation Bill') was tabled in the House of Commons. If passed, it would give the vote to around one million women who were householders, or occupying business premises with a value of £10 per annum or over. This was less than many campaigners wanted, but they believed that it would be a 'wedge', opening the door to more comprehensive legislation in the future. At a Lantern Lecture in the Tunbridge Wells Great Hall on 18 June, Bertha Mason, secretary of the national NUWSS, pointed to signs that the long and weary struggle for the vote was drawing to a close. Another speaker at the same meeting said that the feeling of fair play was now coming like a wave over the country.

On the same day as that meeting, a joint WSPU and WFL procession, under the title 'From Prison to Citizenship', took place in London.[a] It was intended to demonstrate how much support for the cause had grown and celebrate the fact that victory was close. Around 10,000 women, including leaders and local branch members, marched from Blackfriars to the Albert Hall, accompanied by a series of bands. As ever, there was a multitude of banners. Some of these had been made especially for the occasion, including one which read 'The Bill the Whole Bill and the Bill now.'

The WFL's newspaper *The Vote* commented on the range of women taking part:

> *Looking on at the never-ending army which passed steadily in well-marshalled battalions – homemakers, teachers, civil servants, shop assistants, actresses, artists, scientists, writers, nurses, medical women, athletes, sanitary inspectors – no-one could ignore or deny the part taken in the daily work of the State by the sex which has been consistently denied citizen rights.*[115]

The WFL marchers included former prisoners (carrying poles topped with silver arrows), who were led by the organisation's

---

a   The procession had been postponed from 28 May, following the death of King Edward VII.

founder Teresa Billington-Greig. She was followed by a deputy representing Muriel Matters, who carried a banner decorated with a chain, in reference to the Ladies' Gallery protest (Muriel and Violet Tillard were away on a tour of Australia). Next came other members who had been imprisoned, marching in groups according to the number of sentences they had served. Olive Ibbotson would have been in this part of the procession, as would a deputy representing Violet.

Prison to Citizenship Procession (1910)
Women's Library, LSE

Following the procession, there was a meeting at the Albert Hall. Thousands of marchers packed the arena, stalls, boxes, balcony and gallery. All eyes were fixed on the stage and on the tall, straight figure of Emmeline Pankhurst, who paused, surveyed the huge audience and uttered a single word – '*Victory!*'

The conviction that success was around the corner was widespread and strong. A cartoon on the front page of NUWSS newspaper *The Common Cause* on 7 July depicted a woman pushing at an open door. A day later the front page of the WSPU's newspaper *Votes for Women* showed a ship called 'Victory' sailing towards the shore, where a throng of excited suffragettes were waiting.

Amelia Scott, Sarah Grand and other Tunbridge Wells suffragists would not have marched in the Prison to Citizenship procession. Anxious to disassociate themselves from the militant societies and their actions (despite the current truce), the NUWSS refused to take part and declined the offer of a box at the Albert Hall. Instead, they held their own event a few weeks later. On 9 July, women from Tunbridge Wells took part in an NUWSS demonstration in Trafalgar Square, which was attended by around 20,000 women and men. In common with other societies, one of their members carried a banner inscribed with the number of people who had signed their election petition earlier in the year.

On 12 July, the Conciliation Bill passed its second reading by 299 votes to 189 (a substantial majority of 110). However, immediately afterwards MPs voted to refer the bill to a Committee of the Whole House (citing its importance as the reason). As it had in 1908, this meant that time would have to be found for the bill to be debated by the House of Commons and it was unlikely to progress any further in the current session.

Despite having said at election time that reform was needed, Tunbridge Wells MP Herbert Spender-Clay voted against the bill. A few weeks later, the *Advertiser* carried a cartoon under the headline 'Jilted' depicting a Votes for Women campaigner as a distressed bride and the MP as a runaway bridegroom. The text beneath quoted a speech he had made at a local fete. He claimed to have changed his views, having discovered that, if women had the vote, there would be eleven and a half million more of them entitled to vote than men. In addition, at a time when there was a wave of emotion going over the country, he feared many women would record their vote 'without ever thinking over the matter.' [116]

Campaigners in all the three main suffrage organisations were determined that the bill should not be lost altogether and their newspapers made frequent references to the 110 vote majority. On 23 July, the WSPU held a Great Demonstration in Support of the Bill. Two huge processions made their way through the streets to the Park, where there were forty platforms and 150 speakers. (The NUWSS had agreed to take part this time, on the condition that the WSPU did not resume its militant tactics.) Bathed in brilliant sunshine, Hyde Park was filled once again with crowds of demonstrators and an array of banners in the suffrage colours.

The Prime Minister was unmoved by this demonstration of support, however. Towards the end of July, he confirmed that the Conciliation Bill would not be given any more parliamentary time and refused to promise that any would be found in the autumn. Apart from his personal opposition to giving women the vote, this may have been down to his precarious position at the head of a minority government. The fear that property-owning women would vote for the Conservative Party continued to have a strong hold on many Liberal MPs.

Despite this setback, the NUWSS and WFL remained optimistic, through the summer and on into the autumn ,that the bill might be revived. The WSPU, however, were more sceptical. Along with the other organisations, they continued pressing for time to be allowed for it, but at the same time they began collecting the names of members who were willing to take part in a deputation to the Prime Minister. By the end of October, 150 women had signed up, including Kate Le Lacheur.

Chapter 15

Black Friday

Born in 1877, Kate was Lydia Le Lacheur's fifth daughter. She attended Tunbridge Wells High School and was a pupil there in 1889, when Headmistress Mary Moberly and two other teachers signed the national declaration in favour of women's suffrage. After leaving school, Kate studied natural sciences at Newnham College, Cambridge, where she probably attended meetings of the Ladies' Discussion Society on subjects such as women in local government. Certainly the atmosphere at the college favoured women's rights. Suffragist leader Millicent Garrett Fawcett sat on its council and there were staff (such as chemistry lecturer Ida Freund) and fellow students (such as New Zealander Frances Parker[a]) who supported the Votes for Women cause. Kate was awarded a degree by Newnham in 1899, although as a woman she was not able to graduate from the University[b] (unlike her younger brothers, William and Edward, who also studied at Cambridge).

---

a In 1908 Frances (Fanny) Parker would be one the speakers Kate's sisters heard at the Hyde Park rally.

b Cambridge University did not award degrees to women until 1947.

Lovegrove Farm vehicle (with Kate Le Lacheur driving)
State Library of South Australia Ref. PRG 280/1/3/385

In 1902 Kate went to work as manageress of the Lekhampstead Manor Farm School near Newbury and by 1904 she was running Lovegrove Farm and Dairy Farm at Checkendon near Reading, together with Frances Parker. According to an article in the *Kentish Advertiser*:

One of the most enterprising of women dairy farmers is Miss Le Lacheur. She is a Socialist and a Suffragist, and has her farm hands, both men and women, sitting at the same dinner table as herself. To her belongs the distinction of the delivery of milk by motor. She started a chauffeur and a motor-float some time ago, and now a smart motor, with two milk-cans at the back…may be seen moving swiftly along the country roads with milk fresh from the cow.[117]

The caption beneath a photograph published in the *Lincolnshire Chronicle* during 1909, of Kate and other workers with the farm's motor milk-cart read:

The residents of Lovegrove Farm are ardent Suffragettes, and a huge board inscribed "Votes for Women" is intended to intimate to all and sundry that this farm, at least, is not under the thumb of a mere man.[118]

Given her family background, the influence of teachers such as Mary Moberly and her experiences at Newnham College, it is not surprising that Kate became involved in the Votes for Women campaign. She joined the Reading WSPU (Women's Social and Political Union) branch, acting as steward at some of their meetings, and made donations to funds every year from 1907 onwards. Sometimes these were very generous. In the summer of 1908 she donated £60, which represented £5 for each week of the three month sentences served by the stone-throwers who had taken part in 'the rush' on Parliament.

Up to November 1910, Kate's activism seems to have been through making donations, local branch activities, or supporting other women. For example, when Frances Parker was sent to Holloway Prison in February 1908, following a demonstration at Parliament, Kate wrote to the prison governor asking to visit her and claimed that her sentence was 'a gross piece of injustice.' Now, however, she committed herself to taking a more active part and volunteered to take part in the WSPU deputation.

On 18 November 1910, thirty-three-year-old Kate travelled into London and headed to Caxton Hall, up the road from the House of Commons, where a 'Woman's Parliament' had been convened. Around 300 suffragettes, wearing warm winter coats and hats trimmed with feathers, flowers and ribbons, filled the room. A selection of venerable campaigners were on the stage, while in the main body of the hall sat Kate and other women who had volunteered for active service, wearing small white satin badges with the words 'Deputation 1910' on them. The mood was tense and serious.

Soon news arrived. The Prime Minister had announced that, with the Commons and the Lords in deadlock over the budget, Parliament would be dissolved in ten days' time and there would be another general election. He had made no specific reference to women's suffrage, but it was clear that time had run out and the Conciliation Bill was not going to be passed in the current session. The suffragettes believed they had been betrayed. A vital opportunity had been lost and legislation would have to start again from scratch. It was time for action. Emmeline Pankhurst addressed the meeting, saying:

All other kinds of effort having failed, you will now press forward in quietness and peaceableness, offending none and blaming none, ready to sacrifice yourselves even unto death if need be, in the cause of freedom.[119]

At 12.40pm, the first group of women, led by the unmistakable figure of Emmeline, in a full-length fur coat and feather-trimmed hat, emerged into the bitter cold and began walking slowly along Victoria Street to Westminster. They were an impressive set. Eminent physicist Hertha Ayrton, aged fifty-eight, had been the first woman to read a paper at the Royal Society. Pioneering doctor Elizabeth Garrett Anderson (who had delivered the first national petition back in 1866) was now in her eighties. Princess Sophia Duleep Singh, a diminutive figure in a short fur coat, was the daughter of a maharaja and god-daughter of the late queen. Sixty-six-year-old Georgiana Solomon was the widow of a leading South African politician.

The atmosphere was friendly at first, with pedestrians and bus passengers cheering as they passed. But when the group reached Parliament Square, things changed. Their police escort abandoned them to the mob that had gathered there, described by one eye-witness as 'the idle, jostling crowd that flocks to every

London sight, and would as gladly flock to a London hanging if you gave it one to gloat over.'[120] Home Secretary Winston Churchill had been alerted to the demonstration and there were also large numbers of police.

Emmeline and her group were jostled and shoved. When they tried to reach the House of Commons, policemen blocked their path and pushed them back into the crowd. Fortunately some male supporters managed to force a way through and eventually all twelve made it to the St Stephen's entrance. They planned to wait on the steps there until the Prime Minister agreed to see them.

Having failed to stop this first group from reaching their destination, the police turned their attention to WSPU supporters in the crowd. Some were carrying small purple banners, with slogans such as 'Asquith has Veto'd our bill', which the police snatched and ripped to pieces.

Meanwhile, further groups of twelve women (one including Kate) were setting off from Caxton Hall every few minutes.[a] They also carried banners, with messages such as 'Women's Will Beats Asquith's Won't' and 'Where there's a Bill there's a way.' When they reached Parliament Square they tried to join their leaders on the steps of the Commons, but met with a violent response. They were assaulted by uniformed police (many of whom had been brought in from the suburbs and were more used to dealing with rowdy drunks) and by the rough element in the crowd (some of whom later turned out to be plain-clothes policemen).

The police jeered and shouted abuse at the suffragettes as they kicked them, punched them and hit them with batons. Horses were ridden towards the women, reared up and knocked them to the ground. Their arms were twisted and their thumbs bent back. Their skirts were lifted and obscenities spat at them.

---

a Twelve was the maximum number of people for a demonstration to be legal.

The most frequent complaint afterwards was of 'twisting round, pinching, crewing, nipping or wringing the breasts...often done in the most public way so as to inflict the utmost humiliation.'[121] This form of attack was extremely distressing, especially as it was believed that a breast injury could cause cancer.

None of the protestors had experienced anything similar before. They were shocked and terrified. One wrote of being 'tossed about like a cork on an angry sea, turning round and round.'[122] According to another:

> *For hours one was beaten about the body, thrown backwards and forwards from one to another, until one felt dazed with the horror of it – One policeman picked me up in his arms and threw me into the crowd saying 'You come again you B--- B--, and I will show you what I will do to you' – a favourite trick was pinching the upper part of one's arms which were black and blue afterwards –What I complain of on behalf of all of us is the long-drawn-out agony of the delayed arrest.*[123]

Black Friday (1910)
© Museum of London

Undeterred, the suffragettes continued trying to reach the House of Commons, but were repeatedly assaulted and thrown back. This went on for hours. (It was later alleged that, with the Liberal Party anxious to avoid adverse publicity in advance of the general election, Churchill had instructed the police to avoid making arrests as far as possible.) Injured women were taken back to Caxton Hall, where a makeshift hospital had been set up. Meanwhile, further groups continued to set off.

When they saw how the women were being treated, some onlookers changed their opinion. If these women were breaking the law they should be arrested. If they *weren't* breaking the law, they should be allowed to protest in peace.

Finally, at around 3.30pm, Emmeline Pankhurst and the first deputation were invited inside the Commons. However, they were disappointed to encounter only the Prime Minister's secretary, who said that Mr Asquith was not prepared to see them. They returned to the St Stephen's Entrance, where they watched in horror, from behind a police cordon, as the violent assaults on their fellow protestors continued.

In the end the police had no option but to start making arrests. In all, 115 women (including Kate) and four men were taken to Cannon Row Police Station. The scene there was one of mounting chaos, as more and more of them arrived, with black eyes, bleeding noses, bruises, dislocations and torn clothes. They were charged with obstruction and resisting the police, or (in a few cases) assault and wilful damage, and bailed to appear in court in the morning.

Eventually Parliament Square was cleared of people. Gas lamps shone through the fog onto discarded banners and items of clothing, the only evidence that remained of what had just occurred. The demonstration had lasted six hours, during which the suffragettes had met with an unprecedented level of violence.

Next morning, the suffragettes who had been released on

bail arrived at Bow Street Magistrates' Court on foot or by motor car. They were warmly dressed and carried rugs. Assuming that they were likely to be found guilty and sent straight to prison, many had brought suitcases with them. Fellow WSPU members crowded round the court entrance and cheered as they went in. An organ-grinder played *Put me among the girls.*

At 1pm the first in a long line of defendants was ushered into the courtroom and took her place in the dock. Before her case could be heard, the prosecutor made a speech. After referring to the 'unseemly conduct' of many ladies and the 'moderation' of the police, who had taken the women into custody for their own protection, he informed the court that the Home Secretary had determined that 'no public advantage would be gained by proceeding with the prosecution.' As a consequence, no evidence would be offered against any of the defendants. A ripple of laughter and applause went round the court, although the main reaction was astonishment. The women who had been waiting outside were brought into the courtroom in small groups and informed that they were being discharged.

The suffragettes were clear that they had been treated appallingly by the police and the government on the day that soon became known as 'Black Friday.' Many of the women who took part suffered long term effects and two died as a result of the injuries they sustained. *Votes for Women* described it as the worst treatment that had been meted out to any deputation since the conflict between women and the government had begun.

The newspapers, however, were mostly less sympathetic. *The Times* described the protestors as 'suffrage raiders' and referred to 'disorderly scenes'. The *Daily Mirror* published a photograph on their front page showing Ada Wright collapsed on the ground. The caption seemed to direct blame at the suffragettes rather than the police. 'While forcibly endeavouring yesterday to enter the Houses of Parliament, great numbers of suffragettes used more frantic methods than ever before.' Despite this, the government was anxious to avoid adverse publicity and ordered the *Mirror* to suppress the picture and destroy the negative, although many copies of the paper had already been sold. Presenting a rather different view of events, the *Daily News* quoted an eye-witness, who said that, while some policemen had been as gentle as possible under the circumstances, the acts of brutality and unnecessary violence of others had made his blood run cold.

Journalist Henry Brailsford and Dr Jessie Murray interviewed many of the women who had been involved in the demonstration and produced a report on how the police had handled it. The evidence of the officers' violent behaviour was overwhelming, but the Metropolitan Police Commissioner responded by claiming that the worst assaults had been committed by members of the public. Winston Churchill continued to deny having ordered police to hold off making arrests and refused to hold an official enquiry into police conduct.

The following Tuesday, 22 November, the WSPU assembled at Caxton Hall again. They were informed that the Prime Minister had continued refusing to meet their leaders, but had made a statement in the Commons on the subject of Votes for Women. This was now read out:

The government will, if they are still in power, give facilities in the next parliament for effectively proceeding with a Bill which is so framed as to permit of Free Amendment.[124]

The suffragettes had heard similar statements before and this fell far short of what they wanted, especially in the light of previous broken promises. Protests resumed immediately. They marched to Downing Street and to other MPs' homes, en masse rather than in small groups. Their actions, which included throwing stones, were more violent than they had been in Parliament Square the previous Friday. The *Daily News*, less tolerant of their behaviour on this occasion, reported that they struck policemen with umbrellas and fragments of banner poles and described them as 'infuriated women making a savage onslaught on the police.'

The suffragettes' violence ensured that they were arrested more quickly on this occasion. (The police were also anxious not to see a repeat of the previous Friday's events.) Actress Kitty Marion wrote that 'the battle of Downing Street raged like a seething cauldron'[125] and she was thankful when at last, breathless and exhausted, she was arrested. Over 150 women were taken into custody, including Kate Le Lacheur (who had not been deterred by her experience the previous week), Violet Tillard (who had returned from her Australian tour) and her younger sister Irene. (Both the Tillard sisters were now living in London and it seems that they may have transferred their allegiance from the WFL (Women's Freedom League) to the WSPU).

When their cases came up in court, those who had only been charged with obstruction, including Kate and Violet, were released without charge. However, seventy-five women were convicted of assault or damaging property. Among these was Irene Tillard who, together with four other women, was accused of breaking windows at the Colonial Office on Whitehall to the value of £4 15s. All five pleaded guilty, although they claimed that they had taken care to select windows in unoccupied rooms. This did not impress the magistrate, who sentenced them to two months each.

Irene was released at the end of January, having served her sentence in Holloway Prison, and wrote to the editor of *Votes for Women*, asking him to pass on her thanks to WSPU members who had sent her presents of food. The editor commented that her letter was typical and all the released prisoners wanted to thank the many kind friends who had made their imprisonment more tolerable.

* * *

The general election Asquith had announced on Black Friday took place in December 1910 and, as in January, the NUWSS (National Union of Women's Suffrage Societies) were the only suffrage organisation to campaign in Tunbridge Wells. This time they put their support firmly behind Liberal candidate Alfred Hedges, who was hoping to regain his seat. The suffragists distributed several thousand leaflets, sold over one hundred copies of *The Common Cause* and rented a shop at 18 Crescent Road (opposite the Calverley Hotel stables), which they decorated in red, green and white and with what the press described as 'another interesting election picture gallery.' On election day, several of them drove through the town in a car decorated with both their colours and the blue ribbons of the Liberals.

Despite their efforts, Alfred was not re-elected and Herbert Spender-Clay continued as MP for Tunbridge Wells. Nationally the Liberals managed to hang on to power, although with no overall majority. With Asquith still at the head of the government, it was probably not surprising that the King's Speech on 6 February 1911 contained no reference to Votes for Women. However, three days later Liberal MP George Kemp tabled a revised Conciliation Bill (the second one) on behalf of the Conciliation Committee. It passed its first reading and hopes were raised once again. The WSPU resumed their truce, despite the painful memories of Black Friday, and suspended militant activities once again. Soon there would be an excellent opportunity for a more peaceful form of protest.

Chapter 16

No Vote No Census!

'Boycott The Census' read the banner on the front page of *The Vote* on 11 February 1911. An article inside the Women's Freedom League (WFL) newspaper argued: 'Any Government which refuses to recognize women must be met by women's refusal to recognize the Government' and continued: 'We intend to do our best to make [the census] unreliable and inaccurate.'[126]

The census presented an opportunity for the sort of peaceful protest favoured by the WFL, without the potential for violent encounters with the police such as WSPU (Women's Social and Political Union) members had experienced on Black Friday the previous November. At a WFL 'At Home' in Caxton Hall on 9 February, Charlotte Despard announced that she intended to tear up her form and hoped every woman householder would do the same. If women were not full citizens (with the right to vote), she reasoned, why should they comply with the requirement to be counted?

For the NUWSS (the National Union of Women's Suffrage Societies, by far the largest suffrage organisation), the prospect of breaking the law was unacceptable; their leaders declined to join in planning a boycott and at their national AGM in January 1911, they voted not to adopt this form of protest.

However, the WSPU soon joined in. On 17 February they announced in *Votes for Women* that their members would also be refusing to fill in the census forms and that plans were being made to help them avoid it altogether. The paper described this as a unique opportunity for women to make 'a dignified, logical and effective protest against their political disabilities.'[127] When they were criticised for refusing to take part in something so important, the WSPU responded that, if the government undertook to pass the latest Conciliation Bill, they would abandon their protest. In addition, if legislation was passed in the current parliamentary session, members who had withheld information would immediately provide it.

In the weeks leading up to the census, the WFL and WSPU both published detailed advice for their members on how to protest and the potential consequences of doing so. They also printed responses to the numerous enquiries they had received relating to members' specific circumstances and concerns.

There were two main options for protestors – evade or resist. Evading the count would involve spending the night away from home and avoiding the enumerator's attention. (It had to be all night. If someone was away from home at midnight, they were supposed to be counted first thing in the morning.) The WSPU published a list of around thirty towns where a house would be available for protestors to hide out in. Evaders would not be breaking the law. However, it was unusual, and not considered respectable, for a woman to be out late, let alone all night, so this course of action would not be undertaken lightly.

Resisting, on the other hand, meant allowing yourself to be recorded, but refusing to provide any information other than your name. This would be a criminal offence, which could result in a £5 fine, seizure of goods to the same value, or one month in prison. So it would also require a degree of courage.

Aside from the potential consequences for them personally, a further dilemma faced women in deciding to whether to take part in the boycott. On the 1911 form, each married householder was required to enter the length of their marriage, the number of children born, how many were still living and how many had died. If women refused to comply with the census, they could be withholding information which would support the welfare reforms Chancellor Lloyd George was proposing.

Over the last few days of March, 35,000 enumerators walked the streets, delivering around ten million schedules, one to each household in the country. These were to be filled out with a record of everyone present at midnight on Sunday 2 April. It was a huge undertaking. In addition to the enumerators, police constables were issued with forms on which to record homeless people who spent the night in barns, in sheds or in the open air. They were also expected to keep watch on any property where it was suspected that suffragist evaders might be hiding out, making a note of anyone who came or went.

When the night of the count arrived, women found many different ways of evading it. The largest protest took place in London, where the air was chilly and the pavements wet from the rain that had fallen earlier in the evening. Small groups of women walked through the deserted streets and began gathering in Trafalgar Square. At first there were only a handful of witnesses around to observe them – a few policemen and some late night wanderers. However, word got out and by 11.30pm a crowd had gathered. According to *The Times* there were more young men than suffragettes present, but the atmosphere was friendly, with plenty of good-natured cheers and laughter.

Once Big Ben had struck twelve, some protestors drove off in taxicabs, while others headed eastwards, singing *Let's All Go Down the Strand*. The 'Rinkeries', a roller-skating rink on the

Aldwych, was being kept open all night for census protestors. A crowd had gathered outside and when the doors opened, at around 1am, ticket-holders (who were mostly women) had to push their way through to gain admission. Others tried to force their way in too, but the police held them back. Several hundred women, and a few men, skated through the night, accompanied by a band. There was also entertainment – Ethel Smyth conducted *The March of the Women*, the anthem she had composed recently, WSPU leaders made speeches and well-known actresses read suffrage poems. Refreshments were available nearby, in the Gardenia Restaurant, a vegetarian establishment with mahogany counters and mirrored walls, where suffragettes acted as waitresses for the night. Finally, early the next morning, the skaters headed wearily home.

The Aldwych gathering was the largest census protest, but suffragettes spent the night in many different locations, including private homes, offices and public halls, and found many ways to pass the time. In London several women drove around in horse-drawn caravans. At a private home in Manchester, nicknamed Census Lodge, others enjoyed music, dances, games and speeches. In Portsmouth, protestors listened to a reading of Ibsen's banned play *Ghosts*. In Burton-on-Trent, having slept on an office floor, a group of women set off at 6am and rode bicycles through a snowstorm, reaching Lichfield Cathedral, twelve miles away, in time for the morning service.

First thing on Monday 3 April, household heads across the country completed and signed the form. The duty was taken very seriously. The *South Eastern Gazette* noted: 'The King and Queen and other members of the Royal Family set an excellent example to the nation at large in the matter of careful and accurate filling up of the census schedule.'[128]

That same day, enumerators began calling to collect completed forms. They checked for errors and omissions and handed the forms over to local registrars, who inspected and collated them, before forwarding them to the General Register Office. In addition to the usual issues with households who did not have their forms ready, or who had filled them out incorrectly, enumerators had to establish as far as possible, where and how Votes for Women campaigners had tried to subvert the process. When they were aware that women had evaded the count, but had no names or other information, they estimated numbers. The enumerator for the Aldwych recorded that there had been 500 women and seventy men at the skating rink, but listed just a handful of names.

In Hastings a rather nervous enumerator arrived on the doorstep of fifty-five-year-old widow Eliza Harrison, who handed him a return on which she had written 'No Vote. No Information.' The police had been watching her house overnight and knew that a number of suffragettes had stayed there, passing the time by singing suffrage songs. It was probably on the basis of their information that the enumerator estimated there had been five women present, in addition to Eliza and two servants, although he was unable to record any specific details.

At around 2pm a House of Commons cleaner went down into the Chapel of St Mary Undercroft, where she found suffragette Emily Wilding Davison, who had hidden in a cupboard overnight.[a] The police were summoned and arrested Emily, who was detained for a few hours and then released. She achieved her aim and the Clerk of Works recorded her address as 'Found hiding in the Crypt of Westminster Hall, Westminster.' However, her landlady at Coram Street, Bloomsbury, also included her on that household's form, so she ended up being counted twice.

In Tunbridge Wells the vast majority of residents, including the non-militant suffragists, dutifully completed their forms

---

a The cupboard where Emily Wilding Davison hid is marked by a commemorative plaque.

and handed them to the enumerator. At her home on Park Road in Southborough, Amelia Scott listed herself, her sister Louisa, their parlour maid, their cook and the cook's husband and son. At Grosvenor Lodge, Edith Tattershall Dodd, local NUWSS secretary, was recorded as present by her husband Charles. There is no evidence that Sarah Grand completed a form (her cook and parlour maid were the only people listed as present at her home on Grove Hill Road).[a] However, as a law-abiding suffragist, it seems unlikely that she evaded the census and she may well have been abroad on one of her frequent speaking tours. Lydia Le Lacheur completed a return for her household at The Wilderness, which included five female servants and a groom. However, she and her youngest daughter Mabel (aged twenty and recorded as having been 'feeble-minded since birth') were the only family members shown.

There were a few local resisters, who were recorded but made some form of protest on the form. (In some cases, this was the only trace they left behind of their support for the Votes for Women cause.) While Lydia did not make any protest herself, she entered the word 'suffragist' beside the names of two of her servants (both longstanding household members), presumably at their request. Retired bank official Edward Plowright completed the return for his household in Southborough (on the edge of Tunbridge Wells) and wrote in red ink beneath the response for his daughter Catherine, a WFL member, and their servant Elizabeth Tilley: 'This information is given under protest, owing to the fact that, up to the present time, the rights of citizenship have not been granted to women.'[129]

A small number of women in and around Tunbridge Wells refused to provide any information at all, despite warnings that they would be breaking the law. Medical practitioner John Abbott may have been annoyed with Katherine Conway, a nurse

---

a Sarah had moved from Langton Green to Grove Hill Road by this time.

who boarded in his home. He filled in her details, but wrote in a rather tetchy note below: 'Conway is a suffragette and will not inform me of her full name, age or birthplace.' Edith Schweder, a widow living in Lamberhurst, a few miles away, wrote on the form: 'Being a woman householder but having no vote I decline to fill up this paper.' The local enumerator guessed who had been present overnight at her home, estimated their ages and noted at the foot of the form: 'The above information filled in by H F Edwards Registrar, in accordance with instructions received from Census Office.'

Violet Tillard, who was sharing lodgings with Muriel Matters in Kennington, London SW1, by this time, refused to provide any details. She wrote across her return: 'No Vote. No Census. Should women become persons in the eyes of the law this session, full information will be forwarded.'

Any organised evasion by Tunbridge Wells women would not have been through the WFL. Despite Dorothy Le Lacheur's enthusiasm and hard work, the local branch had only been only short-lived and was certainly no longer in existence by 1911. However, a number of local women had been supporting the WSPU for some time (by making donations, for example, and possibly in other ways as well) and would soon be involved in forming a local branch. Most of these were missing from the census records.

Dorothy Le Lacheur was not recorded by her mother at The Wilderness or in any other household.[a] Olive Walton was not at home with her family. (When she drafted her own entry in the *1913 Suffrage Annual and Who's Who* she stated that she had evaded the census.) William Harverson and his three young children (aged ten, seven and two) were at home at 8 Mayfield Road, but there was no sign of his wife Laura. Widow Huldah Wedgwood and her daughter Mary were present at 37

---

a May Le Lacheur had moved away from home by this time and was recorded elsewhere.

Madeira Park, but her two other unmarried daughters, Ethel and Catherine, were not recorded.

With so many of the women who would go on to be active members of the Tunbridge Wells WSPU missing from the count, it seems very likely that they deliberately evaded it.[a] Campaigners from Tunbridge Wells travelled up to London for most major events in the Votes for Women campaign (before and after the census) and some local women probably took part in events on Trafalgar Square and at the Aldwych Skating Rink.

In addition, Tunbridge Wells was on the WSPU's list of places where a home was to be opened up for evaders, so other local women would probably have spent the night together somewhere in or near the town. There is no clear indication of where, although it may have been Landhurst Cottage in Hartfield, a village around eight miles outside Tunbridge Wells. This property, the home of thirty-five-year-old Lilla Durham, was identified as 'uninhabited' on census night and Lilla was not recorded anywhere else. Over the next few months she would take the lead in setting up a local WSPU branch and would host a number of meetings at her home, so it is possible that suffragettes spent the night there. If they did, they managed to escape the attention of the local enumerator Henry Killick.

On 5 April, John Burns, the government minister with overall responsibility for the census, appeared before the House of Commons. He dismissed the suggestion that the Votes for Women protest might have had an impact, saying:

I do not anticipate that the suffragette agitation against the census will have any appreciable effect upon the accuracy of the statistics of population. According to the information that

---

a Local newspapers might have given some clue as to where these women were on census night. However, unfortunately no 1911 editions have survived for either the *Courier* or the *Advertiser* (the town's two main newspapers).

has reached me up to the present, the number of individuals who have evaded being enumerated is altogether negligible.[130]

Official reports on the census, published over the following years, pointed to the efficiency with which it had been run and made no reference to the boycott. This made sense, as evaders and resisters, in Tunbridge Wells and elsewhere, were a tiny fraction of the total population. In addition, no resisters were prosecuted. Burns announced this in the same speech, saying: 'in the hour of success, mercy and magnanimity must be shown.'

Nevertheless, despite being relatively small-scale, the census protest did achieve publicity for the cause. It was also a form of action which was more acceptable to the general public than the WSPU's increasingly militant tactics. (They were currently maintaining their truce, but the violent scenes that had occurred in Parliament Square on Black Friday, and at Downing Street a few days later, were still fresh in many people's minds.)

The WFL and WSPU both claimed that it had been a success and that the numbers participating had been far greater than the authorities anticipated. In *Votes for Women,* the WSPU claimed that it had demonstrated two things: firstly, how many women were prepared to use revolutionary methods to enforce their demand for the vote and secondly, the authorities' impotence in the face of this determined resistance.

Not everyone agreed. In *The Illustrated London News* author G K Chesterton commented:

There seems to be the same ineptness [as with punching policemen] *about the selection of the census as a weapon of protest. It is the sort of thing that annoys men but does not annoy them enough.*[131]

Anti-suffrage campaigners also questioned the protest's effectiveness. An article in *The Anti-Suffrage Review* said that 'few things have been more ineffective, just as few have been more foolish, than the resistance to the census.'

Aside from a few clues in the census, there is little indication of what most women in Tunbridge Wells thought about not having the vote at this time. However, despite the fact that campaigners were a small minority, there was a large and active NUWSS branch in town and a significant number of people had signed their petition at the beginning of 1910. The WFL's campaign had also been very visible for a couple of years, before it came to an end.

Over the following months, people in Tunbridge Wells became aware of a new campaign starting up in the town, run by the WSPU. A Votes for Women poster was put on permanent display at the railway station. Women, wearing purple, green and white accessories, stood on street corners selling copies of *Votes for Women*, which also appeared on bookshop shelves across town. Small groups were seen holding open-air meetings on the Common and at Five Ways and local newspapers reported that a drawing room meeting had been held in Lilla Durham's Hartfield home, when many promises of help were made.

On 20 May sisters Ethel and Catherine Wedgwood rode through the town on two large horses, wearing Votes for Women sashes and carrying placards which advertised a meeting due to take place three days later. Other women walked alongside them, offering newspapers for sale. Local suffragettes had arranged for WSPU leader Emmeline Pethick-Lawrence to come and speak at the Great Hall. They sold tickets (costing from 2s for a reserved seat, to 3d for a place in the gallery), Lilla organised stewards and Lydia Le Lacheur (supportive, despite never joining the WSPU herself) provided flowers to decorate the meeting room.

In her speech at the meeting on 23 May, Emmeline referred to the second Conciliation Bill, which MP George Kemp had tabled earlier in the year and which had passed its second reading on 5 May, with a majority of 167. It would be unconstitutional and undesirable if the cabinet blocked the bill, she said. It was highly important that women's point of view should be taken into account when Parliament was considering subjects such as sweated labour, purity, illegitimacy and maternity. As the meeting ended, the customary resolution was passed and telegraphed to the Prime Minister.

With prospects looking good for the Bill, the WSPU maintained their truce and campaigners' hopes were raised once again. Their optimism continued into June 1911, when a women's procession was held to mark the coronation of George V (a year after he had succeeded to the throne). The procession took place on 17 June. It was organised by the WSPU, but the different wings of the suffrage campaign came together and members of other organisations, including both the WFL and the NUWSS, took part.

The *Common Cause* published instructions from the NUWSS to their members which showed that, as always, the event was organised with military precision. The long list included:

Wear the colours conspicuously
Be punctual
Line up seven abreast
Remain in line once you have found it
Keep in step with the person on your left
Wheel carefully
Hold your head up and square your shoulders
Do not look back or talk to the people behind you
Wear white if possible
Let your dress be short and your hat small

On 17 June (five days before the main coronation procession) an impressive spectacle was seen on London's streets. Led by Flora Drummond, who was on horseback and dressed in green hunting costume, around 40,000 women marched in a procession which stretched for around seven miles. Women of every class and occupation took part, many of them carrying banners and wearing national and historical costumes. Brass bands accompanied suffragettes as they sang the official WSPU anthem, *The March of the Women*, whose first verse went:

> *Shout, shout, up with your song!*
> *Cry with the wind for the dawn is breaking.*
> *March, march, swing you along,*
> *Wide blows our banner and hope is waking.*
> *Song with its story, dreams with their glory,*
> *Lo! They call and glad is their word.*
> *Forward! Hark how it swells*
> *Thunder of freedom, the voice of the Lord.*

Scattered among the marchers were a number of women from Tunbridge Wells, both militants and non-militants. Sarah Grand walked with the Writers Franchise League, while Amelia Scott and local suffragists were in the NUWSS section. Lilla and members of the new WSPU branch marched with a large contingent of suffragettes from across Kent, following behind a magnificent banner on which was displayed the County's white horse on a blue background, together with the word 'Invicta'. Olive Ibbotson, Violet Tillard and Irene Tillard may have been in the parade of 700 or so suffragette prisoners, all dressed in white.

Women's Suffrage Coronation Procession (1911)

Women's Library, LSE

The procession started at 5pm and did not finish until after nine. It brought London to a standstill. Passengers on stranded omnibuses cheered and shouted. There was laughter at some of the historical costumes – especially Queens Boadicea, Henrietta Maria and Elizabeth. According to the WSPU, there was little opposition, apart from a rather forlorn set of sandwich men employed by the anti-suffragists to publicise their message. Marchers were amused to see that several of them were carrying their boards upside down.

Later that evening, meetings were held in the Albert Hall, Hyde Park and Kensington Town Hall. The Tunbridge Wells suffragettes had reserved a box at the Albert Hall, where they heard Emmeline Pankhurst describe the key note of the movement as co-operation with men, with the object of building up a better and brighter type of humanity.[132]

The procession, which was an opportunity both for pageantry and to demonstrate campaigners' dignity and purity, generated a positive reaction in the press. *The Times* commented that it exceeded all other women's suffrage processions in numbers and effect, although the paper also suggested that for many people it was 'a spectacle that troubled and provoked as well as fascinated.'[133] The *Daily News* described it as imposing, inspiring and a powerful demonstration of the movement's strength and unity.'[134]

For the women who took part, it was a stirring experience, as an article in *The Vote* conveyed:

Forty thousand women walking five abreast, with pennants flying, banners held aloft, colours of every hue and shade and gradation blazing in the sun; forty thousand women with faces to the dawn, women of every rank and party and creed and race and colour; women old and young, rich and poor; comrades all in the great cause of freedom…a procession seven miles long, to the inspiring music of a hundred bands…And this procession meant something more than mere pageant and splendour and colour and movement and song. The beating of drums, the call of the music, the sound of many feet, as the rushing of waters, the wonderful organisation – all made a vivid impression upon those who came out to see the biggest and most significant procession of womanhood that has ever walked through the streets of the greatest city in the world.[135]

Through the summer of 1911, and on into the autumn, the Tunbridge Wells suffragettes continued making their presence felt in their home town. They held regular open-air meetings – at Five Ways at the top of town and on Little Mount Sion, just off the High Street. They stood on street corners, offering handbills and copies of *Votes for Women* to passers-by, who were supportive, antagonistic or, in many cases, uninterested. They also placed copies of the paper with local branches of newsagents such as WH Smith (who had a shop at the railway station) and left them lying around in public places, in the hope that people would pick them up.

Even if no-one took a handbill or bought a newspaper, holding them up for inspection helped publicise the cause. The front page of each issue of *Votes for Women* was designed to attract attention. The current state of the campaign was represented in cartoon form, as a chess game, a snowball fight, a castle siege, a scene from Greek mythology, or an episode in the French revolution. Other covers made fun of the unsuccessful attempts by Asquith, Lloyd George and government ministers to avoid suffragette protests. The newspaper sold well – by 1912 its national weekly circulation was 40,000 copies.

The Tunbridge WSPU branch was set up during a truce, which (apart from a short pause after Black Friday) had been in place since January 1910. It was some time since there had been any stone-throwing, mass protests or hunger strikes and the first campaigning activity local suffragettes engaged in was the non-violent census protest. They would have believed, as many others in the Votes for Women movement did, that success was not far off and that they were campaigning to hold the government to its promise. But things were about to change.

Chapter 17

The Argument of the
Broken Pane of Glass

Just a few months later, the jubilation and optimism that campaigners had felt in May, when the latest Conciliation Bill passed its second reading, and in June, as they marched through London's streets in the Coronation Procession, was gone.

When Parliament met in autumn 1911, there was no further reference to the Bill. Instead, on 7 November, Prime Minister Asquith announced that in the next session he intended introducing a new manhood suffrage bill. This would establish a single, straightforward residential qualification for male electors. It would not include women, but they could be added through an amendment. The problem with this was that an amendment would hand the vote to *all* women (not just householders), and they would immediately outnumber male voters. This prospect was unacceptable to most MPs and so an amendment would have no chance of being passed. Both campaigners and the press saw the announcement as a deliberate ploy to prevent women getting the vote. It was a bitter blow, especially when hopes of success had been so high.

On 17 November a deputation from the main suffrage societies went to see the Prime Minister at Downing Street. (For the first time he agreed to see the militant leaders as well as the non-militants.) Christabel Pankhurst, Charlotte Despard and Millicent Fawcett all made lengthy speeches, calling on him to change his mind. Asquith acknowledged the strength and intensity of women's feelings and the fact that a majority in Parliament did not agree with him. But he also confirmed that his own position was unchanged since 1908 (when he first became Prime Minister). Women should not, and would not, be given the vote. In any case, he continued, most of them did not want it. (40,000 women marching in the Coronation Procession had apparently not been sufficient proof).

Despite this setback, the leaders and members of the NUWSS (National Union of Women's Suffrage Societies) and WFL (Women's Freedom League) were hopeful that, although it had been deferred, the Conciliation Bill might still have a chance of succeeding in the next parliamentary session. In January 1912, an article in *The Common Cause* said: 'We are prepared to be patient, but with the patience not of submission, but of watchful courage.'[136] The WSPU (Women's Social and Political Union), however, were less optimistic. Following the unsuccessful deputation to the Prime Minister, their leaders announced an immediate end to the truce and declared war. Several members of the new Tunbridge Wells branch would play a part in the next phase of their campaign, including 25-year-old Olive Walton.

Olive was born in 1886, the third child of seventy-three-year-old wine merchant Charles Walton and his wife Mary Ann. Her father died when she was only seven, after which she had an unhappy childhood, as she was brought up by her very strict mother. Olive, who was described by her family as 'difficult', was not academic (unlike her older brother John and younger sister Mary, who both studied at Oxford University). She

Olive Walton (c1920)
© *National Portrait Gallery, London*

attended a small private school in Germany (where her family lived for a couple of years), did cookery classes, art classes and social work training in London and then returned to live with her family in Tunbridge Wells.

When a local branch of the NUWSS was set up in 1908, Olive became a member, although there is no evidence to suggest she was ever actively involved. It seems that her mother also supported the Votes for Women cause; Mary Ann Walton also joined the NUWSS and in November 1910 she hosted an NUWSS meeting at her home, with Amelia Scott in the chair and a visiting speaker from the national executive. Olive became disillusioned with the lack of progress being achieved by peaceful means. In March 1911, she evaded the census and, when the WSPU began operating in in Tunbridge Wells around the same time, their approach had more appeal and she transferred her allegiance to them.

What attracted women such as Olive to become involved in

the WSPU? In many cases they had become impatient with the sedate campaigning methods of women such as Sarah Grand and Amelia Scott, which seemed to have achieved nothing, and believed that direct action was more likely to get women the vote. But there were other reasons too.

Almost two thirds of the WSPU's members were unmarried and campaigning offered them the chance to escape home lives which could be restrictive, or (as in Olive's case) unhappy. Education for girls had improved, but employment opportunities for young women had not, or at least not to the same extent. Finding a job was still difficult and qualifying in a profession even more so. It was generally assumed that, once a middle-class girl had completed her education (whether at home, school or, in a few cases, university), she would marry and set up home. Militant campaigning gave young, single women an outlet for their energies, as well as a chance to make a difference by challenging an injustice.

The WSPU also offered its members the excitement of serving in an army. They used the language of war (for example, funds raised were known as the 'war chest' and members called each other 'comrade') and their patron saint was Joan of Arc. Medals were issued to those who had taken militant action and worn with pride. Members wore a uniform – the distinctive purple, green and white – and sang marching songs, such as *The Women's Battle Song* (to the tune of *Onward Christian Soldiers*). Suffragettes also hero-worshipped their leaders, especially Christabel Pankhurst, a powerful and inspiring speaker, who inspired passionate loyalty. In return they were expected to devote themselves to the cause.

Olive and other Tunbridge Wells suffragettes may well have been at a rally held by the WSPU in the Albert Hall on 16 November 1911 (the evening before their leaders went to see the Prime Minister), when Emmeline Pethick-Lawrence delivered a call to arms:

After a long period of truce with the Government, we meet tonight a united army on the eve of battle; not because we have chosen to fight, not because we desire militancy, but because the government has broken its terms of peace. The announcement of the intention of the government to bring in a Manhood Suffrage Bill is a declaration of war upon the womanhood of the country.[137]

For many suffragettes participating in the WSPU campaign was also spiritual experience. At the same rally, Christabel told members that, like Joan of Arc, 'their voices were of God' and, in their report on it, *Votes for Women* observed:

To [some] as they listened to the inspired speeches of Mrs Pethick-Lawrence and Miss Pankhurst there was no hall, no city, no century – the figures on the platform, the crowded audience, had gone. They saw only the spirit of womanhood beating its wings against the last barriers that even as they watched seemed to give way. What mattered misunderstanding or abuse, or disappointment or deception – nothing could check, nothing could daunt the spirit of womanhood.[138] [a]

Overall, being involved in the WSPU offered its members a sense of fulfilment. Olive later described this as the happiest period of her life and Emily Wilding Davison wrote: 'Through my humble work in this noblest of causes, I have come into a fullness of joy and an interest in living which I never before experienced.'[139] In addition to this there was a strong sense of comradeship between campaigners and many intense friendships were formed.

Some or all of these factors – the belief that militancy was necessary, the opportunity to escape from home, the excitement of being in an army, a quasi-spiritual experience and a chance

---

a In October 1912, a headline in one of the suffrage newspapers read 'A Sacred Struggle'.

for self-fulfilment – led young women such as Olive to devote considerable time and energy to the WSPU campaign. Their commitment was such that they were willing to demonstrate, break windows, go to prison, hunger strike and even endure the horror of force-feeding. Just a few days later, after the Albert Hall meeting and the fruitless delegation to the Prime Minister, women from Tunbridge Wells had the opportunity to play an active part in the battle for the vote.

On the evening of Tuesday 21 November 1911, WSPU leaders and members gathered at Caxton Hall. For some of them, memories of meeting there on Black Friday (almost exactly a year before) and of what followed in Parliament Square, were still fresh in their minds. A few were still suffering from the injuries they had sustained that day. Speeches were made and Christabel Pankhurst read out a resolution, calling on MPs to withdraw the manhood suffrage bill and replace it with one that offered true equality. The suffragettes cheered enthusiastically, waved handkerchiefs and flags and, when the meeting was over, headed out and walked along Victoria Street towards Westminster.

Five women from Tunbridge Wells – Olive Walton, Lilla Durham, Charlotte Ireland, Kate Conway and Mary Harmer – had travelled up to London to take part in the protest.[a] They may have been at Caxton Hall, although many protestors stayed away because of rumours (false as it turned out) that the police were planning to barricade the building and prevent them from marching. The Tunbridge Wells contingent definitely *were* amongst the hundreds of protestors who converged on Parliament Square from all directions.

Large numbers of policemen, including a squadron on horseback, were ready and waiting. There was also a

---

a There may have been others from Tunbridge Wells too, such as the Wedgwood sisters, but these are the women it is known for certain took part.

detachment of ambulance men in the centre of the square, in case of injuries. When suffragettes began trying to push their way through the police cordon towards the Houses of Parliament, a small group of them were allowed through, while the remainder were pushed back into the crowd. They were jostled and booed as they continued trying to get through. The police, who were far more restrained than they had been on Black Friday, soon began arresting women, including Olive, Charlotte and Kate.

Meanwhile, other suffragettes set off in twos and threes along the surrounding streets. At first sight they appeared peaceful, but every now and then one of them would stop, take a stone out of her pocket and, using a linen bag or handkerchief as a sling, hurl it towards the window of a government building, newspaper office, shop, or private club. The sound of breaking glass signalled the suffragettes' progress, as they walked up Whitehall, circled Trafalgar Square and continued along the Strand, where targets included the Telegraph Office, the Lyons' Corner House and numerous shops. Policemen sounded their whistles and made more arrests. Mary Harmer managed to break two windows at the War Office before she was arrested and Lilla broke several elsewhere (although there is no record of which building she targeted).

Window-breaking was an effective means of getting attention for the cause, but it was also a way to get arrested quickly and avoid the manhandling protestors had experienced on Black Friday. The press noted that on this occasion the suffragettes seemed anxious to get arrested, waiting until a policeman was nearby before throwing their stones and making no attempt at resistance. In her account of the Votes for Women campaign, Sylvia Pankhurst explained the rationale:

Since we must go to prison to obtain the vote, let it be the windows of the government, not the bodies of women which shall be broken, was the argument; for a window-smasher was at once taken quietly into custody.[140]

A series of policemen and suffragettes arrived at Cannon Row Police Station, where a long queue built up outside as the women waited to be processed. A large crowd had gathered and cheered at each new arrival. The loudest cheer of all went up as May Billinghurst was carried in on her wheelchair. In total the police arrested 220 women and three men, mainly for breaking windows.

The following morning, the first cases were heard in Bow Street Magistrates Court. Solicitor Herbert Muskett[a], who prosecuted on behalf of the commissioner of police, began by expressing outrage at the 'disgraceful and discreditable scenes of organised disorder' which had taken place the previous night. Most of the suffragettes defended themselves and took the opportunity to make a speech, so it took some time to work through the long list. A large number of women, including all of the Tunbridge Wells protestors, had their cases adjourned.

On Thursday morning the hearings continued. Olive waited in the Bow Street waiting room, along with thirty or forty other suffragettes who occupied themselves reading newspapers, writing letters, or talking quietly, until their turn came. By midday the court had reached the case before hers on the list, that of Emmeline Pethick-Lawrence, who had led the demonstration. Olive had a long wait, while Emmeline conducted a robust defence to the charge of punching a policeman, challenging the evidence against her, calling witnesses and making a long speech. When she had finished, she was found guilty and sentenced to

---

a Mr Muskett had been prosecuting suffragettes on behalf of the Metropolitan Police for some time – he was the prosecutor after suffragettes protested in the Central Lobby in 1906 and after Violet Tillard protested in the Ladies' Gallery in 1908.

one month in prison. Finally, Olive was summoned. She stood in the dock as a constable gave evidence that he had observed her repeatedly trying to break through the cordon and had no option but to arrest her. In response, Olive stated that her actions had been a protest. After she refused to give an undertaking not to do the same again, the magistrate sentenced her to a ten shilling fine, or seven days 'in the second division.' Olive refused to pay the fine, opting for prison instead.

The cases continued into the following week, with sentences of between five days and two months imposed. Kate's and Mary's cases were heard on Monday 27 November. Kate was accused of hitting a policeman in the face, which she denied. When the policeman appeared as a witness, he conceded that it could have been an accident. Kate told the court that she had done her utmost to break through the police line and reach the House of Commons in order to protest against the government's trickery and dishonesty. She was found guilty and also opted for seven days in prison rather than paying a 10s fine. When her turn came, Mary stated that she had broken the War Office windows 'as a protest at the action of the government and the wretched laws concerning women and children relating to the white slave traffic.' She received the same sentence as Olive and Kate. A day later Lilla was in court. Newspaper reports do not record where she broke windows, but she seems to have broken quite a few. Damages of £2 5s were awarded against her, in addition to a ten shilling fine. The prison sentence she opted for was fourteen days.

Charlotte's case was heard on the Wednesday and she made a lengthy speech, accusing the government of denying women the rights of citizenship and freedom they had been given by the Magna Carta and had exercised until 1832 (when the first Reform Act was passed). She also claimed to be following in the footsteps of the famous tax protestor John Hampden, who preferred imprisonment to injustice and tyranny. Charlotte chose five days in prison, rather than pay a five shilling fine.

The five Tunbridge Wells women served their sentences in Holloway Prison, along with many others. The experience must have been a shock for them, as it had for Violet Tillard back in 1908.

The scale and destructiveness of this latest protest prompted a negative reaction amongst the general public, and the sympathy that the hunger strikers had inspired, and that people had felt during the WSPU truce, now evaporated. Disapproval was heightened by the fact that, for the first time, buildings with no connection to the government had been targeted. Even newspapers who had been previously favourable towards the Votes for Women cause condemned the window-breaking. *The Standard* was generally supportive – it had launched a 'Woman's Platform' section the previous month, in which it promised to end the 'conspiracy of silence' regarding the campaign. But it reported recent events under the headline: 'Wild Rioting Women. Window Smashing Orgy of Disorder at Westminster.' *The Globe* said:

> *...this hysterical stone-throwing only proves, if it proves anything, that there are very large numbers of women who are still quite unfit to be trusted with the vote. It is like the behaviour of a naughty child who stamps and roars and breaks the tea-cups when it is not allowed the jam. What conceivable good can be served by smashing the windows of inoffensive tradesmen who have nothing whatever to do with either giving or refusing the vote?*

When Olive was released from Holloway on 30 November, along with six other women, supporters were outside the prison gates to greet her.[a] A crowd of suffragettes, waiting for one or more of their comrades to emerge, was a familiar sight at the prison. For a more high-profile prisoner there might also be a band playing stirring suffrage songs and a motor car or horse-drawn carriage waiting to whisk her away to a celebratory breakfast. Sometimes two lines of women in white dresses took the place of horses to draw the carriage.

Olive must have found returning home a challenge, especially as her family disapproved of her actions. But her commitment to the campaign had only been heightened. Fresh from their protest and prison sentences, Olive and other local women met for the first formal meeting of the new Tunbridge Wells WSPU branch. It was held at the home of forty-three-year-old married woman Laura Harverson and officers were appointed. Olive and Laura became joint secretaries, Lilla canvassing secretary, and Charlotte a committee member. (Dorothy Le Lacheur was not on the committee; she continued making generous donations to the organisation's funds and played a small part in the new branch, but was not an organiser, as she had been for the WFL.)

In December 1911, *Votes for Women* reported the establishment of the new branch. The involvement of women from Tunbridge Wells in recent events in London was, the paper observed, an indication of the intensity of militant feeling in the area. The branch was an especially active one from this time onwards. Members published regular bulletins in *Votes for Women*, recording their activities, donations and new members. They handed out leaflets supplied by headquarters and paraded through the town wearing sandwich boards. They invited speakers to visit and advertised meetings by chalking advertisements and Votes for Women slogans on pavements in the WSPU colours.

---

a   There is no specific record concerning the release of Mary, Charlotte and Kate on 2 December and Lilla on 11 December.

At Christmas, Lilla Durham entertained a new friend at her home in Hartfield. Kitty Marion was a twenty-one-year-old German music hall actress, with abundant red-gold hair and a strong sense of humour. She would have had plenty of stories to tell Lilla about her experience of campaigning. In 1908 she had taken part in 'the rush' on Parliament. In 1909 she had been sent to Newcastle prison for breaking windows, gone on hunger strike and been force-fed. In 1910 she had experienced police brutality in Parliament Square on Black Friday. Kitty had also taken part in the previous November's protest and she and Lilla seem to have become friends while serving their sentences in Holloway. From this time onwards, she stayed at Hartfield on a number of occasions, which she described in her memoir as 'happy times doing peaceful propaganda.'

During these visits, Kitty joined Lilla, Olive and other local women canvassing door-to-door in Tunbridge Wells. They met with a mixed reception. She later recalled a clergyman who asked them: 'Which lot do you belong to? Mrs Pankhurst's, or those that go around saying "Please sir, it wasn't me, it was the other boy?"' When they visited a leading local anti-suffragist lady to discuss the arrangements for a forthcoming debate, she was rude and hostile, until she discovered that Lilla's late father had been eminent surgeon Arthur Durham, upon which her attitude changed completely.

Money was needed to pay for banners, leaflets, meetings, legal costs and so on, which meant that fundraising was a priority for the Tunbridge Wells suffragettes. Members were encouraged to make donations and many of them did so frequently. (Even Laura Harverson's two oldest children, Clara aged ten and Walter aged seven, were listed as donors.) They also held fundraising events such as fetes and jumble sales.

In January 1912, the WSPU opened a shop at 11 The Pantiles, nestled between the premises of butcher Henry Holyer and beer, wine & spirit merchant William Biggs. There they sold books, pamphlets, postcards, badges, ribbons, sashes and Votes for Women merchandise including tea, cigarettes, calendars and Christmas crackers. They may also have sold games such as Pankasquith (a snakes and ladders-style board game about suffragettes' efforts to reach the House of Commons) and Panko (a card game which pitched pros and antis against each other). 11 The Pantiles acted both as a shop and as an office. With its prominent location, it provided somewhere for suffragettes to meet to organise their campaign and acted as a visible reminder of the cause to the large numbers of residents and visitors who passed by each day.

The Pantiles. (No. 11, which used to be the WSPU office, is on the left.)
© *The Author*

At the start of 1912 a letter published in the Woman's Platform section of *The Standard* described the progress the WSPU were making in Tunbridge Wells:

The militant suffragists are rapidly gaining ground here. The latest advance...is the opening of a permanent office in Ye Pantiles. The purple, white and green flags fluttering over this old world resort appeal to the onlooker against the tyranny of custom which is giving way to a spirit of greater tolerance.[141]

The Tunbridge Wells suffragettes kept in touch with their national organisation by reading their newspaper, listening to visiting speakers and attending events in London. In December 1911, some of them helped run a stall at the WSPU's Christmas Fair in the Portman Rooms on Baker Street. Together with other Kent branches, they sold 'presents for men' – ties, socks, shaving apparatus and 'anything else for the use and comfort of male friends.'

On 6 February 1912, Olive and her fellow protestors may have been amongst 300 WSPU members who attended a dinner at the Connaught Rooms, Kingsway, in honour of the women who had received two-month sentences back in November and who had just been released. (If not, they would have read a detailed account of it in *Votes for Women*.) Emmeline Pankhurst gave an inspiring speech, which began:

I rise to propose the health of our guests, those brave people who have recently come to us from Holloway prison. It is difficult for me to find the right words to express our gratitude, but I say to them from the bottom of my heart, that what they did last November has done more during the last three months to bring this question to where it is than perhaps all the patient work done by women since the movement for the emancipation of women began...We honour these women because having learnt that the argument of the broken pane of glass is the most valuable argument in modern politics, they nerved themselves to use that argument...[142]

172

Chapter 18

An Unannounced Attack

The argument of the broken pane of glass had little impact on
the government. Throughout February 1912, they continued
refusing to make any clear undertaking to give women the vote,
either through the manhood suffrage bill the Prime Minister
had proposed, or through a third version of the Conciliation
Bill, which received its first reading on 19 February.

The WSPU (Women's Social and Political Union) announced
that they would be holding a demonstration in Parliament
Square, on Monday 4 March, calling on the government to act.
They publicised arrangements in *Votes for Women* and circulated
handbills which also gave details.

The Tunbridge Wells suffragettes, however, knew differently.
Each of them had received a circular letter informing her that there
was to be an unannounced protest three days earlier, on 1 March,
and asking her to volunteer for 'danger duty'. It would be the first
time the WSPU had made a group protest without giving any
advance notice and the need for complete secrecy was emphasised.

On Friday 1 March, Olive, Charlotte, Lilla and Kate travelled
back up to London. On arriving at Charing Cross, they walked

along the Strand to the Gardenia Restaurant (a popular place with suffragettes, which many had visited on census night). Each of them was taken in turn to a private room, where she was issued with a hammer, advice on how to throw it in order to avoid broken glass and instructions on where to station herself. (One protestor later said that the hammer given to her was inscribed with the words: 'Better broken windows than broken promises'.) Equipped and briefed, they headed off to their assigned locations.

It had been raining all day, but by early evening the clouds had disappeared and the sun was reflected brightly on wet pavements. Olive made her way along Oxford Street, surrounded by shoppers hurrying to complete their purchases before closing time. She reached the Marshall and Snelgrove department store ('drapers and court dressmakers'), took up position and waited anxiously, careful not to even look in the direction of two other suffragettes who were standing nearby. Meanwhile, Lilla waited towards the bottom of Regent Street, outside a bookmaker's, and Charlotte and Kate were at other (unknown) locations.

At 5.30pm exactly, Emmeline Pankhurst and two other women arrived at 10 Downing Street in a taxi. They threw stones, broke several windows, and were arrested immediately. Fifteen minutes later, Olive launched her hammer hard at one of the huge, twelve foot high, plate glass windows in front of her, which broke with a satisfying sound of smashing. She retrieved her missile and did the same again. Throughout the West End the noise of hammering, shattering glass and splintering wood announced the well-orchestrated protest that was taking place. Liberty's, Debenham & Freebody, Peter Robinson, Dickins & Jones – all the major department stores, with their lavish displays, were targeted.[a]

---

a Several of the stores targeted were regular advertisers in *Votes for Women* and would continue to be, despite having their windows smashed.

There were shouts and screams. Crowds gathered and drivers stopped their cars to watch. Shop assistants emerged and began putting shutters up as fast as possible. In contrast to the previous November, when they had been waiting for protestors in Parliament Square, the police were caught completely unawares. Lone constables, unable to deal with lawbreaking on this scale, sounded their whistles to summon

Window-breaking: Cartoon from *The Gem* (June 1912)

© *March of the Women Collection/ Mary Evans*

help. But no-one came – their colleagues were busy dealing with other similar incidents. The *Daily Chronicle* observed: 'The attack was so astounding and so sudden that it was paralysing.'[143] Police chiefs' attention had been focussed entirely on the protest advertised for the following Monday, and at the very moment Emmeline Pankhurst launched her attack on Downing Street, they were meeting in Scotland Yard, just a few streets away, to discuss the arrangements for policing it.

Eventually, reinforcements arrived and the police began making arrests. Olive managed to break four of Marshall and Snelgrove's windows before she was taken into custody, while Lilla broke three at the bookmaker's on Regent Street, before she too was arrested. In all, more than one hundred suffragettes, who according to the police had caused damage to the value of over £6,000 between them, were arrested. Most of them refused bail, upon which they were crammed into Black Marias and transferred to Holloway Prison, where it took most of the night to book them in and assign them to cells.

The following day Herbert Muskett was back in action at Bow Street Court and outraged once more. He recommended the maximum sentence possible for the window-breakers and opened the first case, saying that 'the scenes which occurred in various streets in the West End…were probably the most outrageous and disgraceful which had yet characterised the woman suffrage movement.'[144]

The first three cases were heard, including that of Emmeline Pankhurst, who made a passionate speech from the dock and concluded by saying that she was prepared to go back to prison, however high the price might be. Most protestors, including the four from Tunbridge Wells, had to wait a few more days in Holloway Prison.

The following Monday, the demonstration which the WSPU had advertised in advance went ahead in Parliament Square. This time the police were prepared. Nearly 3,000 constables were stationed outside the Houses of Parliament and in the surrounding streets and when suffragettes attempted to storm the building, they were able to hold them back. Nevertheless, more windows were broken and there were another hundred or so arrests.

In the following days, a procession of women appeared in the dock at various London courts. Olive, Kate, Lilla and Charlotte all appeared at Bow Street, charged with malicious damage. The first three had destroyed property worth more than £5 and so, instead of being sentenced by the magistrate, they were committed for trial. Having refused the offer of being released on bail, they were sent back to Holloway.

Charlotte's case, however, was heard the following Saturday. She was convicted and, when she refused to pay her fine, sentenced to a month in prison. She made a speech (similar to the one she had given the previous November) saying that:

> ...she took the action she did in order to demand the franchise, which had been taken from women illegally since 1832, and it was to help the outcast women who were daily sacrificed in this country. She was out for a better manhood and a purer womanhood, and God would defend the right.[145]

The reactions of press and public to the latest window-breaking protest were even stronger than they had been the previous November. An article in the *Kentish Advertiser* said: 'It cannot be denied that this sort of thing does serious harm to the women's cause. It will certainly not gain them supporters in the House of Commons.'[146] Labour politician Ramsay MacDonald, a longstanding supporter of women's suffrage, wrote:

> I have no objection to revolution, if it is necessary, but I have the very strongest objection to childishness masquerading as revolution, and all one can say about these window-breaking expeditions is that they are simply silly and provocative.[147]

Under the headline 'Insurgent Hysteria', an article in *The Times*, on 16 March 1912, was scathing about women such as Olive and her friends:

> Women who have not married, who have no domestic duties, or to whom such duties are uncongenial; those who have no aptitude or talents for any profession; the large and, it is to be feared, ever-increasing number of women who find themselves with abundance of leisure and a somewhat vacuous existence – among these are to be found ready recruits for bands of window-smashers and similar would-be hooligans... The

*hysterical, the neurotic, the idle, the habitual imbibers of
excitement are always at the service of those who offer them an
opportunity of gratifying the ruling passion. Some of them are
out with their hammers and their bags full of stones because of
dreary, empty lives and high-strung, over-excitable natures.*[148]

The NUWSS (National Union of Women's Suffrage Societies) suffragists became even more anxious to disassociate themselves from the militants, fearing that window breaking would damage the prospects of the Conciliation Bill currently before Parliament. Millicent Garrett Fawcett wrote a letter to *The Times*, confirming that her organisation strongly disapproved of the suffragettes' actions and reaffirming that she had definitely and finally withdrawn all support and sympathy for the militant movement when they began using violence, back in 1908.

Emmeline Pankhurst was brought to Holloway, but kept separate from the other suffragettes. When they heard about this, the remand prisoners, who included Olive, Lilla and Kate, staged a protest. They broke their cell windows and spent the next two hours calling out their leader's name, banging on cell doors with dustpans and utensils, waving handkerchiefs and singing *The March of the Women* over and over again. (Composer Ethel Smyth had also taken part in the window smashing. During her two-month sentence at Holloway, she would wave a toothbrush through her prison window and conduct as her fellow prisoners marched in the exercise yard and sang the WSPU anthem.)

After a few days, Olive was released from Holloway on bail and went home to prepare herself. On 27 March she arrived at Newington Sessions in Southwark, bringing a packed bag with her in anticipation of a prison sentence. Her brother and younger sister were in court to watch the trial and, when it ended and Olive was found guilty, they offered to pay her fine. She refused the offer, opting to serve a four month prison sentence instead.

Lilla and Kate also appeared in court, but were found not guilty and discharged, leaving Olive and Charlotte the only two of the Tunbridge Wells contingent to go to prison on this occasion.

There was not enough space in Holloway to accommodate the large number of suffragettes who had been sentenced and so, after spending one more night there, Olive and twenty-seven other women were transported, in specially hired omnibuses, to Aylesbury Prison in Buckinghamshire. No doubt they were anxious about what lay ahead.

Chapter 19

A Cruel and Dangerous Practice

On arriving at Aylesbury, the suffragettes were issued with regulation prison clothes and their possessions – combs, books, writing materials and so on – were taken away from them. This indicated that they were not seen as political prisoners. They put in an immediate request to be treated as such, but the prison governor refused. After petitions to Reginald McKenna, the current Home Secretary, were ignored, the women agreed amongst themselves to stop eating food in protest.

It was two years since the last hunger strike, but the suffragettes had a good idea of what they were letting themselves in for. There had been detailed descriptions in *Votes for Women* of previous hunger strikers being force-fed, the violence with which it was done and the injuries it caused to head, teeth, lungs and digestive organs. Olive would also have heard a first account from Kitty Marion, during her visits to Tunbridge Wells (although Kitty later wrote that the most perfect description could not convey the horror and agony she suffered there). So it took huge courage to undertake this form of protest. Women such as Olive only did so out of enormous frustration that their campaign, which had now gone on for so long, was not even being given official recognition.

On the evening of 5 April, eight days after they had arrived at the prison, twenty-five of the Aylesbury suffragettes stopped eating. They concealed this from the authorities for as long as possible, throwing their food out of the window, or finding some other way of hiding it. Despite feeling increasingly tired and unwell, they continued with the routine of needlework, cell cleaning, chapel and exercise, as though nothing unusual was going on. At Winson Green and Holloway Prisons, other suffragettes (including Kitty Marion) were doing the same.

In a statement she wrote later for the WSPU on her experience of being force-fed, Olive wrote:

> *After the first few days I began to lose all desire for food, the only desire I had was the desire and determination at all costs not to give in unless I received the privileges I was fighting for.*

After five days Olive felt weak, but able to continue. However, there were other women who were in a worse state, and another prisoner, a doctor, decided to inform the authorities about the hunger strike. In her statement, Olive described the reaction:

> *The prison and the officials were now in tumult, the governor looked angry, the doctor worried and the wardresses unhappy. The only calm people were the twenty-eight suffrage prisoners, who were at once given solitary confinement.*[149][a]

Olive lay in her cell, waiting. She heard the sound of doors opening and shutting and of the prison doctor's voice. Eventually

---

a Olive kept a diary of her experiences in Aylesbury Prison, a transcript of which is held by the Museum of London. They also hold a copy of a report on the hunger strike she wrote for the WSPU in July 1912.

he arrived at her cell, gave her a brief physical examination and told her how foolish she was being. She confirmed that she was not going to be eating any food. 'Oh aren't you?' said the doctor, with a grin. 'I shall see about that!' He left the cell and she sat for another hour and a half, her heart hammering, and prayed for strength to deal with what was coming. Then it began. One of the other women later described what happened next:

> It must have been a tortured, nerve-wracked body that gave that cry. So it was – and the horror of that night will never pass from my memory. For it went on for hours I think, from cell after cell one heard it, the struggle, the gasping and then the shriek of anguish.[150]

Four hours passed before Olive's turn came. For most of that time she kept her fingers in her ears, trying unsuccessfully to block out the sounds of women choking, pleading and screaming. At the end of each session came silence, which was almost worse. After a while she decided she could make things more difficult if she hung onto the window bars. She put her chair on the table, climbed up and held on for forty minutes, until the wardresses finally arrived at her cell. There were six or seven of them and they soon managed to pull her down, force her into the chair and tie her to it. Her head was pulled backwards by her hair and her mouth prised open.

A hunger striker who was force-fed at Holloway Prison, described her experience of what happened next, which would have been similar to Olive's:

> One [of the doctors] knelt to grip my shoulders, another lifted aloft the funnel that was to receive the liquid, the third knelt by my head and took the long tube in his hand and, little by little, forced the stiff nozzle at the end of the tube up my left nostril.

As the nozzle turned at the top of my nose to enter my gullet it
seemed as if my left eye was being wrenched out of its socket.
Then the food, a mixture of cocoa, Bovril, medicines and a
drug to keep one from vomiting when the tube was drawn out,
was poured into the funnel and down into my aching, bruised,
quivering body.[151]

Olive felt as though she was being choked and suffocated at the
same time and, after the tube had been removed, she vomited.
The process was repeated over the following days. To begin with
the suffragettes were fed twice a day, but this was increased to
three times, which meant that they spent most of their waking
hours in suspense, waiting for the next session to start.

On each occasion, Olive resisted being put in the chair
and struggled violently with the wardresses. She found that
she could make things more difficult by biting onto the tube,
which made the doctor lose patience and feed her into the
stomach instead. At least that avoided the gagging sensation.
She became weaker and suffered from neuralgia, although she
observed later that she was not in as much pain as some others.

Force-feeding: Cartoon from *The Suffragette* (1912)
© *Museum of London*

On 11 April, six days after the hunger strike had started, four Aylesbury prisoners were released on the grounds of ill health. Olive continued her protest, although as time went on she became increasingly anxious, tired and in pain. Sylvia Pankhurst described the effects of being on hunger strike:

> *Each day one's bones seem more prominent, the flesh falling away, the skin shrivelled, the hands and feet a dull purple with bright red streaks. One is always cold...Pain settles in the small of the back and in the chest; occasionally a sharp stinging pain in the right breast. Griping pains seize one suddenly in the stomach and abdomen. The pulse becomes swift and irregular. There are palpitations and pain in the region of the heart. If one rises from bed, one grows faint and giddy, and there comes at last a constant ringing in the ears.*[152]

Events in Aylesbury Prison received wide attention and provoked various reactions. A WSPU meeting at the London Pavilion heard an account from one of the women who had been released early and passed a resolution which included the words:

> *The meeting expresses its admiration for the courage shown by the women in Aylesbury in adopting the heroic hunger strike as a protest against the refusal; and views with horror the attempt to coerce them into submission by recourse to the cruel and dangerous practice of forcible feeding.*[153]

A letter written by Sylvia Pankhurst appeared in the *Manchester Guardian* on 13 April, alleging that force-feeding at Aylesbury was being accompanied by wanton and unnecessary cruelty. When its contents were referred to during a House of Commons debate, the Home Secretary described the letter as a tissue of falsehoods. He made clear where the blame lay and claimed that, when forcible feeding had been necessary, it had been carried out with as little use of force and as much gentleness as the prisoner's conduct would permit.

In Tunbridge Wells the new WSPU branch campaigned in support of Olive. An appeal was published in the local papers, calling on women to write to the Home Secretary and MPs demanding the immediate suspension of the dangerous and barbarous treatment she was being subjected to. Evelyn Billing, the West Kent organiser, stood on a makeshift platform at Five Ways, in the centre of town, telling the assembled crowd, and anyone passing by, about the cruel torture of force feeding. She explained the reason for the hunger strikes and asked her audience to petition their MP and the Home Secretary to put an immediate end to it, in the interests of justice and humanity. Local suffragettes sent letters and petitions as requested, and some made extra donations to WSPU funds, including Ethel Wedgwood who contributed £1 for each week of Olive's imprisonment.

On the evening of 13 April Olive heard, from her cell, the sound of a band playing *The March of the Women*. It came closer and closer and when she peered out of the window, she could see a crowd of demonstrators. The Women's Tax Resistance League (WTRL)[a] had organised a demonstration in Aylesbury to protest at the treatment of the hunger strikers, and around one hundred people had marched from Market Square to the prison. Olive and other suffragette prisoners waved handkerchiefs through the window bars and had a glimpse of flags in the WSPU and WTRL colours being waved

---

a The Women's Tax Resistance League was a national suffrage organisation with links to the Women's Freedom League. There are further details of their activities in Chapter 22.

in return. That evening, Olive wrote in her diary: 'It has all been grand, but oh! what a longing it gives me to be away from this place.'[154]

Finally, on 17 April, the suffragettes heard that, faced with adverse publicity and fearing that a hunger striker might die (creating a martyr for the Votes for Women movement) the Home Secretary had given in. He had announced that the suffragettes were to be treated as political prisoners, although they would only be given the minimum concessions allowable under rule 243a. After twelve days, Olive and the others ended their hunger strike. 'What a victory!' she wrote. The following day, which she described as 'a day of rejoicing', the suffragettes, thinner and with shaky legs, were allowed to take exercise together once again.

From this time onwards, life in prison was much more bearable. The suffragettes were housed separately from other prisoners, in a building which had previously been used as an 'Inebriate Reformatory' (for repeat alcohol offenders), and their cells were larger than those at Holloway. The food was ample and they kept themselves busy with reading, gardening, sewing, musical concerts and games (including rounders and an obstacle race). Sometimes they had to improvise, such as when one of them gave a concert using a comb and when several of them played tennis using dustpans as racket and a small bench as the net. Olive wrote that they had christened the prison an 'Agricultural, Physical Culture, Vegetarian, Theosophical, Social Reform and above all Simple Life Summer School.'

The suffragettes were sent letters and food parcels and were also allowed occasional visitors. Olive's sister Mary and Iris Yeoman, another of the Tunbridge Wells suffragettes, came to see her (in the presence of a wardress, who listened to every word they said). They would have told Olive about events taking place outside the prison. Some of these must have seemed unreal, none more so than the sinking of the unsinkable Titanic, which had occurred ten days into the hunger strike and which was the focus of public interest for weeks afterwards.

Another piece of news, which had reached the prisoners early in their sentence, and which was more relevant to their current situation, was that on 28 March (the day they arrived at Aylesbury) the latest Conciliation Bill had been defeated at its second reading. The bill was essentially the same one that had been passed with a large majority in May 1911. However, recent militant protests had caused some MPs to change their vote (and others to abstain). In addition, Irish MPs had voted against it, in return for Asquith's continued support of home rule.

During the debate on the bill, MP Harold Baker had said: 'I think the breaking of windows has let in a good deal of fresh air on this subject… it goes to show that those who claim to have more power to persuade women are exactly those who are least fitted to exercise political power.'[155] An article in *The Common Cause* observed:

> *These men [MPs who had changed their vote] still believe in the justice of women's suffrage, but they were so dreadfully afraid that people would think the smashing of tradesmen's windows had forced them to vote for the bill that they voted against it to show the women that they weren't the sort of men to be bullied.*

Olive and the others were especially interested in hearing news of WSPU leaders Emmeline Pankhurst, Emmeline Pethick-Lawrence and Frederick Pethick-Lawrence, who were on trial at the Old Bailey for inciting their members to carry out March's window-breaking attacks. On 22 May, all three were found guilty, sentenced to nine months in the second division and ordered to pay costs. On 10 June, the Home Secretary responded to pressure and agreed that they should be transferred to the first division, which highlighted the limited nature of the concession made to the other suffragettes in prison (under Winston Churchill's Rule 243a). In addition, on 22 June, word reached the remaining Aylesbury prisoners that the Pethick-Lawrences were being forcibly fed. They agreed between themselves to resume hunger strikes to protest at this, putting pressure on the government to treat all women's suffrage prisoners the same. Two days later thirteen suffragettes, including Olive, began refusing food again.

Thankfully the force-feeding only lasted five days this time. On 29 June, Olive reached the end of her sentence and was released. She had asked her younger sister to come and meet her, but Mary refused. Olive's family were horrified at her militant activities and prison sentences and, despite the fact that Mary had visited her in prison, it seems their patience had run out. When she returned home to Tunbridge Wells, she would have been weak at first, in need of complete rest and finding it difficult to start eating again. Other physical and psychological effects would have lasted much longer; another suffragette wrote in her autobiography about the searing pain that memories of force-feeding could still conjure up forty years later.[156]

Women such as Olive, who had taken their commitment to the cause to such an extreme, were admired and celebrated by their fellow suffragettes. Like all hunger strikers, Olive was awarded a medal, with a purple, green and white ribbon and her name, date of arrest and 'Hunger Striker' engraved on a silver bar or circle, and the dates she had been force-fed engraved on enamel bars. It was presented to her in a purple box, with a green velvet lining and the wording: 'Presented to Olive Walton by the Women's Social and Political Union in recognition of a gallant action, whereby through endurance to the last extremity of hunger and hardship a great principle of political justice was vindicated.'

WSPU Hunger Striker's Medal
Women's Library, LSE

In late July 1912, the Tunbridge Wells WSPU held an 'At Home' for the released prisoners, at the Grand Hotel on London Road. Ethel Wedgwood called on all those who could not go to prison, to commit themselves to the cause, for example, by selling papers. Lilla described her experiences while on remand in Holloway, which included the humiliation of being 'frogmarched' – held by both arms and both legs and carried face down. Olive and Kitty Marion (who was back in town for another visit) gave their accounts of being force fed.

A *Courier* correspondent described the meeting and wrote:

Those who were privileged to be present gave the most sympathetic, and it may almost be said horrified attention to the experiences related by the Tunbridge Wells lady who was among the sufferers by forcible feeding, and who described with pathetic simplicity and without the slightest affectation of the martyr's pose, her sufferings...Other speakers made further allegations as to the torture caused by forcible feeding, and the whole pitiful story made a very painful impression upon the audience.[157]

A few months later, the Tunbridge Wells suffragettes were pleased and excited when Sylvia Pankhurst, Emmeline's middle daughter, agreed to come and speak at a meeting in the town.[a] Sylvia had worked for the WSPU full-time since 1906, using her skills as an artist in designing logos, leaflets, banners and flags for them. She had already spent several periods in Holloway Prison, where she had gone on hunger strike. A committed socialist, Sylvia was especially involved with the East London suffragettes and had recently moved to live in Bow, setting up a new shop and campaign headquarters there. An article in the *Courier*, advertising the meeting, said:

---

a Sylvia had visited the area previously; she and Keir Hardy stayed at a rented cottage in Penshurst a number of times in 1909.

She has so keen a sympathy with the poor in their hard struggle for life in the midst of the most difficult conditions, that poverty-stricken women speak to her with a frankness and confidence that few investigators are met with.[158]

Lilla, Olive and the others sold tickets for the meeting and placed advertisements, in local newspapers and in *Votes for Women*. Five of them walked through the streets of Tunbridge Wells, carrying sandwich boards to publicise Sylvia's visit. The *Courier* reported:

Heedless of unpleasant weather and muddy roads, they pluckily marched along the principal thoroughfares, having started from the office at the Pantiles. The appearance of well-dressed ladies, belonging to prominent Tunbridge Wells families, adopting this method of promoting the case of women's suffrage, created a mild sensation and gave rise to a small amount of good-humoured chaff.[159][a]

On 18 November, the Great Hall was packed. Charles Grey, who was in the chair for the meeting, reminded the audience that this day marked the second anniversary of Black Friday, the event which had prompted suffragettes to adopt more extreme campaigning methods, including attacks on government and private property. Sylvia then spoke, describing the exploitation of women workers in the East End and the high level of infant mortality that resulted from overcrowded slums. Problems such as these would not be dealt with properly, she said, until women had the vote.

Another subject she touched on was women who were

a The *Courier* identified this protest as being by members of the Women's Freedom League. However, the League was no longer active in the town by this time and the reference to an office on the Pantiles points to the WSPU.

forced into prostitution and the Criminal Law Amendment Bill – known generally as the White Slave Traffic Bill – which had recently gone before Parliament. This legislation was aimed at tightening the law against prostitution, but Sylvia described it as a poor, weak bill that would not achieve much. Once women had the vote, she claimed, they would try to stamp the stain (of prostitution) out of the country.

Sexual morality was an important issue for the WSPU (as it was for the NUWSS (National Union of Women's Suffrage Societies) and their members). Suffragettes believed in the moral superiority of women and the need to protect them from men, whether they were oppressing their wives or forcing women into prostitution. This had been emphasised when white, symbolising purity, was chosen as one of their colours and when members were encouraged to wear white at marches and rallies.

Many suffragettes were especially concerned about enforced prostitution. In November 1911, Tunbridge Wells suffragette Mary Harmer had referred to the white slave trade at her hearing in Bow Street Magistrates' Court. In the same month, Flora Drummond wrote an article in which she pointed out that a man could be punished less harshly for trapping an innocent girl and forcing her to a life of shame than if he had stolen a loaf of bread. In 1913, Sylvia's older sister Christabel would write a series of articles on sexually transmitted diseases and how sexual equality – which could only be achieved by women having the vote – would put an end to them.[a] She put forward an extreme view of men, not shared by all suffragettes, arguing that marriage was 'an appalling danger to women' and to be avoided at all costs.

As 1912 came to a close, the WSPU's militancy reached a new height. One particular target was pillar boxes, into

---

a These articles were reproduced subsequently in a book called '*The Great Scourge and How to End It*'.

which substances such as acid, ink, glue, and even rags
soaked with paraffin, were tipped. It was estimated that over
5,000 letters were damaged between October and December
that year. Tunbridge Wells experienced this form of protest
on the evening of 17 December. Bottles containing what
appeared to be a mixture of gum, ink and acid were tossed
into pillar boxes across the town, where they shattered,
damaging the letters inside. No one was caught, but everyone
was clear that suffragettes, whether local women or others,
were responsible.

This increase in militancy was viewed negatively by many
WSPU supporters, as well as by non-militant suffragists such
as Millicent Garrett Fawcett. Following the window-breaking
in November 1911, veteran campaigner Elizabeth Garrett
Anderson (who had delivered the national petition back in
1866 and marched with Emmeline Pankhurst on Black Friday)
resigned from the organisation. Actress Elizabeth Robins, who
had joined the WSPU following the NUWW (National Union of
Women Workers) conference in 1906 and served as a committee
member, resigned in the summer of 1912, unhappy at the
escalation of tactics. In July 1912, Elizabeth Wolstenholme-
Elmy, another long-standing activist, wrote in the *Manchester
Guardian*:

> *Now that our cause is on the verge of success, I wish to add my
> protest against the madness which seems to have seized a few
> persons whose anti-social and criminal actions would seem
> designed to wreck the whole movement.*[160]

Frederick and Emmeline Pethick-Lawrence, who had been
WSPU leaders from the start and provided significant financial
backing, were also unhappy at the direction campaigning had
taken. After they were released from prison in the summer of

1912, they began speaking more openly about their concerns at methods such as window-smashing. Emmeline and Christabel Pankhurst did not take kindly to this and in October 1912, the couple were abruptly expelled from the WSPU.

Despite losing key supporters such as these, the WSPU continued to campaign actively. The Tunbridge Wells branch stayed loyal and their activities were reported regularly in *The Suffragette*, the organisation's new newspaper (in place of *Votes for Women*, which the Pethick-Lawrences continued to publish).

Chapter 20

Militancy is to be Fiercer than Ever

At the beginning of 1913 it looked, yet again, as though Votes for Women campaigners might be on the verge of success. 450 MPs (out of a total of 670) were believed to have pledged their support. The Franchise and Registration Bill (which Asquith had first proposed back in November 1911) had passed its second reading the previous year, and in January 1913 several amendments were drafted, any one of which, if passed, would give women the vote.

However, the WSPU (Women's Social and Political Union) were not confident of success. On 10 January, the Tunbridge Wells suffragettes, along with other WSPU members, received a private and confidential letter from Emmeline Pankhurst, reminding them that being militant was a moral obligation and duty. It continued:

I know that the defeat of the amendment will prove to thousands of women that to rely only on peaceful, patient methodology is to court failure, and that militancy is inevitable...[161]

Emmeline was correct to assume the latest attempt at legislation would fail. On 23 January the Speaker of the House of Commons suddenly ruled that adding women's suffrage to the Franchise and Registration Bill through an amendment would change it too much. Completely new legislation would be required if women were to have the vote. Following this, the bill was abandoned altogether. The government indicated that time would be given for a private member's bill, but for now there was no prospect of success.

It was not clear why the government had made this decision, but the consequence was a further phase of militancy and violence. Angry and frustrated at the latest in a long line of betrayals and broken promises, the WSPU resumed militant action immediately. Emmeline announced the escalation of tactics in a speech at Holborn Hall on 27 January. According to the *Daily Chronicle*:

> *Simultaneously with the withdrawal of the Franchise Bill yesterday the suffragettes declared war. Militancy is to be fiercer than ever, and Mrs Pankhurst said last night that while they would regard human life as sacred, they would stop at little short of it…they were going to do as much damage to other people's property as they could. As soon as people had enough of it they would clamour to the government to give women the vote.*[162]

In the early days, the main way that suffragettes protested was by disrupting public meetings and getting themselves arrested. (This included the arrest of Adela Pankhurst and others in October 1906 which provoked such a stir at the NUWW (National Union of Women Workers) conference in Tunbridge Wells.) In 1911-12, frustrated that the Prime Minister was repeatedly blocking Votes for Women legislation, their protests became more aggressive and included window-smashing (such as Olive Walton's assault on Marshall and Snelgrove). Now in 1913, when the latest attempt at legislation failed, suffragettes began making even more destructive protests. New targets included railway stations, private houses, sports facilities, churches and stately homes.

Their attacks were continual and relentless. However, they were on a smaller scale than they had been previously. Guerrilla warfare replaced mass protests such as window-breaking and there were no further multiple imprisonments. Instead, a small number of women went from place to place, armed with heavy cans of paraffin, matches, inflammable material such as cotton wool and sometimes even bombs. Suffragette Lilian Lenton later claimed to have burnt buildings at a rate of two a week and boasted that whenever she saw an empty building, she burnt it down. Kitty Marion was another member of this small group of arsonists, going to much further extremes than any of her Tunbridge Wells friends did in the battle to win the vote. She paid a high price for her commitment; it was later estimated that she was force-fed on over 200 occasions.

On 2 February 1913 another well-known figure from the Votes for Women movement visited Tunbridge Wells, when WSPU leader Annie Kenney came to speak at a meeting in the town hall. Members decorated the room with flags in the WSPU colours and large banners were set up on the stage, including one which read 'Strive and Hold Cheap the Strain'. Branch secretary Laura Harverson was in the chair. In her introduction she contrasted the situation in England to that in New Zealand (where she had spent the last eight months and where women had gained the vote twenty years earlier). The *Advertiser* reported her as saying that:

...in England...a woman was a nobody. She was the property of her husband, and was the mother of his children, and if he disagreed with her she had to make the best of it. In New

Zealand the husband and wife were joint guardians of the children, and this led to a spirit of camaraderie between men and women, which was unknown in England.[163]

Laura introduced Annie, who had a lively manner, a mass of golden hair and, even at the age of thirty-four, a slight, child-like figure. When she stood up to speak, those close to the stage could see that her hands were scarred and she had one finger missing – evidence of her past life. (She had begun working in the Lancashire cotton mills as a child and continued until she joined the WSPU in 1905.) They would also have seen, on her face, the strain of her current responsibilities. At a time when the campaign had reached new heights of militancy, Christabel Pankhurst had gone into 'exile' in Paris and Annie was running the organisation under her instructions.

Never known for being shy, Annie was, by now, an experienced public speaker. In a clear, although not very melodious, voice she began by describing working conditions in the East End, very different from anything her listeners had ever experienced. Next she spoke about the need for militant action. The *Advertiser* reported her arguments:

If women had been militant in 1884, women would have been enfranchised years ago. In 1906 they decided that they would not put up with this trickery and dodgery and the bamboozling of women...[Suffragettes] said they must do something to make men realise that they were prepared to do as men had [done previously]...The time would come when the people of this country would realise that the only way to stop militancy was to give the vote to women...They did not like militancy, but she would be prepared to see every pillar box in the country burned if they could save one white slave.[164]

Annie's speech inspired the Tunbridge Wells suffragettes. While they do not seem to have been directly involved in the arson campaign (in common with the majority of WSPU members) they continued publicising the cause on the streets of their home town, fundraising and recruiting new members. They also sold the WSPU's new newspaper *The Suffragette*, shifting around eighty copies a week.

In March 1913 they took part in self-denial week. This was an annual fundraising event which generated financial contributions and allowed women to show solidarity with those who were taking more drastic action and serving time in prison. It involved giving up something (tea, cocoa, milk or sugar, for example), as well as making and selling items such as sweets, soap or clothes. The Tunbridge Wells suffragettes made cakes, sweets and needlework to sell in their office. May Le Lacheur (who had trained at agricultural college and was now running a nursery in Sussex) sent boxes of flowers and another member donated primroses. Olive Walton described the week's activities in a letter published in *The Suffragette*:

> *We made a fair sum by our office sale and afternoon teas. Many strangers paid us a visit, which gave us the opportunity of enlightening them on militant methods, while they were enjoying home-made cakes and 'Votes for Women' tea. One morning I went out with a tray of flowers, expecting hostility from a certain section of the public, but everybody was most decent, and I received sixpences from quite unexpected quarters, many refusing to take any flowers in return.*[165]

Another non-violent way of demonstrating support for the cause, and getting publicity, was to disrupt political meetings, something suffragettes had been doing since the start of their campaign. In March 1913, an opportunity to protest at the

Liberal Party's continued refusal to give women the vote arose in Tunbridge Wells, when the Home Counties Liberal Federation booked the Opera House for a conference.

On this occasion, Olive Walton was joined by fellow suffragette Emily Wilding Davison. Tall and slim, with red hair and green eyes, Emily had been active in the WSPU for some time. Back in 1908 she had been a chief steward at the huge Hyde Park rally which the Le Lacheur sisters and their friends attended. Since then, she had broken windows, set fire to post boxes, protested in the House of Commons and served several prison sentences. Emily did not flinch from the physical pain and suffering incurred as result of her protests; in 1909, while in Strangeways Prison, she had been one of the first women to be force-fed. The reason she took part in a protest in Tunbridge Wells may have been her personal connection with local campaigners – like Kitty Marion, she was a friend of Lilla Durham and had stayed at her house in Hartfield on a number of occasions.

Admission to Liberal Party meetings was by ticket only; organisers were anxious to avoid any suffragette protests. If a ticket was issued to a woman, it had to have her name and address written clearly on it and she had to be a known Party supporter. So the only option for Emily and Olive was to hide overnight. The evening before the meeting they attended a vaudeville show, which included a short play entitled *Over the Border to Gretna Green*, the Letines (a 'novel comical eccentric acrobatic act') and popular comedian Ted Cowan.

When the show was over, the two suffragettes hid until everyone had left. They spent the night exploring the building, until around 5.30am, when they clambered down into a dark, dirty space under the stage. They waited there for the next fifteen hours, concealed by planks of wood and old scenery and with only a few biscuits to sustain them. Emily had previous experience of hiding in cramped conditions from census night in 1911, when she hid in a cupboard in the House of Commons. On this occasion her discomfort would have been even greater; in May 1912, while serving a sentence at Holloway Prison, she had protested at the treatment of her fellow prisoners by throwing herself down an iron staircase. The head and spine injuries she incurred caused her continual pain from that time onwards.

Early the following evening, not long before the conference was due to start, the two women heard sounds of the building being searched. They kept their nerve, stayed hidden and were not discovered. Soon afterwards they heard delegates taking their seats and the opening speeches being made. Goverment minister Lord Beauchamp had only been speaking for a few minutes when Olive, covered in dust, emerged from beneath the stage, into the orchestra pit, where the press were seated. 'When are you going to do something for women?' she shouted. 'We demand women's suffrage. Votes for Women!' There were cries of 'Sit down!' and 'Turn her out', as well as hissing from all directions. A number of stewards clambered over the rails, surrounded Olive and asked her to leave. When she refused, they seized her and ejected her swiftly from the building. Next Emily came out from under the stage, climbed up onto it and shouted, 'No peace until you give the vote.' One of the stewards placed a handkerchief over her mouth to stop her speaking and she was also forcibly removed.

The Earl, apparently unfazed by the protest, assured his audience: 'I am more accustomed to these things than you are. Let us go back to a more interesting topic.' He continued with his lengthy speech, which covered the Welsh Bill and the Plural Voting Bill, but made no reference at all to women's suffrage. After votes of thanks, the meeting concluded with the National Anthem. A journalist from the *Courier* interviewed Olive and asked whether the stewards had handled her roughly. 'More or less,' she said. 'But I was not hurt.'

Tunbridge Wells experienced the WSPU's guerrilla-style campaigning a couple of weeks later, when the cricket pavilion was burnt down in the early hours of 11 April. This was just one of many such actions at this time. The issue of *The Suffragette* published on the same day included a double page spread under the heading 'The Women's Revolution – a Reign of Terror – Fire and Bombs', which included accounts of attacks on a mansion, a race stand, a railway station, pillar boxes and a picture gallery.

Assuming that WSPU secretary Violet Matthews was telling the truth when she assured a reporter from the *Advertiser* that local suffragettes had been away in London for a meeting the previous evening (and there is no reason not to), they had experienced an impressive occasion. The *Daily Chronicle* noted that the Albert Hall was comfortably full, but not overflowing, as it would have been a year or two earlier. However, the audience were as spirited as ever and the building echoed to the sounds of singing, speeches and applause. In the chair for the meeting was Flora Drummond, who had marshalled her troops so effectively at the Hyde Park rally back in 1908. Conspicuous by her absence, however, was Emmeline Pankhurst, who was on hunger strike in Holloway Prison. 'We have no message to give you from Mrs Pankhurst,' Flora announced, 'but we do have a message from her spirit. What does it say? "Fight on! And we will do!"'[166] This was greeted by loud cheers, after which Flora continued, describing the movement's militant arm as a hillside of heather on fire, which was beyond control and could only be stopped by giving women the vote.

The main focus of the meeting, apart from Mrs Pankhurst's current situation, was a piece of legislation going through Parliament, which had been nicknamed the 'Cat and Mouse Bill.' This had passed its second reading on 3 April and was the government's response to the adverse publicity being generated by force-feeding. If it was made law, hunger strikers would be released as soon as their health deteriorated. Once their condition had improved, the authorities would 'pounce' and send them back to prison to complete the rest of their sentence. This could be repeated over and over again. *The Suffragette* had described it as 'surely the most savagely-devised measure ever brought before Parliament in modern times.'[167]

At the end of the meeting, a collection was taken and suffragettes piled money and jewellery onto the plates. An elderly lady gave a bag of farthings and another woman even removed her wedding ring and donated it. The Tunbridge Wells group handed over the money they had raised from their activities during Self-denial Week. The total amount raised was £14,622 – a record. After the meeting, a telegram was sent to Chancellor Lloyd George, which read: 'Please inform the Commons that the suffragists' answer to the Cat and Mouse Bill is the raising of £15,000 towards the campaign.'

Parliament responded by passing The Prisoners (Temporary Discharge for Ill Health) Act (the official name for the Cat and Mouse Act) which received royal assent on 25 April. It seemed that the government could find the time to pass legislation quickly if it chose. The speedy passage of this act was in sharp contrast to the progress of women's suffrage bills, which were continually being delayed.

The meeting on 10 April was the last one the WSPU would hold at the Albert Hall. Season ticket holders and others objected to the building being used by suffragettes and the trustees decided that they would no longer take any booking from them. In any case, the WSPU had changed the way they worked and would hold no further large meetings, mass rallies or marches. The exception to this was one, final spectacular procession, on the occasion of a funeral.

On 4 June 1913, just two months after she had burst out from under the stage in the Tunbridge Wells Opera House,

Emily Wilding Davison attended the Epsom Derby. As horses thundered round Tattenham Corner and towards the crowded stand, she ducked under the rails and ran out onto the course. Emily appeared to reach up to the King's horse (possibly to drape the WSPU colours over him), was knocked to the ground and trampled underfoot. She never regained consciousness and died in Epsom hospital four days later.

Before her death, Emily had fallen out of favour with the WSPU leaders, who considered her to be out of control and her actions too extreme, even for them. However, her funeral provided an opportunity both to present her as a martyr and to demonstrate how much support their organisation still had. The Tunbridge Wells suffragettes received a copy of the circular letter sent to all local societies, which read: 'Your Society will probably feel it an honour to take part in the procession, and in this way testify to their reverence of this woman who has laid down her life for the Cause we all have at heart.' On Saturday 14 June, seven of them travelled up to London, including Isabel Haynes (who had recently taken over as secretary and who had protested outside the Great Hall with Olive Walton earlier in the year) and Lilla Durham.

The Tunbridge Wells women joined the crowds of mourners lining up outside Victoria Station, along Buckingham Palace Road and down every side street. At 2pm the coffin arrived by train from Epsom and the procession set off. To the front was the tall figure of Charlotte Marsh (a friend of Emily's, who had been in Aylesbury Prison with Olive) carrying a large gold cross. She was followed by several young girls dressed in white and carrying laurel wreaths and then London WSPU members: rows of women in black carrying purple irises, in purple carrying red peonies and in white carrying lilies.[a] Next came a large contingent of hunger strikers, also wearing white. (If Olive

---

a   Red, representing martyrdom, had been added to the usual WSPU colours.

attended the funeral, she may have been in this group.) Some of these women were suffragette 'mice' – released from prison, but expecting to be re-arrested at any moment.

At the centre of the procession was the coffin, which was carried on a low dray, drawn by four black horses. It had been draped with a purple cloth embroidered with two large white arrows (symbolising Emily's prison sentences) and laid on top of it was a laurel wreath. The coffin was preceded by a group of clergy and escorted by a guard of honour made up of Emily's close friends, who wore white and carried Madonna lilies. Emily's brother, Captain Henry Davison (one of the few men in the procession), walked behind it.

After Davison came an empty horse-drawn carriage, which conveyed a powerful message. Emmeline Pankhurst had been released from prison a couple of weeks' earlier, in poor physical condition due to the effects of hunger striking. As she left to attend the funeral, she was re-arrested by detectives, who had been waiting outside, and taken back to Holloway.[a]

A series of carriages carrying floral tributes were followed by women doctors and graduates in colourful robes. The Tunbridge Wells suffragettes were amongst the provincial societies who came next, wearing mourning dress and carrying banners. To the rear were members of other suffrage societies (including the Women's Freedom League (WFL), but not the National Union of Women's Suffrage Societies (NUWSS)).

Several thousand women made their way along Piccadilly and up Shaftesbury Avenue. One newspaper observed that, as white succeeded purple and scarlet followed black, the procession resembled the long unfurling of a military banner. As many as 50,000 spectators crowded the pavements, stood in shop doorways, leant out of windows and perched on rooftops. In places the crowd was so dense the police had difficulty keeping

a Emmeline Pankhurst was released again two days later

the road clear. Men raised their hats in respect as the coffin passed. Marchers and crowd were mostly silent and almost the only sound came from bands playing Chopin's funeral march and sombre music by Beethoven and Handel.

Emily Wilding-Davison's Funeral (1913)
© *Museum of London*

When the procession reached St George's Church in Bloomsbury, it halted for a short service, which concluded with the hymn 'Fight the Good Fight.'[a] As the mourners left the church, some of the crowd tried to raise a cheer for the King's jockey. Then, when they got close to King's Cross Station, a group of hooligans made a rush towards the coffin, although, according to Charlotte Marsh, they fell back when they saw the cross she was carrying. The coffin was loaded onto a special train carriage and, accompanied by an escort of suffragettes, taken to Emily's home town, Morpeth in Northumberland, where her burial took place.

Emily's protest, death and funeral attracted attention and divided public opinion. Most of the press condemned her

a The clergy of four other parishes had refused to hold the service.

actions. The *Telegraph* said that her Derby day protest was murderous as well as suicidal and the only charitable verdict was that she was insane. *The Standard* said that 'the militant' had reduced herself to the level of pest and an enemy of society and was no more admirable than an anarchist who blew himself up. *The Globe* described the funeral procession as an 'outrageous blasphemy', saying that Emily had tried to ruin or injure helpless or innocent people in every possible way and never wearied in ill-doing. In Tunbridge Wells, the *Courier* had a more positive slant; it made no specific comment on Emily's action, but described her as 'one of the earliest and most earnest workers in the cause of the enfranchisement of women.'[168]

People living in towns such as Tunbridge Wells now had an opportunity to witness events in a more direct way than they had previously. During June 1913, before the main feature was screened, audiences at the two cinemas on Camden Road in Tunbridge Wells – the Picture Playhouse and Camden Electric – would have watched dramatic Pathé News footage, filmed from several angles, of Emily dashing out onto the racecourse on Derby Day. They would also have seen her funeral procession, with suffragettes resembling a white river forging through a mass of dark-suited onlookers. These powerful images focussed public attention on the Votes for Women campaign, increasing its impact on those who may previously have been uninterested or unaware.

Emily's funeral was the WSPU's last great pageant, but their members continued to find new ways to publicise their cause. On 10 August 1913, Olive Walton and ten other suffragettes set off from the Lincoln's Inn headquarters in a decorated cart, pulled by a horse named Asquith (as the one pulling the WFL caravan had been).[a] They arrived in Tunbridge Wells two days later and, dressed in gypsy costume, walked through the streets selling copies of *The Suffragette*. They also held a meetings at Five Ways and on the Common, which concluded with them singing a selection of rousing suffrage songs. Olive experienced a better reception on this occasion than she had earlier in 1913, when she protested outside the Great Hall. This time there was no need to take refuge in the police station.

WSPU Holiday Campaign (1913)
© *March of the Women Collection/Mary Evans*

There was one further instance of destructive militant action in the Tunbridge Wells area although, as with the pavilion fire, it was never confirmed who was responsible. On the morning of 16 September 1913, occupants of Penshurst Place, a stately home just outside the town, woke to the sound of crackling wood and the smell of smoke. On investigating, they found several windows alight and saw two women running away across the lawn. A large amount of suffrage literature was

---

a   The group may have included other local suffragettes – Olive had been advertising for branch members to join her.

found in the grounds, together with rags soaked in petrol. The fire was soon put out, with the help of hand extinguishers, and little damage had been done, but there was outrage locally. The *Courier* described the attack as 'a dastardly attempt', which was only foiled by the 'promptitude and courage' of the housekeeper and two maids.[169] The paper said that this incident shed a new light on militancy, as there were servants living immediately above the fire who could have been killed if it had not been put out so quickly.

Outrage, which was frequently and robustly expressed in the House of Commons, in the newspapers, in meetings and in private homes, was a common reaction to suffragettes' destructiveness. For some women, this prompted them to join the campaign against women's suffrage.

Chapter 21

Different Gifts and Different Spheres

The protest meeting which took place at the Great Hall, following the pavilion fire in April 1913, demonstrated the strength of local anti-suffrage feeling at that time. Some attended specifically because they were angry about the fire. However, others were regular attenders at anti-suffrage meetings – a campaign against women having the vote had been running in Tunbridge Wells for the previous four years.

At a national level, anti-suffrage campaigning (and sentiment) stretched back much further. For as long as there had been women who demanded the vote, there had been others who did not want it, and indeed believed they should not have it. Even Queen Victoria held this view. Back in 1870 (after the first women's suffrage bill had been derailed, despite passing its second reading) she stated her position in a letter to Prince Albert's biographer:

The Queen is most anxious to enlist every one who can speak or write to join in checking this mad, wicked folly of 'Woman's Rights,' with all its attendant horrors, on which her poor feeble sex is bent, forgetting every sense of womanly feeling and propriety...It is a subject which makes the Queen so furious that she cannot contain herself. God created men and women different – then let them remain each in their own position...[170]

Opposition continued to be expressed from that time onwards, whether it was in press articles, at public meetings or in parliamentary debates, although in the nineteenth century and early twentieth century, it was generally not organised or co-ordinated.

An exception to this occurred in June 1889. With a private member's bill due to go before Parliament, literary magazine *The Nineteenth Century* published an appeal against women's suffrage.[a] It had been launched by writer Mary Ward and was signed by 104 prominent women, including many titled ladies. (Over 2,000 more women, from all over Britain, signed an accompanying protest.) The appeal argued that women were unsuited, physically and otherwise, to participating in politics and concluded:

It is because we are keenly alive to the enormous value of [women's] special contribution to the community, that we oppose what seems to us likely to endanger that contribution.[171]

It was only once the militant activities of the suffragettes began attracting public attention that the opponents of women's suffrage began organising themselves. The Women's National Anti-Suffrage League was formed in July 1908 (soon after stones were thrown at a government building for the first time). Mary Ward, still resolutely opposed to women having the vote, drafted their manifesto, which pointed to the danger that women would

---

a　The response to this anti-suffrage declaration, which was signed by Tunbridge Wells headmistress Mary Moberly, was referred to in an earlier chapter.

gain the vote by default, in which case the country would '…
drift towards a momentous revolution, both social and political,
before it has realised the dangers involved.'[172]

Support grew rapidly; by the end of 1908, the League had
around 2,000 members, who between them had collected over
300,000 signatures on an anti-suffrage petition. Their first
branch was established in Hawkhurst, fifteen miles south of
Tunbridge Wells, with Ethel Harrison (who was also on the
national executive) as its chair. A meeting of the branch, on 4
November 1908, began with all present singing 'The Suffragette
Girl' to the tune of 'Oh What Can the Matter be?' and concluded
with a resolution to the effect that women did not want the vote.

The following year, the movement arrived in Tunbridge
Wells. On 11 May 1909 Mary Angela Dickens – novelist,
journalist, the famous author's granddaughter and an organising
secretary of the Anti-Suffrage League – spoke at a meeting in the
Tunbridge Wells Town Hall. According to the *Courier* she was a
fluent and convincing speaker, with a gift of bright description
like her grandfather, who 'applied a cold douche in the shape of
forcible logic to the pretensions of feminine suffragists'.[173] The
main argument Mary put forward against giving women the
vote was that they would use it irresponsibly. 'Looking at the
militant suffragettes,' she asked her audience, 'do you believe
that such women would approach the great national questions
calmly, sanely, with dignity, and with womanliness?' She
continued by stating that if there were more women voters than
men, the government would become effeminate, and England
only maintained her position in the world because of her 'virile
manly attitude in Imperial Politics.' Women were content to let
men represent them in war, she said, why not be content to let
men represent them in politics?

At the end of the meeting, it was agreed to set up a local
anti-suffrage society and a committee was appointed, with the

Honourable Eleanor Amherst as president and Mary Backhouse as secretary.[a] By September 1909, it was up and running and attracting support. The following summer, the *Anti-Suffrage Review* reported that the Tunbridge Wells Anti-Suffrage Society had held three meetings and there was strong anti-suffrage feeling in the area. (The National Union of Women's Suffrage Societies (NUWSS) and Women's Freedom League (WFL) were both running active pro-suffrage campaigns in the town at the same time.)

In July 1910, when the first Conciliation Bill was about to have its second reading, and seemed likely to succeed, the Society hurriedly arranged a deputation to call on local MP Herbert Spender-Clay. (On the same day, Sarah Grand and other local suffragists were demonstrating in Trafalgar Square in support of the Bill.) The deputation was led by the branch's president, Mrs Abbott, who was backed up by Mary and Margaret Backhouse, other committee members and local councillors. Treasurer Edward Waldon spoke on the ladies' behalf, asking the MP to accept a resolution the Society had passed at their last meeting, which read:

Sir, we urge you to oppose in every possible way this so called 'Conciliation Bill' now before the House of Commons for its Second Reading, which, if passed, must inevitably end in 'Universal Man and Woman Suffrage' thus at once putting the balance of power into the hands of women.[174]

Whether or not it was the anti-suffragists' arguments that influenced him, Captain Spender-Clay complied with their request; three days later he was one of a minority of MPs who voted against the Conciliation Bill when it passed its second reading.

---

a Both Mary and her sister Margaret were enthusiastic anti-suffrage campaigners. Newspaper articles often referred to Miss M Backhouse and it is sometimes difficult to be sure which one is being referred to.

In December 1910 (not long after Black Friday) the national women's and men's anti-suffrage organisations merged to form the National League for Opposing Women's Suffrage (NLOWS). They continued attracting support and seventy-two new branches were opened in the first year of the new organisation. Speakers were despatched round the country, to address anti-suffrage meetings and take part in public debates. These included a small number of women, one of whom had strong connections with Tunbridge Wells – Gwladys Solomon.

Gwladys was born in Swansea in 1877, the daughter of the Reverend George Cowper-Smith. When she was seven years old, her father was appointed to the Mount Pleasant Congregational Church in Tunbridge Wells, a post he held until his retirement in 1912. At the age of fourteen she was a boarder at Milton

Gwladys Solomon
Drawn by Katharine Harper

Mount College in Gravesend, a school for ministers' daughters, and ten years later she was working as an assistant mistress at the Clergy Daughters School in Bristol.

In January 1906, aged twenty-nine, Gwladys was back in Tunbridge Wells for her wedding to William Gladstone Solomon, a Jewish South African who had studied at the Royal Academy and was a successful artist. At the end of the ceremony, which took place at her father's church, guests emerged beneath the building's huge classical-style columns. Amongst them were suffragist Lydia Le Lacheur (a regular worshipper at the church), the groom's elegant mother Georgiana and his younger sister Daisy, a short, plump twenty-two-year-old, who was a bridesmaid, along with Gwladys's older sister.[175]

Gwladys and William made an unlikely couple and it is difficult to guess how they might have met or why they decided to get married. As it turned out, the marriage did not last. Gwladys gave birth to a son, Scott, in Hampstead at the end of 1907, but the couple made separate trips abroad in 1909 and 1910 and, when the 1911 census was taken, they were living apart.

One problem between them may have been the political views of William's family, especially his mother and sister, both of whom joined the WSPU in 1908 and became well-known suffragettes. In February 1909 Daisy and another woman walked along the Strand behind a rather bemused post boy and were delivered as 'Human Letters' to the Prime Minister at 10 Downing Street. A few days later she was arrested and sentenced to a month's imprisonment, which she served in Holloway Prison. In June 1909, Georgiana was arrested after taking part in a deputation to the House of Commons and also sent to Holloway; in November 1910 she was in Parliament Square on Black Friday and in 1912 she took part in the same window-breaking protest as Olive Walton and the other Tunbridge Wells suffragettes.

Gwladys saw things very differently from her in-laws. She joined the Women's Anti-Suffrage League soon after it was formed in 1908 and, in February 1909, she was appointed honorary secretary of their Hampstead branch. Many Votes for Women supporters did not approve of the actions of militants such as Daisy and Georgiana; how much more disapproving must she have been?

Her views also seem to have differed from her father's. Rev. George Cowper-Smith was on the platform at Liberal Party meetings in Tunbridge Wells on a number of occasions when pro-suffrage views were aired. For example, in January 1908 he chaired a meeting of the Women's Liberal Association, at which an NUWSS speaker and MP Alfred Hedges both pressed for women's suffrage.

In October 1909 Gwladys returned to Tunbridge Wells and attended a meeting organised by the local branch of the Postal and Telegraph Guild. After papers for and against women's suffrage, had been read, Miss Peacock, a local WFL member, spoke and made a spirited defence of Votes for Women. Gwladys, who was always happy to enter into debate with pro-suffrage campaigners, challenged her vigorously.

Over the next couple of years, Gwladys was increasingly involved in the anti-suffrage campaign and when she completed her Hampstead household's census form in April 1911, she described her occupation as NLOWS organising secretary. From that time on, she travelled all over the country, speaking and debating on their behalf. She had no training in public speaking and it seems unlikely that her background as a clergyman's daughter and schoolteacher would have equipped her for this role. But she took it up with enthusiasm. She spoke at meetings in locations as diverse as drawing rooms, factories, church halls and hotels, to audiences ranging from shipworkers on the Clyde, to Girl Guides in Bristol and working women in Berkhamsted. One of her busiest campaigns was in the summer of 1911, when she addressed eleven open-air meetings in South Wales in just two weeks.

What did people make of this minister's daughter from Tunbridge Wells? Gwladys was generally given a better reception than suffragettes who went on similar tours. She was heckled occasionally, but never on the scale they experienced and there are no reports of anything being thrown at her. Meetings concluded with a resolution against women's suffrage, which was invariably passed with little or no opposition, indicating that most audience members were receptive to her message.

Anti-suffragists had various reasons for believing that women should not have the vote and Gwladys covered most of them in her speeches.

Like many anti-suffragists, Gwladys believed that women did not need the vote, as Parliament already protected their interests effectively. In August 1911, as she stood in a motor car addressing an audience of several hundred in Cirencester, she argued that forty years' agitation had already brought women many rights and privileges. These would be extended further, without any need for women to be directly represented in Parliament.

Another key argument was that a woman's primary role was as homemaker and voting would distract her from this. In May 1911, around one hundred workmen in a North London canteen listened attentively and applauded enthusiastically when Gwladys said the 'the greatest privilege a woman could have was peace and leisure to bring up her children properly.'[176] At an adult education group in Hampstead Garden Suburb that evening, she claimed women were needed in the home to ensure their babies survived and grew up safely. And, in a letter to *The Standard* in October 1911, she stated that Christ clearly taught two things: firstly, that certain spheres of men's work were closed to women and secondly, that for women 'motherhood' was the highest work.

Gwladys also considered that women should not have a say in electing a parliament that was responsible for the Empire, the Army and the Navy. These institutions were dependent on physical force, she argued, and should therefore be run by men. In June 1912, while campaigning in Wales, she wrote in a letter to David Lloyd George, Chancellor of the Exchequer:

As a typical woman householder and rate and taxpayer I beg you – a typical man – to take upon your stronger shoulders the burden of responsibility for the safety of the Empire, the Army and Navy, Trade, Shipping, Mining, Railways etc. I am too thankful to pay my taxes in return for your protection, if only you will leave me to look after my home and child.[177]

On 9 August 1912, the *Courier* published a letter from Glwadys in which she wrote that giving the vote to all women would be 'dangerous to the Empire'. Since Parliament controlled the Army, Navy, the State and the Empire, which were all great businesses run by men, would it be fair or wise to let women control them?[178]

From the start, one of the main arguments against women having the vote was that, as well as being physically weaker, they were emotionally unstable and not capable of voting wisely. (Suffrage campaigners frequently pointed out that many men were not capable of this either.) Glwadys and other anti-suffrage speakers cited the suffragettes' disruptive behaviour as evidence that some women at least could not be trusted with the vote. During a tour of North Wales in November 1912, she repeatedly expressed disgust at their actions, especially when they disrupted the National Eisteddfod and heckled David Lloyd George. In a meeting of the Cambridge University Anti-Suffrage Society in March 1913, she said that the suffragettes' methods were 'the most degrading and debasing the world had ever known.'

Tunbridge Wells anti-suffrage campaigner Margaret Backhouse had a similar point of view, believing that women could not be trusted with power and responsibility. On 10 January 1912, *The Standard* published a letter from her which read:

...we contend that a preponderating female vote would lead to hasty and unnecessary wars, among many other follies... The emotionalism of women alone would...be a grave danger to the state.[179]

In the same letter, Margaret also referred to another anti-suffrage concern. Prime Minister Asquith and some in his party feared that, if property-owning women were given the vote, they would use it for the Conservatives. On the other hand, many anti-suffragists feared that if all women were given the vote, this would open the door to socialism. Staunch Conservative Margaret claimed that 'underneath the suffragist robe of high-sounding ideals lurks the cloven hoof of socialism.' These fears may have seemed justified in 1912, when the NUWSS made a pact with the Labour Party and began supporting their candidates in by-elections.

The arguments against women's suffrage cited by Gwladys, Margaret and other anti-suffrage campaigners often focussed on the negative consequences if women were given the vote. However, a few leading female anti-suffragists, including Mary Ward and Ethel Harrison, framed things in a more positive way. In an approach that became known as 'The Forward Policy', they argued that women had a distinctive and important role to play in areas such as local government, care for the poor and education. These activities rather than the vote, they suggested, would allow women to have an influence in the aspects of life that mattered to them most.

Finally, in addition to the various reasons they believed women should not have the vote, anti-suffragists were confident that they represented the 'silent majority' and that most women did not want it. Votes for Women campaigners were a minority, they claimed, and not representative of the general population. Gwladys concluded her August 1912 letter to the *Courier* by saying: 'The truth is that women who want the vote are in a very, very small minority, and they have no earthly right to try to impose their will on the majority.'[180]

The Spectator, which was consistently anti-suffrage, agreed. In January 1913, after the latest attempt at Votes for Women legislation had failed (when the Speaker announced that an amendment to the Franchise and Registration Bill would change it too much) an article stated:

> *We fancy...that women as a whole dislike the thought of woman suffrage even more than men do. So far from looking upon women suffragists as champions of their sex, they feel that suffragists are undermining the whole position of women... They do not admit the relevance of any silly talk about the 'inferiority' of their sex. All they admit is a difference, and they frankly accept that difference.*

Anti-suffragists claimed to have evidence that many men and women supported their views. They regularly collected large numbers of signatures on petitions and carried out surveys, by canvassing door-to-door and sending out pre-paid postcards. In 1911 the NLOWS said that, of around 30,000 people they had canvassed to date, 65% had been opposed to women's suffrage and another 16% indifferent, leaving only 19% in favour.

It is impossible to be sure how accurate this assessment was. Votes for Women campaigners also claimed to represent the views of most women and they also cited survey results, which in their case showed that a majority of people believed women should have the vote. Each side was very critical of the other's methodology.

Despite heated debates and the criticisms they made of each other, the views of anti-suffrage campaigners and women's suffrage supporters were not completely different. Most women in both movements believed that women's natures and abilities were essentially different from men and that women had a particular role to play. And, although anti-suffrage campaigners believed women should not vote, the majority did not believe they were inferior. At a meeting in Leamington Spa in 1913, Gwladys said that the fact that women were as intelligent as men did not mean they could do the duties of men.

There were also similarities between the campaigning styles of the anti-suffrage campaigners and those of the non-militant suffragists. Members of the Tunbridge Wells NLOWS branch were also active in selling their newspaper, *The Anti-Suffrage Review,* around the town; they employed a man on an occasional basis to do so and placed copies with local booksellers. Some of their meetings would have felt quite similar to pro-suffrage ones. On 14 March 1911, the branch held an 'At Home' at the Christ Church parish room, with speeches, entertainment and refreshments. Just as at pro-suffrage meetings, leaflets were handed out, postcards, badges and the organisation's newspaper were offered for sale, petition signatures were collected and new members signed up. If someone had walked in off the street, they might have thought for a moment that they were at a meeting of the NUWSS.

The national NLOWS did not have the same flair for organisation as suffragists or suffragettes. Their meetings were less colourful events and they generally did not hold large marches or mass meetings. An exception to this occurred on 28 February 1912, when they held a meeting at the Albert Hall, which was as large and impressive as any of the pro-suffrage ones held there. (The NUWSS had held a meeting at the same venue only five days earlier and the WSPU would meet there a month later.)

At the time of the meeting, anti-suffragists considered their campaign was more necessary than ever. The previous November the WSPU had suspended their truce and resumed militant action with the window-smashing protest that Olive Walton took part in. And there was always the threat that legislation might succeed; the latest Conciliation Bill had been shelved when the Prime Minister announced that there would be a manhood suffrage bill, but it could be revived at any time.

Around 20,000 ticket applications were received, double the number of seats available. Gwladys and members of the

Tunbridge Wells NLOWS branch, such as the Backhouse sisters, may well have attended, if they were able to get tickets.

Sylvia Pankhurst later observed that on the platform that evening were seven cabinet ministers, five dukes, fifteen earls, five viscounts, forty-four barons, thirteen Members of Parliament and one woman. The last was Violet Markham, a social and education reformer and leading anti-suffragist, and it was her speech that made the most impact. Violet's message was 'the great principle' that men and women were different beings, with talents that were complementary, not identical. There was already a natural route by which women could participate in public affairs, she argued:

> *If the work of the Imperial Parliament belongs more naturally to men, the work of local government, with its splendid opportunities for civic betterment and the uplifting of the race, belongs more naturally to women.*[181]

Violet's speech was greeted by prolonged cheering and a standing ovation. *The Spectator* noted the Albert Hall audience's calmness and sense of a common purpose and observed that the meeting had drawn back the curtain and showed the granite barrier which would prevent women getting the vote – in other words the strength of opposition.

On 22 October 1912, the Tunbridge Wells NLOWS organised an anti-suffrage 'At Home' which was held at the town hall. The speaker was well-known anti-suffragist Gladys Pott (who would be back in town the following April, after the pavilion fire). NUWSS leaders Amelia Scott and Sarah Grand both attended, along with other local suffragists. Amelia spoke up, asking the speaker whether women should accept the current decline of religion and moral standards, just because they were women, and therefore considered incapable of good judgement. At the end of the meeting, the Chair proposed a vote of thanks and reflected the general anti-suffragist view on militancy. 'The suffragettes are doing all they can to degrade their sex,' he said, 'and to drag all that has been regarded as pure, holy and lovely in women in the dirt.'

As militancy became even more extreme, anti-suffrage sentiment and support for anti-suffrage organisations increased. The window-breaking of November 1911 and March 1912, together with the arson attacks over the following year or so, led more people to join the NLOWS and by 1914 their total membership had risen to around 42,000. In Tunbridge Wells there was a sharp increase in numbers after the pavilion was burnt down; at their 1914 annual meeting, a year later, Secretary Mary Backhouse reported that the branch's membership had grown by over one hundred, to 391.[a]

While suffragists and anti-suffragists in Tunbridge Wells were generally very polite towards each other, things could get heated at times. In April 1913 (soon after the fire) Mary wrote a letter to the *Courier*, alleging that there was a close connection between the militants and non-militants in the town, despite what the latter claimed to the contrary. NUWSS Secretary Gertrude Mosely wrote to the paper denying this allegation. She emphasised that hers was a non-militant organisation, which had always condemned violent methods and that support should not be withheld from them, because people disapproved of the WSPU. The dispute continued with further letters published over the following weeks.

Suffragists in Tunbridge Wells were anxious to prove that, contrary to Mary's claim, they had nothing to do with the militants. Soon they would be marching through the streets of Tunbridge Wells, as a demonstration of their different approach.

---

a This was very similar to the membership of the local NUWSS branch.

Chapter 22

The Women's Pilgrimage

While the Tunbridge Wells suffragettes were marching through London's streets, breaking windows, getting themselves arrested and going to prison, local suffragists such as Amelia Scott, Sarah Grand and Lydia Le Lacheur had continued their more low-key campaign (especially during the general elections in January and December 1910). While their activities attracted less attention, debate and press coverage, they were part of a huge movement, far larger than the WSPU (Women's Social and Political Union) or the WFL (Women's Freedom League). By 1910, the NUWSS (National Union of Women's Suffrage Societies) had over 400 branches and around 50,000 members. In a speech she made in 1911, Millicent Garrett Fawcett likened them to a glacier – slow and unstoppable. (Sylvia Pankhurst put it rather differently, describing them as 'so staid, so willing to sit, so incorrigibly leisurely'.)

Following their 1910 election campaign, the Tunbridge Wells suffragists continued to hold regular 'At Homes', hosted by a member, but usually held in a public venue. These featured well-argued addresses in favour of women's suffrage, describing the benefits of giving women the vote and the experiences of other

countries where this had already happened. Refreshments were
provided and there was either an admission charge or donations
were requested towards funds. They also organised entertainments
and ran fundraising events such as white elephant sales.

In February 1911, the NUWSS branch opened a shop and
club at 18 Crescent Road (this was the property from which they
had run their election campaign the previous December). On
sale was a range of goods similar to those the suffragettes would
offer at their shop on the Pantiles, when it opened later the
same year. These included postcards, tea, chocolates, suffrage
literature and their newspaper *The Common Cause*. Members
could also visit for teas and light refreshments.

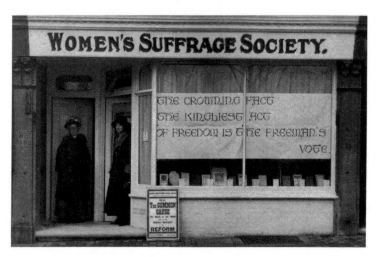

The NUWSS shop at 18 Crescent Road
Women's Library, LSE

However, despite the large membership and many campaigning
activities of the NUWSS, it was the suffragettes who continued
to attract the most attention, locally and nationally, and their
protests dominated any discussion on Votes for Women, whether
it took place in the press, at public meetings, or in private homes.

The suffragists were frustrated by this and feared that the chance of success was being undermined. The WSPU's actions, they argued, allowed Asquith and the government to treat women's suffrage as a law and order issue, with public safety rather than women's rights as the main focus. It also provided support for the anti-suffragists, who could point to the suffragettes' actions as proof that women were emotional and illogical and could not be trusted with the responsibility of voting.

On 7 March 1913 Amelia Scott wrote to the *Advertiser*, quoting Millicent Garrett Fawcett, who had described the outrages committed by suffragettes as 'detestable and deeply injurious to the cause.'[182] She continued in her own words: 'It seems to us, who are working for this great cause by constitutional methods, that no victory is worth gaining at the expense of honour.'

On 8 May 1913, speaking at an NUWSS meeting at the town hall, Sarah Grand also commented on the negative effect of militancy. The *Courier* reported her words:

There were amongst the militant party women whose courage and devotion had never been exceeded in the world...But she was bound to say, speaking personally, that militancy had been a great enemy to the women's movement. She was quite sure if it had not been for militancy, women would have been enfranchised by this time.[183]

Sarah's attitude towards the suffragettes had changed. In 1908 she had attended the WSPU rally in Hyde Park and in 1911 she had marched alongside their members in the Coronation Procession. Since then, however, their actions had diverged far from those of the noble and virtuous 'new woman' who featured in her books, articles and talks and, as a result, her opinion had changed. He speech in the town hall had made this clear and in

June 1913, when she heard that the Women Writers' Suffrage League was to take part in Emily Wilding Davison's funeral procession, Sarah resigned in protest.

But, whatever suffragists such as Sarah and Amelia thought of the WSPU, the organisation's campaign was a powerful one. What was to be done to counter its negative impact? The NUWSS decided to arrange a huge pilgrimage, starting from seventeen different cities and following eight main routes. Local women would join them for short distances, as well as holding their own events. The marchers and other supporters would converge on London towards the end of July, where there would be a huge celebration. The sight of suffragists on the streets would remind the public that, as well as the militant WSPU, there was a large, constitutional organisation campaigning for the vote by peaceful means. According to *The Common Cause*, the keynote of the march, which would involve around 400 local societies, would be 'the joyousness of self-dedication to the cause.'

The Kent marchers were to set off from Margate and follow a route that would take them through Canterbury, Rochester, Maidstone and Tonbridge, where they would join up with a second group who had set out from Folkestone. It does not seem that any Tunbridge Wells suffragists took part in the whole pilgrimage, but they did hold meetings to plan how they could be involved. Members were asked to provide hospitality for walkers and to advertise the event by putting up posters and giving out handbills. It was also decided that there would be a short march by local suffragists, which would meet up with the pilgrims in nearby Tonbridge. Over recent years both suffragists and suffragettes from Tunbridge Wells had marched on London's streets. Now, for the first time, some of them would march through their home town.

Poster advertising NUWSS Pilgrimage (1913)
Women's Library, LSE

Having left Margate on 1 July, the Kent pilgrims arrived in Canterbury on the 10th. Several women from Tunbridge Wells, including Sarah, Amelia, Lydia Le Lacheur and Gertrude Mosely, travelled there and joined them as they marched through the city's narrow streets. Afterwards, they attended a service at the cathedral and took afternoon tea with the marchers. Amelia later recalled an ostler in a hotel doorway calling out to her, 'Go it, mother! You'll win through!'

The Tunbridge Wells procession took place on 21 July, the day the pilgrimage was due to arrive in Tonbridge. At mid-day around a hundred women gathered outside the office on Crescent Road. Local suffragists were joined by others who had come up on the Hastings train, or travelled by road from surrounding villages. The women wore black, grey, navy or white, as instructed by the NUWSS, and each had a satchel slung over her shoulder, with a red, green and white strap and 'Kent Pilgrims Way' written on it in red letters.[a] They also displayed the colours on pennants, coat badges and rosettes pinned on their hats. A report in the *Courier* commented that, to a short-sighted spectator, the sight would have resembled a green, red and white kaleidoscope. The *Advertiser* observed that the colourful assembly looked as picturesque as a Sunday school procession and chattered just as much. At one point the sound of their chatter was drowned out, when a barrel organ and three male singers, standing across the road, struck up a rendition of *I'm Dreaming of You*. However, to the women's relief, the musicians soon departed.

At around 2pm, Gertrude Mosely brought the procession to order and the marchers set off, walking in pairs. They turned into Calverley Road, passed the town hall and headed up Grosvenor Hill. To the front was a constable, together with two young lady suffragists pushing brightly decorated bicycles. They were followed by a banner advertising a meeting to be held part way along the route with 'Non Militant' written in large letters at the top. Next came Sarah, elegant in black satin trimmed with black lace. She was followed by committee members, including Gertrude, Amelia and Lydia. The 'rank and file' followed behind, among whom was Olive Walton's younger sister. (Mary had rejected Olive's style of protest, but evidently did believe that women should have the vote.)

A few of the suffragists carried banners, including one with the Tunbridge Wells borough motto 'Do Well, Doubt Not.' This was also an opportunity for fundraising, and others collected donations to the cause, in small boxes painted in the NUWSS colours, and sold copies of *The Common Cause*. To the rear was a bold red banner, with the words 'Votes for Women'. The *Tunbridge Wells Gazette* noted that some of the town's best-known and most influential residents were amongst the marchers

---

a Amelia Scott's satchel can be seen at the Women's Library.

and that the quality of the material in their dresses indicated that the procession was almost entirely middle-class.[184] Some of them were elderly, so progress was slow and steady.

Thankfully, the Tunbridge Wells pilgrims met with a better response than those marching through East Grinstead, who were pelted with eggs and tomatoes and had to take refuge. The reaction here was more respectful; the *Advertiser* described passers-by stopping, looking, murmuring, 'H'm Suffragettes again', and moving on. According to the *Gazette:*

One could not help remarking upon the absolute respect and deference with which the crowds who lined the kerbs at various busy spots treated the pilgrims. Salutations and encouraging utterances were frequent; coarse criticism entirely absent.

It was not exactly a rapturous response, but the march's dignified nature, and the respectful way in which it was received, were just what the suffragists had hoped for. Their reception was in sharp contrast to the scene outside the Great Hall a couple of months earlier, when Olive Walton and her fellow suffragettes had been mobbed and were taken to the police station for their own safety.

When they reached St John's Road, a short distance along the route, five carriages and a motor car joined the procession, to act as transport for some of the less mobile marchers. It was here that one solitary protest was made. Silas Edwards (a picture dealer) and his brother Tom (a local councillor) had put up a banner outside their house, which read: 'The majority of women in this Country do not want the vote.'

As the marchers arrived in Southborough, part-way to Tonbridge, contingents from Tonbridge and Langton Green, carrying an array of banners, joined them and were greeted by cheers. The *Gazette* observed that all Southborough turned out

for what had, by this point, become a 'triumphant procession.'
The marchers stopped at the Royal Victoria Hall, a local
municipal building, where they held a meeting.

Sarah Grand opened proceedings. By taking part in the
march they were making history, she said, and changing
perceptions:

> *The Suffrage movement has done away with many*
> *misconceptions of womankind, particularly the fallacious*
> *opinion that women are not good for much. It has abolished*
> *many of the prejudices which were the cause of many*
> *reasonable people opposing the movement.*[185]

Sarah continued: 'One has only to tell a woman that she cannot
do any particular thing and she will straightaway,' and pointed
to women's success in education and the medical profession.
There were a number of weaknesses women had outgrown, but
she would only mention one – the fear of mice! When mice
had been released at women's suffrage meetings, instead of
fleeing, women picked them up and used them to illustrate their
arguments.

Amelia, who spoke next, began by proposing a resolution:

> *This meeting, believing that the exclusion of women from the*
> *Parliamentary franchise is unjust and contrary to the principle*
> *of representative government, calls on His Majesty's ministers*
> *to introduce a measure removing this injustice without further*
> *delay.*

She reminded her listeners of the march's purpose:

> *The object of this pilgrimage is not pleasure, or excitement,*
> *but to demonstrate to those persons who still maintain that*

*quiet home-loving women are against this movement that this
is not true; for here, before their very eyes, are such women on
the road.*[186]

Amelia's public speaking skills and confidence had developed
through her suffrage activities, as well as through her role as poor
law guardian and on numerous local committees. In a stirring
speech, she talked about how the world had changed for women.

*Woman no longer only competes with her fellow woman in the
marriage market, in order to gain an 'establishment'; she now
competes with men and women in the labour-market for her
daily bread, and not only in the labour-market but in almost
every field of activity, such as art, literature, medicine, science
and many other professions.*

Next she described the motivation which had driven many
campaigners from the start, especially non-militant suffragists.
They were prompted to act, she said, not just by a belief that they
had the right to access something they were excluded from, but
also by a belief that if they had the vote, women would be able
to bring about change and create a more compassionate society.
Amelia had in her mind her experiences as a social worker.
Whose business was it, she asked, to protect the women who
did 90% of the sweated work in England, the child mother made
pregnant by her own father, the wife of a drunken husband,
or the 240 illegitimate children born in the twelve and a half
years she had been a poor law guardian? The answer was clear.
'We women who are so safe, so protected, whose lives are so
comfortable, in a backwater – safe from the waves of this
troublesome world – the duty is ours.'

Amelia finished by calling for women to be given political
power:

We need power – political power. We have had women's power of influence all these ages, and yet these evils still exist. So much for this vaunted influence... Why should we shrink from political power?

Malcolm Mitchell, secretary of the national Men's League for Women's Suffrage, seconded the resolution, which was passed without opposition. After a vote of thanks, refreshments were served and around twenty-five suffragists (including Amelia and Gertrude) continued walking down the road to Tonbridge, where the local suffrage society held an open-air meeting. This time the atmosphere was rather less peaceful. The *Advertiser* reported that one of the speakers aroused the indignation of men in the crowd and was hassled as she walked along the High Street afterwards.

The Kent pilgrims continued walking, through Sevenoaks, Sidcup and Blackheath and then on to central London, where all the various pilgrimages converged on 26 July. The marchers had come from far and wide, including one group who had walked all the way from Land's End and, despite incidents such as in East Grinstead, they had generally been well-received. They were joined in London by other suffragists and merged into four processions, which started from Maida Vale, Kensington, Bloomsbury and Trafalgar Square. The last location was where seventeen women from Tunbridge Wells met up with marchers and campaigners from across Kent. Together they headed for Hyde Park, arriving there at around 5pm, at the same time as the other processions.

The papers estimated that there were 50,000 people in the park that day, gathered around twenty platforms, and reported that Millicent Garrett Fawcett, the main speaker, was especially well-received. In an echo of the WSPU rally back in 1908, a bugle was sounded at exactly 6pm and a resolution read out at each platform, calling on the government to give women the vote.

Some of the Tunbridge Wells suffragists stayed on in London overnight. The following day they returned to Trafalgar Square and joined a long queue of women who marched along the Strand and Fleet Street to St Paul's, where around 500 people attended a church service. For the text of his sermon, Canon Simpson chose 1 Kings XIX verse 15 – 'Go, return on thy way to the wilderness of Damascus.'

A couple of weeks later, on 8 August, the Prime Minister received an NUWSS deputation at Downing Street (the first he had agreed to see since November 1911). However, even at this stage, his position on Votes for Women remained unchanged. This was enormously frustrating for campaigners. Women's rights, responsibilities and opportunities had continued to grow through the early twentieth century – for example the 1907 Qualification of Women (County and Borough Councils) Act meant that women could now sit as councillors, aldermen, mayors and chairmen on county and borough councils. Yet they were still being denied the vote.

One specific injustice, which dated back to the previous century and which continued to anger many women, was that they paid tax, yet were not allowed to vote for the government that levied, collected and spent their money. A few of them, including Maud Roll from Rotherfield near Tunbridge Wells, protested against this by refusing to pay the money they owed.

Chapter 23

Taxation Without Representation is Tyranny!

On a sunny afternoon in June 1914, the Sussex Assembly Rooms, at one end of the Pantiles, were the scene of an unusual auction. Herbert Banks, of local estate agents Carter and Banks, was more used to bringing his hammer down on a property, or the entire contents of one. Only that morning he had conducted a lengthy sale of goods 'removed from various residences across the town' including mahogany bedroom furniture, hair mattresses and pianos. In the afternoon sale, which had attracted a great deal of attention, there was just one lot – a small silver dish which had been 'seized in distraint' from forty-five-year-old Maud Roll.

From the beginning of the Votes for Women campaign, a connection was made between tax and suffrage; it seemed an obvious injustice to campaigners that women who paid taxes had no say in how the money was spent. In 1832, when Henry Hunt presented the first petition to parliament on behalf of widow Mary Smith, he stated that since she paid taxes, she did not see why she should not have a share in the election of a representative. In her application to join the Northern Reform

Society in 1858, Matilda Biggs pointed to the injustice of being taxed like men and yet denied a voice. When Lydia Becker spoke in Tunbridge Wells back in 1879, her subject was 'Taxation and Representation'.

It was an injustice that campaigners continually referred to, and through the nineteenth and early twentieth centuries a few individual women chose to withhold the tax they owed, as a way of protesting at not having the vote.

One notable example of these women was Henrietta Muller, a well-known suffrage campaigner. In 1884, bailiffs called at her home on Cadogan Place and seized several pieces of furniture. Henrietta, who was described as a 'veritable volcano of temper and pluck', claimed they had chosen the items most precious to her, but continued defiantly: 'they did not collect the rates, and they never will if they rob me of every stick of my furniture and pull the doors and windows out of my house. I shall continue this fight if I am the only woman left in England to do so.'[187]

Another famous protest began on 23 May 1906, when suffragette Dora Montefiore, who had refused to pay income tax, barricaded the doors and gates of her Hammersmith villa to keep out the tax collector and bailiff.[a] A six-week siege followed and attracted a great deal of publicity. Suffragettes, together with large numbers of police, press and public, gathered regularly outside Dora's home, which became known as 'Fort Montefiore' and protest meetings were held in the street, which she addressed from an upstairs window. A red banner with white lettering, which was displayed on the terrace, proclaimed: 'Women should vote for the laws they obey and the taxes they pay.' Eventually, on 3 July, the bailiff, accompanied by a police constable, forced entry and seized several items of furniture. These were auctioned at a

---

a In October 1906, Dora would be one of the WSPU protestors whose arrest at the House of Commons caused such a stir at the NUWW conference in Tunbridge Wells.

crowded sale and bought back by Dora herself. Other similar, although less dramatic, protests followed.

In October 1909 the Women's Tax Resistance League (WTRL) was founded, with the motto 'No Vote No Tax' and official colours of grey and silver. The organisation had close links with the Women's Freedom League (WFL) and adopted a similar approach to campaigning – like the WFL, they advocated direct action and law-breaking, but stopped short of violence. Tax protests, which appealed to people's sense of fairness, were more acceptable to the general public than window-breaking or arson.

The WTRL recruited women who were willing to campaign for the vote by refusing to pay tax, advised them on their legal position and supported them in their protests. By July 1910 the League had over one hundred members, including some who were prepared to withhold taxes immediately and others who had committed to doing so once membership reached 500. They withheld a variety of dues – including dog licences, servants' licences, carriage licences, property tax and inhabited house duty. The authorities responded by seizing goods to the value of the unpaid tax and selling them. The sales, which were held in public places such as auction rooms, village halls, public houses and village greens, offered an excellent opportunity for publicity. Fellow WTRL members and other supporters attended and often bought back the confiscated goods.

Women's Tax Resistance League Badge
Women's Library, LSE

Tax resistance was not restricted solely to the WTRL. The WSPU (Women's Social and Political Union) adopted it as a form of protest from November 1910, although it was not one their members used all that much, preferring more drastic campaigning methods.

The NUWSS (National Union of Women's Suffrage Societies) national executive, on the other hand, decided not to adopt tax resistance as a policy, although some of their members supported it. In Tunbridge Wells, Sarah Grand and Amelia Scott, while not choosing this form of protest themselves, seem to have approved of it. In a letter to the Hastings WTRL organiser in 1912 (apologising for being unable to attend a meeting) Sarah wrote: 'Tax-Resistance is an heroical form of protest, with which I have very much sympathy and more admiration.'[188] Amelia once commented: 'Equality is only recognised by the State when the tax collector comes around.'

The Tunbridge Wells NUWSS branch gave tax resistance some consideration; on 7 July 1911 WTRL organiser Margaret Kineton Parkes spoke at a meeting in the Crescent Road office.

Lydia Le Lacheur took the chair and the meeting was followed by 'a most animated and instructive discussion'[189] However, members came to the conclusion that breaking the law would be a step too far. At a meeting in January 1912 it was decided that, in the interest of law and order, they would pay the tax owed on their office, although it was also recorded in the minutes that: 'at the same time the committee instructed its treasurer to emphasise to the authorities its sense of injustice [at] the compulsory fulfilment of the obligations of citizenship by those to whom its rights are denied.'[190]

The WTRL's national membership grew slowly and never reached 500 members, but its protests attracted attention and generated publicity for the suffrage cause. During the five years it was in existence, over 220 women took part in its campaign. The more well-known the protestor, the greater the publicity. In July 1911 a diamond ring was seized from Princess Sophia Duleep Singh, after she had refused to pay the dues owing on her five dogs, a male servant and a carriage. It was sold at auction for £10, bought by a WTRL member and returned to the Princess. In April 1913, a silver cup was seized from the Duchess of Bedford, who had refused to pay the Imperial taxes she owed in relation to the Prince's Skating Rink in Knightsbridge. The cup was also purchased by a fellow protestor and returned to her.

Advertisement for WTRL Sale
Women's Library, LSE

Former Tunbridge Wells resident Kate Le Lacheur belonged to the WTRL, as well as to the WSPU. In November 1911 (a year after she took part in the 'Black Friday' protest) three pieces of furniture, including a roll top desk, were confiscated from her and sold at auction in Reading. WTRL members attended the sale to support her and, when it was over, a protest meeting was held in a public hall nearby. In April 1912 Kate had a dogcart confiscated for failing to pay agricultural land tax, which was also sold in Reading. When she returned home from the sale, she discovered that bailiffs had visited the farm again in her absence and seized a cow for non-payment of further taxes. However, after they had led it a few miles down the road, the cow had bolted and returned to the farm. When the same thing happened a second time, the bailiffs had given up and left the cow in a shed, together with a copy of the distraining order.

Maud Roll, whose silver dish was on sale on the summer's day in 1914, was another regular tax protestor. Maud was born in Kensington in 1866, and in 1901 she was living in Hove, Sussex, with her widowed mother and a brother who was a doctor. At some point in the next few years, she moved to Rotherfield (a few miles south of Tunbridge Wells) where she lived in Oakdene, a large timbered house owned by Honnor Morten, a nurse, journalist and social reformer. In 1905 Honnor had used a legacy to purchase the property and established a community there, together with a number of other women. As well as Maud, these included Olive Ibbotson, who had been living at Oakdene in May 1908 when she was arrested while delivering the WFL resolution to the Prime Minister at Downing Street.

Maud was secretary of the North Sussex NUWSS and treasurer of the Rotherfield women's suffrage society. However, she also supported the WFL and in 1912 she walked in two stages of a march they organised, from Edinburgh to London. Tax resistance seems to have been a form of protest that appealed to Maud and she joined the WTRL soon after it was founded in 1909.

Maud's first protest took place in July 1912. A set of silver spoons, which had been confiscated from her for non-payment of taxes, was sold in 'The Square' in Rotherfield, in front of a large crowd, who were good natured and mostly supportive. A few people made speeches, including Margaret Kineton Parkes of the WTRL. She pointed out that the Liberal government had always talked about taxation and representation going together, so they should either remove the burden of taxation from women or give them the vote. The spoons were purchased by local suffragists and returned to Maud that evening.

The following May, a silver salver and a gold ring were seized from Maud and Honnor and auctioned at the crossroads in Mark Cross by Mr Playfoot, an income tax inspector from Crowborough. After the salver had been sold for £2 2s and the ring for 31s, a protest meeting was held. One of the speakers said that the refusal to give women the vote was like a workman stealing another's tools so that he could keep the work for himself. Another pointed out that taxes paid by women went towards paying MPs' salaries. Maud vowed to continue resisting until women got the vote. This was not a WSPU protest, but some of the Tunbridge Wells suffragettes attended the sale to support her. They waved banners, handed out leaflets and offered copies of *The Suffragette* for sale. After the meeting, members of the crowd made a bonfire of their leaflets.

Sadly, Honnor had been suffering from throat cancer when the 1913 sale took place and she died just a few weeks later. However, Maud continued refusing to pay tax. In June 1914, after attempts had been made to recover more unpaid taxes, a silver salver, estimated to be worth the same as the amount she owed, was seized from Oakdene. (It may have been the same one that had been confiscated the previous year.) It was announced that the salver would be auctioned on 19 June at the Assembly Room, a public building close to the Pantiles.

The WTRL had a policy of getting as much publicity as possible when members' goods were confiscated and sold, so Margaret Kineton Parkes travelled to Tunbridge Wells ahead of the sale to drum up support. She claimed afterwards that she had met with a good reception and local tradesmen had been happy to display her organisation's posters in their windows. Margaret was back in town again when the sale took place and, before Herbert Banks started proceedings, she made a short speech. (Auctioneers were generally willing to allow this.) The question of taxation was a serious matter for women, she said. Women contributed over twenty million pounds a year towards the country's revenue, but received no representation in return.

Bidding was brisk on the silver salver, which was eventually sold to one of Maud's supporters for £5 5s. ('Take it back where it came from,' someone called out.) Maud and the other protestors left the auction room, crossed over London Road and walked onto the Common. Two of them were holding banners which read 'No Vote No Tax' and several others carried white parasols inscribed with the same message. A trolley, decorated in the WTRL colours, had been set up in an open area and Maud climbed up onto it to address the small crowd that had gathered.

'I look on taxes in the same light as bills,' she said. 'I want to know what I'm paying for. To pay tax without having the vote is like going into a shop, putting down one's money, and leaving the shopkeeper to give one just what they liked for it.' Margaret, who spoke next, referred to the old Liberal cry of 'Taxation without Representation is Tyranny!' and asked why a Liberal government was unable to apply it to women. She finished by proposing a resolution:

> *That we protest against the seizure and sale of Miss Roll's goods, and consider the women taxpayers of this country are justified in refusing to pay all Imperial taxes until they have the same control over Imperial expenditure as the male taxpayers possess.*[191]

All present voted in favour, apart from one man. Newspaper reports did not name him, but it seems likely that he was sixty-two-year-old picture dealer Silas Edwards, a well-known local character. (It was he and his brother who had displayed the lone anti-suffrage banner outside their home as the NUWSS pilgrimage passed by the previous year). This would have been rather ironic. Silas was a Passive Resister, who had regularly had goods confiscated after refusing to pay the portion of his rates used to fund church-based education. Certainly it was Silas who spoke up next, asking whether it was intended that women should become MPs.

Margaret responded crisply, asking him, 'Can't you trust women?'

'Not some of them.'

'You haven't had the right sort.'

'I haven't yet had any sort,' said Silas (a long term bachelor).

'That explains it.' (Which prompted laughter.)

After another (anonymous) male speaker had asked a couple of questions, Silas interjected again:

'Won't some ladies ask a question?'

A woman responded, 'I should like to know why there are always so many men at these meetings who ask silly questions?'

Anonymous: 'They have to make up for the silence of the ladies.'

There was more laughter as a woman got the last word: 'Ladies never open their mouths unless they have something worth saying.'

Maud concluded the meeting by reminding the crowd that she could have found a more pleasant way of spending the afternoon than standing on a trolley in the hot sun. However, she and her co-workers were engaged in a fight which, despite being long, was certain to result in victory.

This was only a small meeting, although it was covered in detail by the local press, which was what Maud had been aiming for. A month earlier, a much larger event had taken place in Tunbridge Wells, when the local Conservative and Unionist Association organised a demonstration against home rule for Ireland. It began with a large procession that set off from Calverley Parade and headed along Crescent Road (past the NUWSS office where local suffragists had lined up for their Pilgrimage the previous year). The *Courier*'s report commented on the extraordinary number of women who took part; they were four deep in their section, which extended over a quarter of a mile, and they:

...presented a cheerful spectacle of colour, every lady bearing
a small flag, whilst some, not content with a single expression
of their sentiments, wore hat ribbons or sashes of the national
colours.[192]

The procession eventually reached the Common, where numbers swelled to around 10,000. There were songs and speeches from three platforms, erected close to Wellington Rocks, with the greatest number of people gathered round Rudyard Kipling, who made an inflammatory speech, accusing the government of sacrificing the people of Ulster in order to stay in power. At the conclusion a resolution that home rule should be put to the people was greeted with prolonged cheers.

The scale of this event, compared to the WTRL protest and to the NUWSS pilgrimage the previous year, suggests that interest in home rule was much greater than in Votes for Women. On the other hand, women's participation in such large numbers provides clear evidence that they were interested in politics and actively involved in political movements.

The issue of the *Courier* that reported on the auction of Maud's dish also contained accounts of a suffragist garden party, a Grocers' Association conference and a car company's staff outing. There was no reference at all to the possibility of war. There were plenty of rumours, but it seems unlikely that any of those listening to Maud on that hot summer day would have guessed that just over a month later their country would be at war. Or that, by the time peace came, the world would have changed and women would finally get the vote.

Chapter 24

The Dark Shadow of War

On the morning of Thursday 30 July 1914, the band of the Royal Irish Rifles were setting up for that day's performance on the Pantiles bandstand. (They had been booked to play each day for a week.) A telegram was handed to the bandmaster, who read it and instructed his men to pack up their instruments. They did so and headed to the station to catch the first possible trains back to their Wiltshire barracks. For months there had been rumours of war and now it had become a reality.

The following day, an article in the *Courier* observed:

The dark shadow of War hangs heavily over us. Its oppressive adumbration reaches even to Tunbridge Wells, where the holiday season has been temporarily disturbed by the cancelling of leave to local naval and military men... Trifling as [cancelling the band concert] might be, it startles us out of our insular complacency and brings us home to what might otherwise be but a distant echo of the dimly-realised Armageddon for which Europe is silently and swiftly arming.[193]

At midnight on 4 August, as Britain's ultimatum to Germany expired, war was declared. Local reserve forces began mustering immediately and the following day soldiers marched through the streets of Tunbridge Wells, with crowds of people looking on, cheering and singing patriotic songs. By night-time 400 territorial soldiers in local units, the 4th Battalion of the Royal West Kents and the Yeomanry, had left for the front.

On the same day, forty-one-year-old Annette Matthews, the final 'disgusted lady', began writing a diary, which she would keep throughout the war. She wrote it to help her children understand the events, but it also provides a vivid and detailed picture of the war and its impact on the lives of women in Tunbridge Wells.

Annette was born in 1873 in Leeds. Her father, locomotive manufacturer James Kitson, was a mayor, alderman and magistrate and her older half-brother, also called James, became a Liberal MP and was made a peer in 1902. Like them, Annette was active in public life; she volunteered in a women's settlement in the East End of London and served as a poor law guardian in Scarborough.[194] In 1910, aged thirty-seven, she married widower John Bromhead Matthews, chief justice of the Bahamas, who was twelve years older than her. The following year the couple moved to Tunbridge Wells with their baby son Stephen and a daughter, named Esther, was born soon afterwards.

Annette Matthews
Courtesy of the Tate family

While most of the 'disgusted ladies' were single, the first (Matilda) and last (Annette) were married. However, their situations were very different. Annette's rights within marriage were much greater than Matilda's; she had control over her own income and assets and, if she had wished to divorce, it would have been easier to do so (although it would still have been more difficult for her than for her husband). She also had more opportunities outside home, although as a middle-class woman this was likely to take the form of voluntary work. One thing remained unchanged, though: Annette could not vote. And, like Matilda, she considered this an injustice.

When she arrived in Tunbridge Wells Annette was already an experienced suffrage campaigner, having been secretary of the Scarborough Women's Suffrage Society. She soon joined the local NUWSS (National Union of Women's Suffrage Societies) branch and, by February 1913, she had been appointed as their vice-president.

The day after war began, she wrote her first diary entry:

> *For a week we have lived in a strange and ugly dream. At first it seemed impossible that War, which has darkened central Europe for forty years, should have really come...The people are quiet, sad & very earnest to meet everything with the best spirit. There is no enthusiasm. The chief feeling is horror that such a cataclysm of conditions should come from the aggression of one race and among workers and women there is a deepest grief at the thought of the privations that must befall the poor.*[195]

The reality of war was brought home by the frequent sight of soldiers around town. Tunbridge Wells' location and rail connections made it a good place to station and train troops before they headed off to the front and soon soldiers began arriving from other parts of the country. Lines of tents appeared on the lower Common, as the Royal Engineers set up camp there. When the autumn arrived, bringing colder weather, troops were billeted in church halls, public buildings, private homes and the skating rink. From late September onwards, wounded soldiers were treated in the town's larger homes and in local hospitals.

Huge numbers of men left to fight in the war. Shop assistants, factory workers, bank officials, milkmen, postmen, solicitors – they came from every walk of life (although working-class men predominated). Many of them would not return and soon the local papers were filled with long lists of men killed or injured in their country's service, often accompanied by photos of fresh-faced young men in uniform. The number of local losses rose sharply in November 1915, when HMS Hythe collided with another ship at Cape Helles, Gallipoli, and sank. Casualties included men from Tunbridge Wells and nearby Southborough, and Annette wrote:

The newspapers tell us nothing, but the cruel telegrams are coming through to women in the neighbourhood, telling them of the loss of their men. The only son of Sir David Salomon was among the drowned. This is the first naval disaster that has directly struck at local homes.

On the night of 13 October 1915, the town had its one direct experience of warfare. Censorship meant that there was no reference to it in the newspapers, but in her diary Annette described hearing three violent explosions. Her husband went to investigate and discovered that a Zeppelin, on its way back from London, had dropped bombs. 'No-one has been killed or even scarcely injured,' she wrote. 'It is truly a miracle. Many people were greatly frightened.'

In November 1916, there was a further influx of soldiers, with estimates of the number billeted in town ranging from 8,000 to 15,000. According to Annette, the Common was busy with men doing drills, practising bayonet charges, stabbing suspended sacks and doing physical exercises.

The war had a profound effect on daily life. Food and petrol were rationed and blackouts were enforced. Gardens were given over to growing vegetables and horses requisitioned. Families had to cope without husbands, fathers and sons, who had often been the main breadwinners. Shops, factories and businesses lost employees. In 1917, Annette wrote in her diary: 'Raids, explosions, casualty lists, rations, high prices are all part of our lives now and no longer cause us excitement.'

Women faced the challenge of looking after their own households in these circumstances. But they also played a vital role in meeting other people's needs, whether these were troops billeted in the town, wounded soldiers back from the front, local families in difficulty, or Belgian refugees escaping the German army. Tunbridge Wells had a strong tradition of volunteering and for women, such as Amelia Scott and Annette Matthews, war work was an extension of the voluntary work they had already been doing.

With minds and energies focussed on the war, campaigning for the vote was halted, for the time being at least. Immediately after it began, the NUWSS suspended all political activity, so that members could devote themselves to war work. Millicent Garrett Fawcett wrote to local branches on 5 August, informing them of this, and Sarah Grand replied on behalf of the Tunbridge Wells Society:

We heartily agree with you as to the advisability of ceasing propaganda work in the present crisis, and we are prepared to co-operate in whatever scheme the Borough or other existing agency may undertake for the relief of those who suffer from the commercial strain.[196]

In a postscript to her letter she recognised that in practice the war was likely to help in finally achieving the suffragists' aim:

> *May I venture to suggest that now is the time for us to show our colours, both literally and figuratively...Once associated with works of mercy [our colours] would be likely to win more hearts to the cause of the Enfranchisement of Women than all our talking has won heads as yet. It is hearts that turn the scale.*[197]

The Tunbridge Wells NUWSS branch announced in the newspapers that, in common with societies throughout the country, they were suspending propaganda work in order to assist those suffering distress as a result of the war. The *Courier* described this as a step which would win them the heartfelt thanks and respect of all English people, whatever their views regarding the women's cause. The suffragists placed a notice in the window at Crescent Road which read 'All Political and Propaganda Work is suspended' and contacted Mayor Charles Emson to offer their services and the use of the property.

The WSPU (Women's Social and Political Union) also suspended their local campaigning activities once the war had begun, although they had already become much less active over recent months. On 10 August, the Home Secretary announced the release of all WSPU prisoners under an amnesty, and shortly afterwards the Tunbridge Wells suffragettes received a circular letter which was sent to all members by Emmeline Pankhurst. In it she wrote:

> *It is obvious that even the most vigorous militancy of the WSPU is for the time being rendered less effective by contrast with the infinitely greater violence done in the present war...*

Under all the circumstance it has been decided to economise the Union's energies and financial resources by a temporary suspension of activities.[198][a]

The Tunbridge Wells WSPU branch had continued campaigning through 1913 and 1914, at a time when support was waning and many other branches closed. However, soon after the war began they ceased operating. On 21 August the *Courier* noted that local organiser Ursula Hartley had informed them that the WSPU were suspending all activities and closing their shop.

In contrast to the suffragists, local suffragettes did not take a leading role in war work, either collectively or individually. After Ursula's announcement there were no further references to the WSPU in the local papers and no evidence that she, or other local suffragettes such as Violet Matthews, Charlotte Ireland or Lilla Durham participated in any wartime activities. (Olive Walton and the Wedgwood sisters had moved away from Tunbridge Wells.) It is of course possible that they made a contribution to the war effort which went unrecorded, especially as most of their members did not have the high profile that women such as Amelia, Sarah and Annette did.

The National League for Opposing Women's Suffrage (NLOWS) also ceased campaigning soon after the war began. (In any case, they had lost support and momentum by this time, unable to counter the fact that a clear majority of MPs supported women's suffrage.) The Tunbridge Wells anti-suffragists placed an announcement in the *Advertiser*:

Having regard to the outbreak of War, the local branch committee of the NLOWS has decided to stop all anti-suffrage

---

a Not all members of the WSPU agreed with their leaders' support for the war. For example, in 1916 the East London Federation of Suffragettes, led by Sylvia Pankhurst, split from the WSPU and campaigned against the war.

work in Tunbridge Wells for the present, and is directing all its
energies towards relieving distress caused by the War, and in
giving all possible aid to the Red Cross Society.

While some individual members of the NLOWS branch became involved in organisations such as the Red Cross and the Soldiers and Sailors Families Association, the organisation itself did not undertake any war work.

So the NUWSS was the only local suffrage organisation (pro or anti) to do so. This was something suffragists saw as their duty (even those who were pacifists). The national organisation now had over 50,000 members and a well-organised network of around 500 local societies, which meant they were able to make a significant contribution. Millicent Garrett Fawcett wrote in *The Common Cause:* 'Let us show ourselves worthy of citizenship, whether our claim to it be recognized or not.'[199]

At the Mayor's suggestion, 18 Crescent Road was re-opened as a clothing depot, where donations could be left, mended if necessary and distributed to convalescent soldiers and local families who were in need as a result of the war. The suffragists placed appeals in the local papers, asking for contributions which could be of any 'fashion, shape or size', providing they were in a good condition. Specific items that were in demand were boots (preferably well-mended and ready to wear), shoes, children's clothes, men's suits, women's nightdresses and underwear. Households across Tunbridge Wells rummaged through their wardrobes, and garments began arriving at the depot, where a well-organised team of volunteers sorted and folded them. They were distributed directly to applicants and through local hospitals and charities such as the Red Cross and the Salvation Army.

From late October 1914, the depot also assisted the Belgian refugees who had begun arriving in town; on 11 December the

Courier reported that, in its first three months, it had supplied them with 659 items of clothing. Demand from the Belgians diminished during 1916, although the depot continued operating until the end of 1917, by which time the needs of local families had also reduced. In three years over 11,000 garments passed through the suffragists' hands.

Their assistance was much appreciated. In April 1916 the *Courier* published a letter to suffragist Gertrude Mosely, who was acting as clothing depot secretary, from a Monsieur Raes, whose wife had been helped by them during her stay in Tunbridge Wells. He wrote (in French): 'I take this opportunity to thank you, as well as the other 'Misses' and ladies of the depot, for all you did for my wife during her exile in England, and am also grateful for your kindnesses which greatly reassured her during those unhappy times.'[200]

The depot was the main focus for local suffragists during the war. However, they also supported a national project – the Scottish Women's Hospitals. These were set up by Scottish suffragists as voluntary, women-only organisations and treated wounded soldiers, across Europe but especially in Serbia. In January 1916, Annette Matthews organised a meeting in support of the hospitals, which she described as being 'crowded to suffocation.' In her diary she observed: 'These suffrage women, Doctors [and] Nurses, have done marvels of work [and] undoubtedly have gained the sympathy and admiration of everyone, whether for women's franchise or not.'[201]

Lydia Le Lacheur and Amelia Scott both played a key role in the town's support for Belgian refugees (in general and not just through the NUWSS clothes depot). At the beginning of October 1914, Lydia was responsible for receiving some of the earliest arrivals at Grosvenor Lodge. (Edith Tattershall Dodd and her husband had moved out of their home so that refugees could be accommodated there.) When the mayor established a Belgian

Refugees Committee on 15 October 1914, to co-ordinate local support, Lydia and Amelia were both members and Amelia was on the executive committee.[a] The war often brought people of different outlooks together and this was so on the Committee; in addition to the suffragists, members included Mayor Charles Emson, his wife Margaret and Louisa Lushington, who had all been actively involved in the local anti-suffrage society since it was founded four years earlier.

The Refugees Committee made regular appeals for donations of money, accommodation, furniture and other household goods and ensured that Belgian refugees sent to Tunbridge Wells were provided with accommodation in lodging houses and private homes across the town.

Some suffragists, including Annette Matthews and Amelia Scott, were involved in war work through the National Union of Women Workers (NUWW). At the start of the war they opened a recreation tent on the Common, jointly with the National British Women's Temperance Association, where they served refreshments to soldiers. They also sold them a wide range of provisions – including tea, coffee, Bovril, cakes, meat pies, candles, tobacco, matches and postage stamps – and provided a piano, gramophone, games, magazines and facilities for writing letters. In her diary entry for 18 September 1914, Annette described spending three hours in a draughty tent handing out tea and cakes and washing up. Over the course of the war, the NUWW would run eighteen canteens in Tunbridge Wells, providing around 720,000 meals in total to soldiers camped or billeted in the town and to wounded soldiers and their visitors.[202]

In autumn 1914, NUWW members, including Amelia, approached the town's Watch Committee and asked them to appoint women police officers. When troops began arriving in

---

a After the war Amelia was awarded a Palme D'or by the King of the Belgians, in recognition of her work supporting Belgian refugees.

town, they had soon become a focus of interest for young women and girls suffering from 'khaki fever.' The *Courier* observed: 'The military are quite an attraction to the feminine portion of the community and the 'glad eye' is used with great effect when the shades of night are falling fast!'[203]

The committee turned down the women's request. However, the government had authorised the NUWW to set up voluntary patrols, and this is what happened in Tunbridge Wells. Thirty-three women enrolled and, from October 1914 onwards, pairs of patrollers, wearing special arm badges, walked the town's streets at night, especially in the area around Camden Road and Calverley Road. Their aim was to befriend young women and persuade them to avoid the moral dangers posed by soldiers. Amelia described this activity as 'a protest against rowdyism and a plea for decency.'[204] The *Courier* reported:

> *For several months past, a number of very devoted lady residents have been patrolling the streets at night, endeavouring…to 'make friends' with the young and excited girls, and protect them, as far as possible, from the dangers and difficulties which must arise under the existing abnormal conditions of the district.*[205]

The young women were not all grateful for this protection. One of them was quoted as saying that the patrollers were 'just a lot of old maids who don't like to see girls happy, because they can't get husbands for themselves.' Nevertheless, patrols continued until the end of the war.

The *Courier* also pointed out their limitations:

> *It has, however, been borne in upon these ladies that their work is incomplete, and to a certain extent, unsatisfactory, because, up to the present moment, they have not been able to*

offer these girls – girls who are frivolous not bad – a counter-attraction from dark streets and lanes.

In an effort to offer a 'counter attraction' to khaki fever, the Leisure Hour Club, which had been founded by the NUWW in 1901, was promoted as a place where soldiers and girls could socialise, away from the dangers of the streets. In addition, in March 1915 the patrol committee set up the Comrades Club at 13 Quarry Road, where soldiers and locals could meet for non-alcoholic refreshments and entertainments. A social evening in February 1916 featured name-guessing, apple bobbing and hat-decorating competitions.

Another NUWW project, a laundry, was set up in June 1915 at 44 Grosvenor Road, to wash and mend the uniforms of soldiers billeted in the town. (It was also intended to discourage the 'undesirable' women who were hanging around soldiers' billets, in the pretence of offering to do their washing). At around the time the laundry opened, local NUWW president, Lady Constance Coote, wrote an appeal for funds, which was published in the *Courier*. In it she said:

Though we cannot fight at the Front, we can wage war in the background against uncleanliness and un-mended garments, and prevent our soldiers suffering from these unnecessary miseries, besides providing paid employment for a number of women who are in need of work.[206]

The laundry had 200 voluntary helpers and forty paid staff (many of whom were women who had lost their jobs at local laundries when people cut back on using them after the war began). Managing it was a huge task and Amelia Scott studied book-keeping so that she could undertake the role. At their busiest period, they washed, mended and sorted as many as 20,000 garments for over 2,000 men each week. It was not always pleasant work – soldiers often came back from the front with clothes that were filthy and infested with vermin.

NUWW Laundry
Women's Library, LSE

In addition to the NUWSS and the NUWW, there were numerous other women's organisations – some of which had already been in existence and others which were set up specially – who became involved in the war effort. And many women who had not previously been involved in voluntary work now took it up.

At the beginning of 1915, a local branch of the Women's Emergency Corps (WEC) was established. Their aims were to co-ordinate women's war work in Tunbridge Wells and to assist women who were out of work due to the war. Soon afterwards, a local branch of the WEC's military wing, the Women's Volunteer Reserve (WVR), was formed and began training women in activities such as motor mechanics, signalling and first aid. Their members, wearing khaki uniforms, became a regular sight, marching through the streets of Tunbridge Wells. After the National Registration Act was passed in July 1915, all civilian men and women aged between fifteen and sixty-five (who were expected to be available for work or military service) were required to register. WVR members acted as enumerators, sending out and collecting the forms (blue for men and granite white for women), issuing registration cards and collating the results.

Other organisations active in wartime included the Red Cross, who formed Voluntary Aid Detachments (VADs) and trained women as medical reserves, freeing up qualified nurses for other work. They also opened hospitals, including several in and around Tunbridge Wells. In October 1917, a local branch was formed of the Women's Auxiliary Army Corps (WAAC), which provided cooks, domestic workers and clerks for the army (Annette Matthews was involved in their recruitment drives).

The war also had an impact on women's paid employment. Most working-class women had already been working outside the home. However, as the war progressed and increasing numbers of men headed for the front, they began taking on jobs that had previously been done by men. Between 1914 and 1918, around two million women replaced men in jobs from bus driver to factory worker. In July 1915, the South Eastern and Chatham Railway began employing women as booking clerks and trained the daughters of ticket collectors to take on their father's role. In May 1915, Annette Matthews noted in her diary that the household's milk was now being delivered by a girl. In November 1916 there were appeals published in the *Courier* for women to train as munitions workers. They were assured that work such as screw-cutting, turning, metal plate work and soldering was well within women's physical powers and that there would be carefully-managed hostels for them to lodge in if they wished.

Women were proving that they were capable of holding down jobs other than those in traditionally 'female' roles, such as shop work and domestic service. However, employers still considered that their work was worth less than men's and frequently their wage packets did not match.

While the war opened up new employment opportunities for women, others were closing down. Firstly, there was a tendency for people to cut back on consumption, which reduced the work available for workers such as servants, seamstresses and shop assistants. Secondly, there was a danger that middle-class volunteers would undertake work that would otherwise have been done by wage earners. Local activists were aware of the potential for this, and the WEC in particular tried to avoid taking on the sort of work that would otherwise have earnt a woman a wage. When they were approached with requests for paid employment, they did their best to find opportunities.

So a large number of women in Tunbridge Wells, including some of the town's leading local Votes for Women campaigners, were playing a key role in the war effort. This was recognised and valued. In April 1916, an article in the *Advertiser* commented:

There is much cause of satisfaction at the way in which women have come forward to serve their country, in almost every capacity, and the consequent quickening of public opinion in favour of granting to them the full rights of citizenship.[207]

Chapter 25

The Hour of Victory for
Our Great Cause

The women's suffrage campaign was never completely suspended and for some women, the key role they were playing in the war effort made them feel even more frustrated at not having the vote. On 22 July 1915, Annette Matthews wrote in her diary:

> Our best blood is being spilt at the front [yet] our women [are] still not admitted to the Nation's Councils, their wisdom lost, [and] their experience unused...and the enemy hammering at our gates.[208]

Campaigners also began to be concerned about what would happen once the war was over. From autumn 1915, there were rumours that the government was considering legislation to protect soldiers serving overseas who were in danger of losing the right to vote. The NUWSS (National Union of Women's Suffrage Societies) were anxious to make sure that any legislation also included women and so, during 1916, they resumed active campaigning. On 4 May, Millicent Garrett Fawcett wrote to the Prime Minister. She pointed to the shift in public opinion towards women having the vote and the general recognition of their contribution during the war, continuing:

> *When the government deals with the franchise, an opportunity will present itself...and we trust that you would include in your Bill clauses which would remove the disability under which women now labour.*[209]

From the summer of 1916 onwards, the Tunbridge Wells NUWSS branch began meeting again. In June, a meeting was held at Lydia Le Lacheur's home, when a Mrs Streeter spoke of 'the increased urgency of the need for the enfranchisement of women'.[210] In October, during a meeting at Grosvenor Lodge, Annette Matthews spoke about the impact the war was having on their cause. The *Advertiser* reported her arguments:

> *It almost seemed that it needed the awful blaze of war to convince some people that women were imbued with a deep sense of patriotism and possessed powers of endurance and organisation, which have proved to be of real value to the nation. But she wondered whether the country was not still half blind to the women's true claim to the vote. Their claim is not based upon the fact that they do men's work, that they are able to clamber up and down the steep steps of a London omnibus, that they hoe and dig, tend horses, carry out intricate engineering operations on heavy shells in munition factories. Women seek recognition, as they have always done, on account of their particular share of the nation's life – their homekeeping, their feeding of the workers, their care of the sick, their motherhood and the upbringing of the young, a magnificent work to which no termination will be put at the close of war.*[211]

In November 1916, the NUWSS held a meeting at the town hall. Amelia Scott was in the chair and the speaker was Millicent Garrett Fawcett. Her subject was the way that women had contributed to the war effort, by taking over men's work in this country and in hospitals abroad. Women had shown their ability in almost every department of labour, she said, and the war should make the comradeship of men and women deeper and stronger. According to the *Advertiser*, she continued by talking about the impact of this war work on the prospect of women getting the vote:

> She thought women's work in the war had created a great impression on the public mind. She did not say they should have the vote as a reward. They had always looked upon it as a right...After the war there would be great problems to settle between the men who came back from the Army, employers who wanted to get cheap women's labour, and women who were now doing the work previously done by men. How could women put forward their case if they had not the vote?...The prospects for the future, she thought, were good.[212]

However, some people continued to be opposed to women having the vote. An additional argument they now raised was that, since women were not directly involved in fighting for their country, they should not have a say in electing a government that could take the country to war.

A cross-party conference on electoral reform in late 1916 and early 1917 considered the position of men serving their country overseas, including soldiers who would no longer meet the residential qualification for a vote and working-class men serving their country overseas who were not eligible to vote, because they did not meet the property ownership criteria. (Despite the extension of voting rights by the 1884 Reform

Act, 40% of men aged twenty-one and over still did not have a vote.) The continued exclusion of women, many of whom had contributed to the war effort at home, was also considered.

One of the main barriers to women's suffrage was removed in December 1916, when Herbert Asquith was replaced by David Lloyd George as Prime Minister. Millicent Garrett Fawcett later wrote: 'It was Mr Asquith, more than any other one person, who prevented the Liberal Party becoming a Reform Party.'[213] While Lloyd George had been opposed to giving the vote to all women and had strongly condemned the militants' actions, he had always supported the principle of giving some women the vote.

On 15 May 1917, the Representation of the People Bill was tabled, on 22 May it passed its second reading and on 19 June MPs debated Clause 4, which proposed giving the vote to a limited number of women. Not all MPs had been won round and, in the lengthy debate that followed, some still argued against the move. Anti-suffragist Sir Frederick Banbury raised a series of objections – women did not want the vote, they did not need it in order to have influence, their role was different from men's and, most tellingly, they were 'hysterical' and 'likely to be affected by gusts and waves of sentiment' and would therefore not use their vote wisely.[214] These were remarkably similar to the objections John Stuart Mill had demolished back in 1867 and which had been cited by anti-suffragists ever since. Most MPs did not agree with Sir Frederick, however, and Clause 4 was approved by a substantial majority, with 385 votes in favour and fifty-five against. Tunbridge Wells MP Herbert Spender-Clay had finally been won round and voted in favour. 'The hour of victory for our great cause has struck,' wrote Millicent Garrett Fawcett in *The Common Cause*. On 23 August 1917 a further, more symbolic, step was taken when the grille at the front of the Ladies' Gallery was removed.[a]

---

a Part of the grille is on display in the Central Lobby and part in the Museum of London.

In the past legislation to give women the vote had passed its second reading, but failed at a later stage. However, the Representation of the People Act made it through all subsequent stages and finally received royal assent on 6 February 1918. The Act gave the vote to all men over twenty-one and to women over thirty who owned a house worth at least £5 a year, were married to a man who did, or were graduates. There were around 8.4m women who met the criteria and they made up 44% of the total electorate. (One reason for limiting the vote to certain women was that, if women had the vote on the same basis as men, they would have outnumbered male voters. This was still unacceptable to many people.)

On 13 March 1918 Annette Matthews attended the 'Women Suffragists' Celebration' at the Queen's Hall, Langham Place, London, organised jointly by the NUWSS, the WFL (Women's Freedom League) and other non-militant suffrage societies. The concert hall, which had space for 2,500 people, had been decorated with flowers and foliage and with banners made by the Artists' Suffrage League, including a large representation of Joan of Arc close to the stage. A standing ovation greeted Millicent Garrett Fawcett as she opened the event, with a bouquet in red, green and white on the table in front of her. Now seventy-one years old, it was more than fifty years since Millicent had listened from the Ladies' Gallery as Mill proposed his amendment to the 1867 Reform Bill. Now she said that she rejoiced, not just for campaigners and not just for women, but for the great country which had done a great thing in a great way. The searchlight of war had shown things in their true light and the government had given women the vote with open hands.

Maude Royden, editor of *The Common Cause* and a former member of the NUWSS executive, also spoke. She thanked the representatives of the three political parties who had supported the struggle and described 'the great troop of men who had been longing for some dignified way of retreat from the impossible anti-suffrage position, and had found in the sight of women clipping bus tickets, a great broad avenue down which they trooped in willing thousands.'[215] The London Symphony Orchestra played Beethoven's Leonora Overture and were joined by the Bach choir in Bach's *Awake Thou Wintry Earth*. At the end of the meeting Hubert Parry conducted *Jerusalem*, his setting of William Blake's words, with the audience joining in for the last two verses.

Back in Tunbridge Wells, women began preparing to exercise their new right to vote. The lead in this was taken by a new organisation, the Women Citizens Association (WCA), an affiliation of around sixteen local societies, including the NUWSS.[a] The *Courier* described its purpose as being 'the education of women in questions of import to their country, questions upon which they are now called to express their opinion in their capacity as parliamentary voters'.[216] Amelia Scott, who was at the heart of things as usual, was appointed treasurer.

From the end of November, the WCA placed advertisements in the local papers, encouraging women to check at the enquiry office that they were registered to vote and to use their vote when the time came. NUWSS Secretary, Edith Tattershall Dodd was in charge of the office, at 52 Grosvenor Road, which was also opened as a 'non-party' information bureau, with volunteers available to answer any questions women electors had in advance of the election. A letter to the *Courier* after the election had taken place thanked the volunteers for their help and 'sympathetic attention' and commented on the happy atmosphere at the bureau.

---

a   The NUWSS continued to exist, under the new name of the National Union of Societies for Equal Citizenship, but was less active, nationally and locally, from this time onwards.

Chapter 26

Full Citizenship at Last

On Monday 11 November 1918, the Great War finally came to an end. Church bells sounded out. Flags, banners and strings of bunting were raised. Children were let out of school, soldiers were excused from drill and the streets filled with crowds. Many people headed to the *Courier's* office to read the wording of the Armistice, which had been relayed to the paper by telephone and posted up outside. Bands of soldiers, some of them the worse for drink, paraded through the streets, singing patriotic songs. According to the *Courier*, they were frequently joined by the 'inevitable girl.' In the evening, large numbers of people gathered on Calverley Road, outside the town hall, where fires were lit and fireworks let off.

A report in the *Advertiser* observed:

As the day wore on, the joy-making became more boisterous. Itinerant flag-vendors were besieged with customers, staid businessmen threw away their cares for the rest of the day. The children had the time of their lives with fireworks and confetti and the whole populace let itself go.

And Annette wrote in her diary:

This has truly been a Great Day...everyone greeted everyone else with smiles, & sometimes tears. It was the gayest and most thrilling of times...No more need we curtain our windows, no more need we picture the horrors of bloodshed & our prisoners are free!

The following day was declared a holiday and in the morning a procession, including organisations who had been involved in the war effort[a], set off from the town hall, watched by crowds of people, many wearing patriotic red, white and blue. They made their way, by a circuitous route, to the Lower Cricket Ground, where a thanksgiving service was attended by several thousand. The mayor, Alderman Gower[b] gave a rousing speech: 'the Beast of Berlin, with all his abominations has been overthrown' he declared.[217] Proceedings concluded with *Rule Britannia* and the National Anthem, accompanied by the band.

Celebrations continued over the following days, with thanksgiving services held in many of the local churches. However, on the whole they were muted. News of casualties was still arriving and there were many injured servicemen in the town. Nearly 3,000 men – family members, friends and colleagues – had gone to fight in the war, of whom almost 800 had been killed. Many others had been scarred, physically and mentally, by their experience.

In her diary, Annette reflected:

The war has taught Rich and Poor to know and respect one another and it has taught men and women Comradeship. It

---

a The NUWSS and other women's groups do not seem to have taken part in the procession.

b Alderman Gower had replaced Charles Emson as mayor in November 1917.

has nearly brought woman to her right place in the State. The
war has discovered nobility and high courage in the humblest
and least regarded persons. We find we have rubbed shoulders
with heros [sic] and heroines in the dull routine of daily life.
We feel we have been through a time of great exaltations,
desolate as it has made many and we come out of the war with
high hope for humanity and human purposes.[218]

Just over a month later, on 14 December 1918, women had the opportunity to vote in a general election for the first time. Out of a total electorate of 37,448 in Tunbridge Wells, 16,124 were women.

It was a grey, wet day, but there was an atmosphere of celebration across the town. The *Courier* commented that it was a woman's election and reports from polling stations indicated that a large number of women voted. Most did so early in the day (apart from shop assistants, who had to wait until their lunch hour). The *Courier* noted that married women often came with two or three female friends, rather than with their husbands. Women's reactions as they voted included confusion, triumph and surprise. 'Is that all?' said one.

Not all the 'disgusted ladies' had the chance to vote. Some did not live long enough. Laura Crompton Jones, who had attended the town's first suffrage meeting back in 1873 and who had been a member of the NUWSS (National Union of Women's Suffrage Societies) branch when it was established in 1906, died in 1915, aged eighty-two. Gertrude Mosely (NUWSS secretary for several years) died in November 1916. Dorothy Le Lacheur died of pneumonia in September 1917, aged only thirty-four, missing the conclusion of the campaign she had fought for so enthusiastically. Others were too young. For example, Isabel Haynes, who had been WSPU (Women's Social and Political Union) branch secretary during 1913, protested with Olive

Walton outside the Great Hall, attended Emily Wilding Davison's funeral and been awarded a medal for her work as a Red Cross orderly during the war, was still only twenty-six.

For many campaigners, though, the day they had been waiting impatiently for had finally arrived. At the NUWSS offices on Crescent Road a procession assembled (as the Pilgrimage had done at the same spot five years earlier). Watched by a small crowd, including the mayoress and deputy mayoress, the suffragists walked to the town hall, with Sarah Grand (aged sixty-four) at their head, carrying a bouquet of red, green and white flowers. Amelia Scott (fifty-eight) and Annette Matthews (forty-five) walked on either side of her and others followed, carrying banners. When they reached the town hall, the women went inside to cast their vote. According to the *Courier*, when Sarah emerged afterwards, she was:

> *...received with cheers by the ladies, whose faces showed how profound was the satisfaction felt by them that the long struggle for political freedom was over, and that women had at last entered into full citizenship.*[219]

Postscript

It certainly had been a long struggle. As far back as 1866, when a third of MPs voted for an amendment that would have given women the vote, many women believed success was not far off. They could have had no idea that so many years of raised and shattered hopes would follow. Over the following fifty years, huge advances were made in women's daily lives, legal rights, employment opportunities and role in public life. Yet, despite all this, women continued to be denied the vote until 1918.

I am inspired by the stories of women such as Matilda, Louisa, Amelia, Sarah, Lydia, Olive and Annette. These were ordinary women who did extraordinary things and they are just as significant in the Votes for Women story as national figures who generated more headlines. Their commitment, energy and capacity for organisation were amazing.

As a keen researcher, I could have continued for years trying to find more information about these women. I am especially intrigued by the ones who have left only faint traces in the records and who may have only been briefly involved in the campaign. Women such as Constance Brock, who carried the banner with Dorothy Le Lacheur in the Women's Freedom League's protest at 10 Downing Street in 1909. What impact did the suffrage campaign have on her life? When she got married a few weeks later, did that end her involvement? (Her name never appears again.)

Despite all the information I have collected, some aspects of the campaign are difficult to understand when viewed through a twenty-first century lens. Even after reading the reasons Gwladys put forward, I am not completely clear why she thought it would be such a bad thing for women to have the vote. Or why so many people (men and women) agreed with her. Women's purity, which was such an important issue for suffrage campaigners in the past, is not a key factor these days (although their right not to be subjected to abuse is). And when women finally won the vote, their reaction was not necessarily what we would expect. On the day that the legislation was passed, Annette Matthews wrote in her diary: 'The relief... was enormous. Now, we can devote ourselves to our home life, because we are a recognised part of the Nation even in that quiet sphere.'

The campaign did not end in 1918. It was not until 1928 that the Equal Franchise Act gave the vote to all women over twenty-one, and therefore on the same basis as men. And even now, in 2018, the year we celebrate the 100th anniversary of the first women being able to vote, there continue to be inequalities. The anniversary is an opportunity to remember what is owed to women such as the 'disgusted ladies' and to commit following their example, by working to ensure that in the future there will be equal rights for all people.

What Happened Next for the Disgusted Ladies?

Sarah Grand moved to Bath in 1920. In 1922, when widower Cedric Chivers was appointed as mayor, she became his lady mayoress, supporting him in his civic responsibilities over the next six years. By this time her fame as a novelist had faded and many in Bath were unaware of her past history. She died in Wiltshire in 1943, at the age of ninety-two.

Annette Matthews continued her involvement in women's causes after the war had ended, campaigning for women police. In 1919, she was appointed as a justice of the peace. She was president of the local branch of the National Council of Women (NCW), formerly the National Union of Women Workers (NUWW) and of the Equal Citizens Society. In 1923 she gave evidence before a government enquiry into the Conditions of Domestic Service.

In 1912, two years after her Black Friday experience, **Kate Le Lacheur** married farmer Godfrey Atkinson, although she kept her own surname, which was unusual for the time. He seems to have supported her in her suffrage campaigning and suffered injuries when a suffragette meeting on the green at Checkendon was ambushed by a group of local men. Early in the war, when her husband was sent overseas, she returned to Tunbridge Wells to stay with her mother, bringing her two young sons with her. Godfrey died in action at the Dardanelles in August 1915 and the following February Kate gave birth to a third son, James, at The Wilderness, her mother's home. After the war she lived in Henley-on-Thames and died there in 1959.

Tax protestor **Maud Roll** was elected to Uckfield Rural Council in 1921 and became a justice of the peace in 1931.

In 1919 **Amelia Scott** (together with one of the NUWW women's patrollers) attended a Buckingham Palace garden party for war workers. In the same year she and her friend Susan Power were elected as the first female members of Tunbridge Wells District Council. Amelia stood as a candidate for the Women Citizens Association, rather than for any political party. The issues on which she based her campaign included women police, up-to-date maternal provision and a hostel for children and mothers. She remained a councillor for many years and continued to fight for women's rights. Amelia ran the local branch of the NCW (along with Annette Matthews) and was secretary of their national Public Services Committee from 1913 to 1930. She also continued to be a poor law guardian for many years.

In the 1920s **Gwladys Solomon** began writing plays and foreign language stories for children. In 1938 she changed her surname by deed poll back to her maiden name of Cowper Smith. (Her son Scott also changed his name to Cowper Smith.) She spent some time living with Scott, a doctor, in Durban, South Africa, but died in North Wales in 1964.

Violet Tillard travelled to Germany in 1919, on a Quaker mission to help people recover from the effects of the war. In October 1921 she moved on to famine-ravaged Buzuluk, in Russia, to help organise relief work. There she encountered famine on a huge scale. (By the time the food shortage ended, it was estimated that around five million people had died.) Sadly Violet contracted typhus while nursing fellow relief workers, and she died on 19 February 1922, aged forty-eight.

Olive Walton served as a Woman Police Volunteer during the war, along with other militant suffragettes. After the war ended she stayed on in the force and in 1920 she was sent to Ireland during the Civil War, where she took part in raids in search of Irish rebels. Her police career ended after she was injured in a motor bike accident in Canterbury. She remained loyal to the Pankhursts (after many had been alienated by their approach) and she was one of a small group of women who watched over Emmeline Pankhurst's coffin on the night before her funeral in 1928.When she adopted a daughter some years later, she named her Christabel.

Key Events

	Tunbridge Wells	National
1830-1870	*1866* Several women from Tunbridge Wells sign the first national petition. *1869* Petition calling for the extension of the suffrage to women from thirty-one residents in Tunbridge Wells presented to Parliament by Peter Taylor MP. (There are further petitions in 1872, 1873 and 1881.)	*1832* The First Reform Act increases the number of men eligible to vote and excludes women by using the term 'male.' *1832* The first women's suffrage petition is presented by Henry Hunt MP, on behalf of Mary Smith. *1865* The Kensington Society debates women's suffrage. *1866* The first national petition for women's suffrage is presented to Parliament by John Stuart Mill MP. *1867* Mill proposes an amendment to the Reform Bill which would include women. It is unsuccessful, although seventy-three MPs vote in favour. *1867* Second Reform Act extends the vote to more men. *1869* The Municipal Franchise Act gives some women the vote in local elections and allows them to become poor law guardians.

	Tunbridge Wells	**National**
1871-1890	*1873* The first women's suffrage meeting is held in Tunbridge Wells. *1879* Manchester campaigner Lydia Becker speaks at a meeting in Tunbridge Wells. *1889* Mary Moberly (local headmistress) and two other teachers sign the *Declaration in Favour of Women's Suffrage.*	*1870* The first women's suffrage bill passes its second reading, but then fails. *1889* An appeal against women's suffrage by 104 well-known women is published in magazine *The Nineteenth Century.* 2,000 women sign a *Declaration in Favour of Women's Suffrage* in response. *1884* The Third Reform Act extends the vote to more men. Approximately 60% can now vote. *1888* County Electors Act allows women to vote for the new County Councils.
1891-1900	*1890* The Tunbridge Wells Women's Liberal Association (WLA) is founded and discusses women's suffrage at one of their first meetings. *1893* Louisa Twining appointed as the first female guardian on the Tonbridge Union. *1895* A Tunbridge Wells branch of the NUWW is formed.	*1895* The National Union of Women Workers (NUWW) is founded. *1897* The National Union of Women's Suffrage Societies (NUWSS) is founded.

	Tunbridge Wells	National
1901-1905	*1903* Five women sit on the first Education Committees in Tunbridge Wells.	*1903* The Women's Social and Political Union (WSPU) is founded in Manchester, led by Emmeline Pankhurst. *1905* Christabel Pankhurst and Annie Kenney are arrested and imprisoned after protesting at a Liberal Party meeting in Manchester.
1906	*Jan* Liberal Alfred Hedges is elected as MP for Tunbridge Wells. *Oct 22nd-25th* Tunbridge Wells hosts the NUWW annual conference at the Opera House. *Nov* A petition committee is formed and a women's suffrage petition made available for signing.	*January* The Liberal Party win the general election by a landslide. *May 19th* A deputation from all the main suffrage societies goes to see Prime Minister Henry Campbell-Bannerman, who advises patience.
1907	*Jan 8th* A deputation from the local WLA goes to see MP Alfred Hedges.	*Feb 9th* NUWSS members walk from Hyde Park to Exeter Hall in the 'Mud March.' *Feb 13th* The WSPU hold their first 'women's parliament' and arrests are made outside the Houses of Parliament.

	Tunbridge Wells	**National**
1908	*Jun 21st* Women from Tunbridge Wells attend the WSPU's Hyde Park rally. *Jun 29th* WFL caravan arrives in Tunbridge Wells. Muriel Matters speaks at meeting on the Common. *Oct 28th* Violet Tillard takes part in the Ladies' Gallery protest and is sent to Holloway Prison. *Oct* Branches of the NUWSS and WFL are founded in Tunbridge Wells.	*Apr* Herbert Asquith becomes Prime Minister. *Jun 21st* The WSPU hold a rally in Hyde Park. *Oct 13th* The WSPU organise 'the rush' on the House of Commons. *Oct 28th* WFL members Muriel Matters and Helen Fox chain themselves to the grille at the Ladies' Gallery.
1909	*May 11th* Angela May Dickens addresses the first anti-suffrage meeting in Tunbridge Wells and a local anti-suffrage society is founded.	*July 5th* Marion Wallace Dunlop is sent to prison and starts the first hunger strike. *Jul-Oct* The WFL maintain 'The Great Watch' – a continuous picket outside the House of Commons.

	Tunbridge Wells	National
1910	*Jan* Conservative Herbert Spender-Clay is elected as MP for Tunbridge Wells. *Nov 18th* Kate Le Lacheur is arrested at the Black Friday protest.	*Jan* The Liberals are re-elected, with a reduced majority. *Jan* An all-party Conciliation Committee is formed to draft a women's suffrage bill. *Feb 14th* The WSPU suspend militancy while the Conciliation Bill is before Parliament. *Jul* The Conciliation Bill passes its second reading. *Jul 23rd* Asquith announces there is insufficient time to progress the bill. *Nov 18th* Police assault WSPU protestors in Parliament Square on 'Black Friday.' *Dec 6th* The NLOWS is formed, as an amalgamation of women's and men's anti-suffrage societies. *Dec* A further general election is held, due to disagreements over the budget, and the Liberal Party is re-elected.

	Tunbridge Wells	National
1911	*Apr 2nd* Local suffrage campaigners take part in the census protest. *Jun 17th* Local women take part in The Women's Coronation Procession. *Nov 21st* Five women from Tunbridge Wells take part in a WSPU demonstration at the House of Commons and are arrested. *Dec 1st* The Tunbridge Wells WSPU branch is founded.	*Apr 2nd* A census protest is organised by the WFL and WSPU. *May 5th* The (second) Conciliation Bill passes its second reading, with a large majority. *June 17th* The WSPU organise the Women's Coronation Procession, with all the main campaigning organisations taking part. *Nov 7th* Asquith announces a manhood suffrage bill, effectively killing the Conciliation Bill. *Nov 17th* A deputation from the main suffrage societies visits Asquith at Downing Street. *Nov 21st* WSPU members protest in and around Parliament Square.
1912	*Mar 1st* Four Tunbridge Wells suffragettes are arrested for window-breaking. *Mar 27th* Olive Walton is sent to Aylesbury Prison, where she goes on hunger strike.	*Mar 1st* The WSPU makes its first unannounced major protest in London. Windows are broken across the West End and hundreds of arrests made. *Mar 28th* The (third) Conciliation Bill is defeated.

	Tunbridge Wells	National
1913	*Mar 14th* Olive Walton and Emily Wilding Davison disrupt a Liberal Party conference at the Opera House. *Apr 11th* The Nevill Cricket Pavilion is burnt down. *Apr 28th* A meeting is held at the Great Hall to condemn suffragettes for causing the fire. *Jul 21st* NUWSS members march through Tunbridge Wells and meet marchers on the Women's Pilgrimage in Tonbridge. *Aug 9th* Tunbridge Wells WSPU members join a group which walks around Kent in gypsy costumes. *Sep 17th* An arson attack takes place at Penshurst Place.	*Apr 25th* The Prisoners (Temporary Discharge for Ill Health) Act is passed. Known as the Cat and Mouse Act. *Jun 4th* Emily Wilding Davison dies at the Epsom Derby. *Jun 14th* Emily's huge funeral procession processes through London. *Jul 18th-26th* The NUWSS Women's Pilgrimage starts out from 17 cities and converges on London.

	Tunbridge Wells	**National**
1914-17	*Jun 19th 1914* A protest meeting is held on Tunbridge Wells Common, after the sale of goods confiscated from Maud Roll for non-payment of tax. *Aug 1914* The local branches of the NUWSS, WSPU and NLOWS suspend their activities in order to focus on war work.	*Aug 4th 1914* War declared. *Aug 5th 1914* The NUWSS announces that campaigning has been suspended. *Aug 10th 1914* With all WSPU prisoners released, the WSPU announces the suspension of campaigning. *July 7th 1915* The WSPU organise the 'Great Procession of Women' in London.
1918 onwards	*Mar 13th 1918* Annette Matthews attends a Votes for Women victory celebration at Queen's Hall. *Dec 14th 1918* Sarah Grand leads a procession of women to the town hall, where they vote for the first time.	*Feb 6th 1918* The Representation of the People Act gives the vote to some women over thirty. *Nov 21st 1918* The Parliament (Qualifications of Women) Act allows women to be elected as MPs. *Dec 14th 1918* Women vote for the first time in a general election. *1928* The Representation of the People Act gives the vote to all men and women over eighteen.

Notes

1   *Courier* 15th November 1912

2   Annie Kenney *Memoirs of a Militant* (1924), p.220

3   Emmeline Pankhurst *My Own Story* (2015 edition), p.252

4   *Advertiser* 18th April 1913, p.6

5   *Advertiser* 18th April 1913, p.6

6   Quoted in the *Courier* 25th April 1913, p.5

7   *Courier* 25th April 1913, p.5

8   *Courier* 25th April 1913

9   *Advertiser* 18th April 1913, p.6

10   *Courier* 2nd May 1913, p.5

11   Elizabeth Crawford (ed) *Campaigning for the Vote: Kate Parry Frye's Suffrage Diary* (2013)

12   *Courier* 2nd May 1913, p.5

13   *Tunbridge Wells Gazette* 30th April 1913, p.2

14   *Advertiser* 18th April 1913, p.6

15   *Advertiser* 2nd May 1913, p.9

16   *Advertiser* 2nd May 1913, p.9

17   Robert Owen *The Book of the New Moral World: Sixth Part* (1841)

18   Letter from Eliza Ashurst, quoted in Kathryn Gleadle *The Early Feminist*, p.40

19   Cady Stanton (ed) *History of Woman Suffrage. Vol 3. Chapter XVI*, by Caroline Biggs, p838

20   Cady Stanton *Eighty Years and More* (1898), p.82

21   Helen Blackburn *Women's Suffrage* (1902), p.19

22 Helen Blackburn *Women's Suffrage* (1902), p.19

23 *Newcastle Guardian* 19th February 1859, p.2

24 Sarah Richardson *The Political Worlds of Women* (2013), p.112

25 John Stuart Mill *Considerations on Representative Government* (1861), p.182

26 'The Ladies' Petition' *Westminster Review* 1867 vol. XXI, p.63

27 *Daily News* 29th June 1866

28 *The Spectator* 9th June 1866, p.8

29 Emily Davies to Barbara Bodichon, in Davies, Murphy & Raftery (eds) *Emily Davies: Collected Letters*, 1861-1875, p.199

30 Millicent Garrett Fawcett *The Women's Victory and After: Personal Reminiscences*, 1911-1918 (1920)

31 Helen Blackburn *Women's Suffrage* (1902), p.68

32 Both quoted in *Englishwoman's Review* No. IV July 1867, p.199

33 Quoted in Richard Reeves *John Stuart Mill: Victorian Firebrand*

34 *Kentish Gazette* 4th May 1869, p.6

35 Emily Davies to Lydia Becker *Emily Davies: Collected Letters 1861-1875*

36 Quoted in Helen Blackburn *Women's Suffrage* (1902), p.110

37 Sutherland Menzies *Political Women* (1873), Vol 1:vii

38 *Courier* 10th Oct 1873, p.4

39 *Tunbridge Wells Weekly Express* 11th March 1879, p.2

40 *Courier* 7th March 1879

41 *Courier* 25th December 1891, p.6

42 *Fortnightly Review* 52 (1889), p.131

43 *Courier* 21st April 1886, p.3

44 *Women's Local Government Society Annual Report*

45 Louisa Twining *Guidance to Women Guardians* (1895)

46 Louisa Twining *Workhouses and Pauperism* (1898), p.129

47 Louisa Twining *Recollections of Life and Work* (1893)

48 Louisa Twining *Recollections of Life and Work* (1893)

49 *Courier* 10th March 1893

50 *Courier* 15th February 1893, p.3

51 *The Churchwoman* 23rd October 1896

52 Louisa Twining *Workhouses and Pauperism* (1898), p.152

53 *Courier* 4th October 1912

54 Barbara Bodichon *Reasons For and Against the Enfranchisement of Women* (1872)

55 *Times* 12th July 1897, p.6

56 Amelia Scott *The History of the National Council of Women in Tunbridge Wells for the last 35 years* (1931) Women's Library 7ASC/2

57 *Courier* 31st May 1895

58 *Courier* 29th November 1893, p.7

59 Amelia Scott (*Speech notes*) Women's Library 7ASC/2/2/2

60 *National Union of Women Workers Occasional Papers.* London School of Economics Reserve Periodicals

61 Amelia Scott *Passing of a Great Dread* (c 1942), Published in instalments in *Social Work* magazine

62 Amelia Scott *Passing of a Great Dread* (c 1942)

63 *Courier* 28th October 1890

64 *Courier* 12th May 1905, p.8

65 *Courier* 12th May 1905, p.8

66 *Courier* 5th January 1906, p.6

67 *Advertiser* 16th March 1906, p.9

68 *Advertiser* 16th March 1906, p.9

69 *Courier* 6th April 1906, p.8

70 Quoted in Ray Strachey *The Cause* (Virago edition 1978), p.301

71 *Courier* 26th October 1906, p.8

72 *Courier* 26th October 1906, p.8

73 *London Daily News* 25th October 1906, p.6

74 *Courier* 26th October 1906, p.9

75 Amelia Scott *The History of the National Council of Women in Tunbridge Wells for the last 35 years* (1931), Women's Library 7ASC/2

76 Evelyn Sharpe *Unfinished Adventure* (1933)

77 *Courier* 30th November 1906, p.5

78 Sarah Grand *Heavenly Twins* (1893), p.11

79 Quoted in Heilmann and Forward (eds) *Sex, Social Purity, and Sarah*

Grand (2000), p.297

80   Quoted in Marks *Bicycles, Bangs and Bloomers* (1990) p.10

81   *Punch* 106 26th May 1894, p.252

82   Sarah Grand *In the Days of My Youth* (1901)

83   Sarah Grand *The Beth Book* (Virago edition 1980), p.473

84   *Courier* 26th April 1907, p.8

85   *Votes for Women* June 18th 1908, p.250

86   *Votes for Women* November 1907, p.13

87   *Courier* 5th June 1908

88   *Courier* 19th June 1908, p.9

89   *Yorkshire Telegraph and Star* 22nd June 1908

90   Sylvia Pankhurst *The Suffrage Movement* (Virago edition, 1977), p.285

91   Quoted in Emmeline Pethick-Lawrence *My Part in a Changing World* (1938), p.184

92   *The Manchester Guardian* 22nd June 1908, p.7

93   Muriel Matters *Biographical account of the Suffragette Violet Tillard* (MOL reference 57.116/28), Museum of London Suffragette collections

94   *Courier* 3rd July 1908, p.7

95   *Courier* 3rd July 1908, p.7

96   *Courier* 3rd July 1908, p.7

97   *Courier* 3rd July 1908, p.7

98   *Cork Examiner* 29th July 1910, p.5

99   *Hansard* HC Deb 28 October 1908 vol 195 cc404

100 Muriel Matters *Unpublished manuscript memoir of Violet Tillard* (1930) Museum of London, Suffragette Fellowship Collection

101 Dora Montefiore *From a Victorian to a Modern* (1927), p.97

102 *Courier* 13th November 1908, p.10

103 *Courier* 4th December 1908

104 *Courier* 12th October 1917, p.5

105 *Courier* 12th February 1909, p.5

106 *Courier* 26th February 1909

107 *London Evening Standard* 28th August 1909, p.10

108 *Courier* 3rd December 1909, p.7

109   *Unpublished autobiography of Kitty Marion*, Women's Library 7KMA

110   *The Standard* 15th October 1908

111   *Times* 27th October 1906, p.8

112   Herbert Gladstone *Letter to Sir Edward Grey* 10th October 1909

113   *The Common Cause* January 27th 1910, p.8

114   *Courier* 21st January 1910, p.6

115   *The Vote* 25th June 1910, p.98

116   *Advertiser* 10th August 1910, p.13

117   *Kentish Advertiser*, 3rd December 1909, p.2

118   *Lincolnshire Chronicle* 2nd July 1909, p.6

119   Quoted in Raeburn *The Militant Suffragettes*, p.153

120   *Votes for Women* 25th November 1910, p.120

121   *Memorandum* by H N Brailsford, Treatment of the Women's Deputation by the Police. Women's Library 7EWD/D/1/2

122   Elizabeth Crawford (ed) *Campaigning for the Vote: Kate Parry Frye's Suffrage Diary* (2013)

123   *Votes for Women* 25th November 1910

124   Sylvia Pankhurst *The Suffragette Movement* (1977 edition), p.344

125   *Unpublished autobiography of Kitty Marion* Women's Library 7KMA

126   *The Vote* 11th February 1910

127   *Votes for Women* 17th March 1911

128   *South Eastern Gazette* 4th April 1911, p.5

129   All information on responses taken from 1911 census returns via www.Ancestry.com

130   *Hansard* HC Deb 05 April 1911 vol 23 cc2193-52193

131   *Illustrated London News* April 8th 1911, p.492

132   *Shoreditch Observer* 24th June 1911, p.2

133   *Times* 19th June 1911, p.33

134   *Daily News* 19th June 1911, p.1

135   *The Vote* June 24th 1911, p.10

136   *The Common Cause* January 11th 1912, p.687

137   *Votes for Women* 17th November 1911

138   *Votes for Women* 24th November 1911, p.118

139 *Votes for Women* 11th June 1909, p.781

140 Sylvia Pankhurst *The Suffrage Movement* (Virago edition, 1977), p.309

141 *The Standard* 8th January 1912, p.11

142 *Votes for Women* 23rd Feb 1912, p.319

143 Quoted in *Votes for Women* March 8th 1912, p.354

144 *Times* 4th March 1912, p.12

145 *Poverty Bay Herald* Volume XXXV111 4th May 1912. Supplement.

146 *Kentish Advertiser* 8th March 1912, p.2

147 Ramsay MacDonald, *Leicester Pioneer* 9th March 1912

148 *Times* 16th March 1912, p. 9

149 Olive Walton *Statement Sent to the Women's Social and Political Union London* (July 1912) Suffragette Fellowship Collection, Museum of London

150 *Bucks Herald* 11th May 1912, p.8

151 Mary Richardson *Laugh a Defiance* 1953, p.84

152 Sylvia Pankhurst *The Suffrage Movement* (Virago edition, 1977), p.474

153 *Votes for Women* 19th April 1912, p.459

154 *Olive Walton's prison diary* (MOL reference 50.82/1131), Museum of London Suffragette collections

155 *Hansard* HC Deb 28 March 1912 vol 36 cc615-731

156 Mary Richardson *Laugh a Defiance* (1953)

157 *Courier* 2nd Aug 1912

158 *Courier* 15th November 1912

159 *Courier* 8th November 1912, p.7

160 *Manchester Guardian* 18th July 1912

161 *Daily Chronicle* 28th January 1913, p.1

162 *Daily Chronicle* 28th January 1913, p.1

163 *Advertiser* 14th February 1913, p.7

164 *Advertiser* 14th February 1913, p.7

165 *The Suffragette* 14th March 1913, p.344

166 *Daily Chronicle* 11th April, p.1

167 *The Suffragette* 4th April 1913, p.399

168 *Courier* 13th June 1913, p.7

169 *Courier* 19th September 1913, p.2

170 Theodore Martin *Queen Victoria as I Knew Her* (1901), p.69

171 'An Appeal Against Female Suffrage' *Nineteenth Century* 25 (June 1889), p.781-8

172 *The Spectator* 25th July 1908

173 *Courier* May 14th 1909

174 *Advertiser* 15th July 1910, p.5

175 *Advertiser* 12th January 1906, p.14

176 *Anti-Suffrage Review* June 1911 No. 13, p.126

177 *Gwladys Solomon letter to Lloyd George* National Archives PRO ref: T 172/968B

178 *Courier* 9th August 1912, p.10

179 *The Standard* 10th January 1912, p.11

180 *Courier* 9th August 1912, p.10

181 Violet Markham, *Miss Violet Markham's Great Speech at the Albert Hall*, National League for Opposing Woman Suffrage), 1912

182 *Advertiser* 7th March 1913, p.13

183 *Advertiser* May 1913

184 *Tunbridge Wells Gazette* 23rd July 1912, p.2

185 *Courier* 25th July 1913

186 Amelia Scott (*Speech notes*) Women's Library 7ASC/2/2/2

187 *Buffalo Express* 3rd July 1884

188 *Courier* 12th June 1914, p.7

189 *The Vote* 8th July 1911, p.8

190 *The Standard* 8th January 1912, p.11

191 *Courier* 24th June 1914

192 *Courier* 22nd May 1914

193 *Courier* 31st July 1914, p.7

194 Annette Matthews *Notes for obituary if required*. Imperial War Museum 09/36/1

195 This quote and those that follow are from *Annette Matthews War Diary*. Imperial War Museum 09/36/1

196   Heilmann and Forward (eds) *Sex, Social Purity and Sarah Grand* (2000)

197   Heilmann and Forward (eds) *Sex, Social Purity and Sarah Grand* (2000)

198   Emmeline Pankhurst circular letter, quoted in Elizabeth Crawford *The Women's Suffrage Movement: A Reference Guide*, p.754

199   *The Common Cause* 14th August 1914

200   *Courier* 17th April 1916

201   *Annette Matthews War Diary*. Imperial War Museum 09/36/1

202   Amelia Scott *Women and War Work* Women's Library 7/ASC/2/1/4/1

203   *Courier* 30th October 1914, p.3

204   Amelia Scott *Women and War Work* Women's Library 7/ASC/2/1/4/1

205   *Courier* 5th March 1915

206   *Courier* 11th June 1915, p.5

207   *Advertiser* 28th April, p.8

208   *Annette Matthews War Diary*. Imperial War Museum 09/36/1

209   *The Common Cause* 19th May 1916, p.84

210   *Advertiser* June 23rd 1916, p.7

211   *Courier* 20th October 1916

212   *Advertiser* 10th November 1916, p.5

213   Millicent Garrett Fawcett *The Women's Victory and After* (1920), p.13

214   *Hansard* HC Deb 15th May 1917

215   *The Common Cause* 22nd March 1918, p.6

216   *Courier* June 14th 1918

217   *Courier* 15th November 1918, p.6

218   *Annette Matthews War Diary*. Imperial War Museum 09/36/1.

219   *Courier* 20th December 1918, p.6

Select Bibliography

ARCHIVES
Imperial War Museum
Annette Matthews *War Diary*. Imperial War Museum 09/36/1

Museum of London, Suffragette Fellowship Collection
Typescript copy of Olive Walton's prison diary (MOL reference 50.82/1131), Museum of London Suffragette Collections
Olive Walton *Statement Sent to the Women's Social and Political Union London* (July 1912) Museum of London Suffragette Collections
Biographical account of the Suffragette Violet Tillard, written by Muriel Matters (MOL reference 57.116/28), Museum of London Suffragette Collections

Women's Library, London School of Economics
Amelia Scott, papers
Kitty Marion, unpublished autobiography
National Union of Suffrage Societies (NUWSS), papers
Women's Freedom League, papers
Women's National Anti-Suffrage League, papers
Women's Tax Resistance League, papers

National Archives
Home Office records
Prison Office records

WEBSITES
http://hansard.millbanksystems.com (Hansard archive)
https://www.kent.ac.uk/sspssr/womenshistorykent (produced by a partnership between Kent University and Tunbridge Wells Museum and Art Gallery)

NEWSPAPERS AND MAGAZINES (LOCAL)
Kent & Sussex Courier (The Courier)
South Eastern Gazette
Tunbridge Wells Advertiser (The Advertiser)
Tunbridge Wells Gazette

NEWSPAPERS AND MAGAZINES (NATIONAL and LONDON)
Daily News
Illustrated London News
Manchester Guardian
The Spectator
The Standard
The Times

SUFFRAGE PUBLICATIONS
The Anti-Suffrage Review
The Common Cause
The Suffragette
The Vote
Votes for Women
Women's Franchise

BOOKS
Blackburn, Helen. *Women's Suffrage*, Williams and Norgate, 1902

Bush, Julia. *Women Against the Vote: female anti-suffragism in Britain*, Oxford University Press, 2007

Chalkin, C.W. *Royal Tunbridge Wells: a history*, Phillimore, 2008

Crawford, Elizabeth (ed) *Campaigning for the Vote: Kate Parry Frye's Suffrage Diary*, Francis Boutle, 2013

Crawford, Elizabeth. *The Women's Suffrage Movement: a reference guide 1866-1926*, Routledge, 2001

Crawford, Elizabeth. *The Women's Suffrage Movement in Britain and Ireland: a regional survey*, Routledge, 2008

Fawcett, Millicent Garrett. *What I Remember*, T. Fisher Unwin, 1924

Harrison, Brian. *Separate Spheres: the opposition to women's suffrage in Britain*, Croom Helm, 1978

Hawksley, Lucinda. *March Women March!*, Andre Deutsch, 2013

Hollis, Patricia. *Ladies Elect: women in English local government 1865-1914*, Clarendon, 1987

Holton, Sandra Stanley. *Suffrage Days: stories from the women's suffrage movement*, Routledge, 1996

Jackson, Sarah and Taylor, Rosemary. *East London Suffragettes*, The History Press, 2014

Kenney, Annie. *Memories of a Militant*, Edward Arnold, 1924

Liddington, Jill. *Rebel Girls: their fight for the vote*, Virago, 2006

Liddington, Jill. *Vanishing for the Vote: suffrage, citizenship and the battle for the vote*, Manchester University Press, 2014

Marlow, Joyce (ed) *Suffragettes: the fight for votes for women*, Virago, 2015

Pankhurst, Emmeline. *My Own Story*, 1914, reprinted Vintage, 2015

Pankhurst, Sylvia. *The Suffragette Movement: an intimate account of persons and ideals*, 1931, reprinted Virago, 1988

Pethick-Lawrence, Emmeline. *My Part in a Changing World*, Gollancz, 1938

Phillips, Melanie. *The Ascent of Woman: a history of the suffragette movement*, Abacus, 2004

R., A.J. (ed) *The Suffrage Annual and Women's Who's Who*, Stanley Paul, 1913

Raeburn, Antonia. *The Militant Suffragettes*, Joseph, 1973

Rendall, Jane (ed.) *Equal or Different: women's politics 1800-1914*, Basil Blackwell, 1987

Royal Tunbridge Wells Civic Society. *The Shock of War: Tunbridge Wells: life on the Home Front 1914-1919*, Local History Monograph No. 13

Savidge, Alan. *Royal Tunbridge Wells*, Midas, 1975

Scott, Amelia *The History of the National Council of Women in Tunbridge Wells for the last 35 years* (1931)

Smith, Harold. *The British Women's Suffrage Campaign 1866-1928*, Routledge, 2014

Steinbach, Susie. *Women in England 1760-1914: a social history*, Weidenfeld & Nicholson, 2004

Strachey, Ray. *The Cause: a short history of the women's movement in Great Britain*, 1931, reprinted Virago, 1978

Twining, Louisa. *Recollections of Life and Work*, E Arnold, 1893

Illustrations

Image of the NUWSS Pilgrimage used on the cover, courtesy of
Tunbridge Wells Museum & Art Gallery

1. Nevill Pavilion Fire. Mary Evans Picture Library
2. Great Hall, Tunbridge Wells (copyright the Author)
3. Matilda Biggs. Drawn by Katharine Harper
4. First National Petition, 1866. Women's Library, LSE
5. Louisa Twining (1906). Elliott & Fry, via Wikimedia
   Creative Commons.
6. Amelia Scott (c1930). Women's Library, LSE
7. Opera House, Tunbridge Wells. (copyright the Author)
8. NUWSS Rally at the Albert Hall (1908). Royal Albert Hall
9. Sarah Grand (1916). National Portrait Gallery
10. WSPU Rally, Hyde Park (1908). Women's Library, LSE
11. WFL Caravan (1908). Women's Library, LSE
12. Violet Tillard. Drawn by Katharine Harper
13. WFL Ladies' Gallery Protest (1908). *Illustrated London News*
14. Christabel Pankhurst, Flora Drummond and Emmeline
    Pankhurst at Bow Street Magistrates' Court (October 1908).
    Women's Library, LSE
15. Prison to Citizenship Procession (1910). Women's Library,
    LSE.

16. Lovegrove Farm Vehicle with Kate Le Lacheur driving. State Library of South Australia

17. Black Friday (1910). Museum of London

18. Women's Suffrage Coronation Procession (1911). Women's Library, LSE

19. Olive Walton (c1920). National Portrait Gallery

20. The Pantiles, Tunbridge Wells (copyright the Author)

21. Window-breaking: cartoon from *The Gem* (June 1912). Mary Evans Picture Library

22. Force-feeding: cartoon from *The Suffragette* (1912). Museum of London

23. WSPU Hunger Striker's Medal. Women's Library, LSE

24. Emily Wilding Davison's Funeral (1913). Museum of London

25. WSPU Holiday Campaign (1913). Mary Evans Picture Library

26. Glwadys Solomon. Drawn by Katharine Harper

27. The NUWSS shop at 18 Crescent Road. Women's Library, LSE

28. Poster advertising NUWSS Pilgrimage (1913). Women's Library, LSE

29. Women's Tax Resistance League Badge. Women's Library, LSE

30. Advertisement for WTRL Sale. Women's Library, LSE

31. Annette Matthews. Tate Family Private Collection

32. NUWW Laundry workers at 44 Grosvenor Road. Women's Library, LSE

Acknowledgements

Many people have helped and encouraged me while I have been writing this book and I am grateful to them all. I would like to say an especially big 'thank you' to:

- Anne Logan of the University of Kent, for her generosity in letting me 'take over' her ladies and her helpful feedback on draft text.

- All those who have given me feedback on the text, especially Christine Carwardine, Hannah Houghton-Berry and Amanda Scott.

- The Festival Hall writers, Patta, Sarah and Rebekah, for their feedback and support. And above all Lulu, whose generous support and detailed feedback have been incredible and essential.

- Writing friends, including Sarah Salway, her Tuesday morning group and the Café Writers, who have given me encouragement and support.

- Staff at the libraries and archives I have visited, including the Women's Library (at the London School of Economics), the Museum of London, and the British Library.

- The Tunbridge Wells Museum and Art Gallery, for permission to use the photograph of the NUWSS Pilgrimage on the book's cover.

- The Museum of London, for permission to quote from Muriel Matter's unpublished biography of Violet Tillard and from Olive Walton's Prison Diary.

- The Women's Library, for permission to quote from Kitty Marion's unpublished autobiography.

- David Tate and family, for permission to quote from the War Diaries of Lady Annette Matthews.

- Katharine Harper for providing line drawings of Matilda Biggs, Violet Tillard and Glwadys Cowper-Smith.

- Sarah Hodder, for giving me the benefit of her design expertise.

- Amanda Scott for proof reading.

- Heidi Hurst at Troubador for all her help and for her patience.

And to all the other friends and family who have been so kind with encouragement and support over the past few years.

Index